D1360930

· T R O P H I E S ·

Intervention
TEACHER'S GUIDE
Grade 5

Harcourt

Orlando   Boston   Dallas   Chicago   San Diego

Visit *The Learning Site!*
www.harcourtschool.com

ISBN 0-15-325347-9

9 10 048 10 09 08 07 06

Table of Contents

What are Intervention Strategies?

Intervention strategies are designed to facilitate learning for those students who may experience some difficulty no matter how well we have planned our curriculum. These strategies offer support and guidance to the student who is struggling. The strategies themselves are no mystery. They are based on the same time-honored techniques that effective teachers have used for years—teaching students on their instructional reading level; modeling previewing and predicting; directed and giving direct instruction in strategic-reading, vocabulary, phonics, fluency, and writing.

Intervention works best in conjunction with a strong core program. For an intervention program to be effective, instruction should focus on specific needs of students, as determined by systematic monitoring of progress.

Components of the Intervention Program

The goal of the *Trophies* Intervention Program is to provide the scaffolding, extra support, and extra reading practice that below-level readers need to succeed in the mainstream reading program. The program includes the following components:

- *Skill Cards* to preteach and reteach the Focus Skill for each lesson
- *Intervention Practice Book* with the following practice pages for each lesson:

    Fluency Page with word lists and phrase-cued sentences that parallel the reading level of the *Intervention Reader* selection

    Phonics Practice Page that reinforces prerequisite phonics/decoding skills and can be used as a teacher-directed or independent activity

    Comprehension Practice Page that gives students an opportunity to respond to the *Intervention Reader* selection and show that they have understood it

    Focus Skill Review Page that provides an additional opportunity to practice and apply the focus skill for that lesson

- *Intervention Reader* to provide reading material at students' instructional reading level
- *Vocabulary Game Boards* and related materials to provide additional practice and application of vocabulary skills
- *Intervention Assessment Book* opportunities to monitor progress and ensure success

Using the *Intervention Teacher's Guides* with *Trophies*

The *Intervention Teacher's Guide* gives support for below-level readers in key instructional strands of *Trophies*, plus prerequisite phonics skills and oral-reading fluency. Each *Intervention Teacher's Guide* lesson includes the following resources:

- The **Phonics/Decoding Lesson** reviews prerequisite phonics and word analysis skills. Each skill is systematically applied in the corresponding *Intervention Reader* selection.

- **Preteach/Reteach Vocabulary** activities to teach key vocabulary that appears in both the *Intervention Reader* selection and the corresponding *Trophies Pupil Edition* selection.

- **Fluency Builders** reinforce important vocabulary while providing reading practice to promote oral reading fluency. You may also wish to use the *Oral Reading Fluency Assessment* periodically to measure student progress.

- **Preteach/Reteach Focus Skill** activities reinforce the objective of *Trophies* Focus Skills, ensuring that below-level readers get the in-depth instruction they need to reach grade skill-level standards.

- **Preview and Summarize** provide support for comprehension of each main selection in *Trophies Pupil Editions*.

- **Directed Reading Lesson** for the *Intervention Reader* selection that reinforces basic comprehension skills, using questions and teacher modeling.

- **Writing Support** for writing lessons in *Trophies* provides interactive writing experiences for the key aspects of the corresponding writing forms and skills.

- **Weekly Review** provides additional support as students review phonics, vocabulary, and focus skills and prepare for testing.

- **Self-Selected Reading** suggests titles that students can read independently with success and also offers specific suggestions for encouraging student expression and participation through conferencing.

The *Intervention Teacher's Guide* lessons clearly identify the most appropriate times during the *Trophies* lesson plan to provide supplemental instruction. Look for the BEFORE or AFTER tag that appears next to each of the key instructional strands, along with page numbers from the core program. For example:

> **BEFORE**
> **Skills/Strategies**
> *pages 305I–305J*

This tag alerts you that *before* you teach the Skill and Strategy lessons that appear in *Trophies* on pages 305I–305J, intervention strategies may be useful. Appropriate preteach activities are provided. Reteaching activities are indicated by the AFTER tag.

Depending on your individual classroom and school schedules, you can tailor the "before" and "after" instruction to suit your needs. The following pages show two options for pacing the instruction in this guide.

Suggested Lesson Planners

Option 1:

DAY 1

BEFORE — Building Background and Vocabulary

Review Phonics
- Identify the sound
- Associate letters to sound
- Word blending
- Apply the skill

Introduce Vocabulary
- Preteach lesson vocabulary

AFTER — Building Background and Vocabulary

Apply Vocabulary Strategies
- Use decoding strategies
- Reteach lesson vocabulary

Fluency Builder
- Use *Intervention Practice Book*

DAY 2

BEFORE — Reading the *Trophies* Selection

Focus Skill
- Preteach the skill
- Use Skill Card Side A

Prepare to Read the *Trophies* selection
- Preview the selection
- Set purpose

AFTER — Reading the *Trophies* Selection

Reread and Summarize

Fluency Builder
- Use *Intervention Practice Book*

Option 2:

DAY 1

AFTER — Weekly Assessments

Self-Selected Reading
- Choosing books
- Conduct student-teacher conferences

Fluency Performance
- Use passage from *Intervention Reader* selection

BEFORE — Building Background and Vocabulary

Review Phonics
- Identify the sound
- Associate letters to sound
- Word blending
- Apply the skill

Introduce Vocabulary
- Preteach lesson vocabulary

DAY 2

AFTER — Building Background and Vocabulary

Apply Vocabulary Strategies
- Use decoding strategies
- Reteach lesson vocabulary

Fluency Builder
- Use *Intervention Practice Book*

BEFORE — Reading the *Trophies* Selection

Focus Skill
- Preteach the skill
- Use Skill Card Side A

Prepare to Read the *Trophies* selection
- Preview the selection
- Set purpose

DAY 3

BEFORE — Making Connections

Directed Reading of *Intervention Reader* selection
- Read the selection
- Summarize the selection
- Answer *Think About It* Questions

AFTER — Skill Review

Focus Skill
- Reteach the skill
- Use Skill Card Side B

Fluency Builder
- Use *Intervention Practice Book*

DAY 4

BEFORE — Writing Lesson

Writing Support
- Build on prior knowledge
- Construct the text
- Revisit the text
- On Your Own

AFTER — Spelling Lesson

Connect Spelling and Phonics
- Reteach phonics
- Build and read longer words

Fluency Builder
- Use passage from *Intervention Reader* selection

DAY 5

BEFORE — Weekly Assessments

Review Vocabulary
- Vocabulary activity

Review Focus Skill
- Use *Intervention Practice Book*

Review Test Prep
- Use the core *Pupil Edition*

AFTER — Weekly Assessments

Self-Selected Reading
- Choosing books
- Conduct student-teacher conferences

Fluency Performance
- Use passage from *Intervention Reader* selection

DAY 3

AFTER — Reading the *Trophies* Selection

Reread and Summarize

Fluency Builder
- Use *Intervention Practice Book*

BEFORE — Making Connections

Directed Reading of *Intervention Reader* selection
- Read the selection
- Summarize the selection
- Answer *Think About It* Questions

DAY 4

AFTER — Skill Review

Focus Skill
- Reteach the skill
- Use Skill Card Side B

Fluency Builder
- Use *Intervention Practice Book*

BEFORE — Writing Lesson

Writing Support
- Build on prior knowledge
- Construct the text
- Revisit the text
- On Your Own

DAY 5

AFTER — Spelling Lesson

Connect Spelling and Phonics
- Reteach phonics
- Build and read longer words

Fluency Builder
- Use passage from *Intervention Reader* selection

BEFORE — Weekly Assessments

Review Vocabulary
- Vocabulary activity

Review Focus Skill
- Use *Intervention Practice Book*

Review Test Prep
- Use the core *Pupil Edition*

Fluency

"So that students will understand why rereading is done, we have involved them in a discussion of how athletes develop skill at their sports. This discussion brings out the fact that athletes spend considerable time practicing basic skills until they develop speed and smoothness at their activity. Repeated readings uses this same type of practice."

S. Jay Samuels
The Reading Teacher, February 1997
(originally published January 1979)

In the years since S. Jay Samuels pioneered the technique of repeated reading to improve fluency, continuing research has confirmed and expanded upon his observations. Ideally, oral reading mirrors the pacing, smoothness, and rhythms of normal speech. Fluency in reading can be defined as a combination of these key elements.

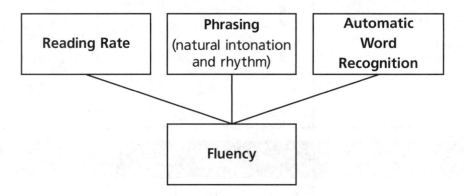

How Do Students Become More Fluent Readers?

Research and the experiences of classroom teachers make it clear that certain practices can and do lead to significant improvements in reading fluency. Techniques that have been shown to be successful include

- **Teacher modeling**

- **Repeated reading of short passages**

- **Daily monitoring of progress**

A program that incorporates these three elements will help struggling readers gain fluency and improve their comprehension.

Using Fluency Builders in the *Intervention Teacher's Guide*

The plan for each lesson in the *Intervention Teacher's Guide* includes daily fluency practice that incorporates the elements of teacher modeling, repeated reading, and self-monitoring.

The fluency portion of the lesson is designed to be completed in five or ten minutes, although you may adjust the time according to students' needs and as your schedule allows.

About the *Intervention Practice Book* Fluency Page

The *Intervention Practice Book* Fluency page is designed to correlate with the phonics elements taught in the *Intervention Teacher's Guide*, as well as with key vocabulary from the *Trophies* and *Intervention Reader* selections. A total of twenty words that fall into these three categories are listed at the top of the Fluency Page for each lesson.

On the bottom half of the page, you will find a set of numbered sentences that incorporate the words from the lists. Slashes are used to divide each sentence into phrases. To help students improve natural phrasing, model reading each phrase smoothly, as a unit, and encourage students to follow the same procedure in their repeated-reading practice.

This chart gives an overview of the fluency portion of the Intervention Program.

Day	Materials	Explanation
1	*Intervention Practice Book* Fluency Page	Teacher models reading aloud word lists. Students then practice reading aloud the word lists with partners.
2	*Intervention Practice Book* Fluency Page	Teacher models reading aloud the phrased fluency sentences. Students then practice repeated rereadings of the sentences with partners.
3	*Intervention Practice Book* Fluency Page	Students read the fluency sentences on tape, assess their own progress, and then reread the sentences on tape to improve pacing and tone.
4	*Intervention Reader* selection	Students read aloud a selected short passage from the *Intervention Reader* selection three times, monitoring their progress after each reading.
5	*Intervention Reader* selection	Students read the same passage aloud to the teacher. Both teacher and student assess the student's progress.

Phonemic Awareness

Rhyming Activities

Rhyme-a-Day

Start each day by teaching students a short rhyme. Periodically throughout the day, repeat the rhyme with them. Say the rhyme together, have them say it alone, pause and leave out words for them to insert, or ask volunteers to say each line. Students will develop a repertoire of favorite rhymes that can serve as a storehouse for creating their own rhymes.

Rhyme Sort

Place on a tabletop pictures of items that rhyme. Have students sort the pictures into groups, according to names that rhyme. You may also want to try an "open sort" by having students create categories of their own to sort the picture cards

Rhyme Pairs

To assess students' ability to recognize pairs of words that rhyme, say a list of twenty or more pairs of words. Half of the word pairs should rhyme. Students tell which word pairs rhyme and which do not. Have students indicate *yes* with a card marked *Y* or another symbol.

If working with **one child** (or small group), have students use one of the Game Boards. From each correct response, the player can move a marker ahead one space. Provide word pairs until the player has completed the game.

What Word Rhymes?

Use theme-related words from across the curriculum to focus on words that rhyme. For example, if you are studying animals, ask: *What rhymes with snake? bear? fox? deer? ant? frog? goat? hen? fish? whale?* If a special holiday is approaching, ask: *What rhymes with flag, year, or heart?* Use these word groups for sound-matching, sound-blending, or sound-segmenting activities.

Sound-Matching Activities

Odd Word Out

Form a group of four students. Say a different word for each group member to repeat. The student with the word that does not begin (or end) like the other words must step out of the group. For example, say *basket, bundle, cost, bargain.* The student whose word is *cost* steps from the group. The odd-word-out player then chooses three students to form a new group and the procedure continues.

Head or Toes, Finger or Nose?

Teach students the following rhyme. Be sure to say the sound, not the letter, at the beginning of each line. Recite the rhyme together several times while touching the body parts.

> /h/ is for *head.*
> /t/ is for *toes.*
> /f/ is for *finger.*
> /n/ is for *nose.*

Explain that you will say a list of words. Students are to touch the head when you say a word that begins with /h/, the toes for the words that begin with /t/, a finger for words that begin with /f/, and the nose for words that begin with /n/. Say words such as *fan, ten, horn, hat, feet, nut, ham, nest, toy, fish, note, tub, nail, time, fox,* and *house.*

Souvenir Sound-Off

Have students imagine that a friend has traveled to a special place and has brought them a gift. Recite the following verse, and ask a volunteer to complete it. The names of the traveler, the place, and the gift must begin with the same letter and sound.

- My friend [person]
  My friend Hannah
- who went to [place]
  who went to Hawaii
- brought me back a [gift].
  brought me back a hula skirt.

After repeating this activity a few times, ask **partners** to recite the missing words. As an alternative, you can focus on words with initial blends and digraphs. Students can focus on social studies and phonics skills by using a world map or globe to find names of places.

Match My Word

Have students match beginning or ending sounds in words. Seat students in pairs, sitting back-to-back. One student in each pair will say a word. His or her partner will repeat the word and say another word that begins with the same sound. Repeat the activity, reversing the roles of partners and focusing on ending sounds.

Sound Isolation Activities

What's Your Name N-N-N-Name?

Invite students to say their names by repeating the initial phoneme in the name, such as *M-M-M-M-Michael* or by drawing out and exaggerating the initial sound, such as *Sssss-erena.* Have students say the names of others, such as friends or family members.

Singling Out the Sounds

Form groups of three students. Students can decide who will name the beginning, the middle, and the ending sounds in one-syllable picture names. Given a set of pictures, the group identifies a picture name, and then each group member isolates and says the sound he or she is responsible for. Group members can check one another.

Chain Reaction

Have students form a circle. The student who begins will say a word such as *bus.* The next child must isolate the ending sound in the word, /s/, and say a word that begins with that sound, such as *sun.* If the word is correct, the two students link arms, and the procedure continues with the next child isolating the final sound in *sun* and giving a word that begins with /n/. You will want all students to be able to link arms and complete the chain, so provide help when needed.

Sound-Addition, Deletion, or Substitution Activities

Add-a-Sound

Explain that the beginning sound is missing in each of the words you will say. Students must add the missing sound and say the new word. Some examples follow.

Add:

/b/ to *at* (bat)	/f/ to *ox* (fox)	/k/ to *art* (cart)
/f/ to *ace* (face)	/p/ to *age* (page)	/h/ to *air* (hair)
/w/ to *all* (wall)	/j/ to *am* (jam)	/r/ to *an* (ran)
/b/ to *and* (band)	/d/ to *ark* (dark)	/f/ to *arm* (farm)
/d/ to *ash* (dash)	/s/ to *it* (sit)	/s/ to *oak* (soak)
/h/ to *eel* (heel)	/b/ to *end* (bend)	/m/ to *ice* (mice)
/n/ to *ear* (near)	/f/ to *east* (feast)	/b/ to *each* (beach)
/f/-/l/ to *at* (flat)	/sk/ to *ate* (skate)	/t/-/r/ to *eat* (treat)
/g/-/r/ to *ill* (grill)	/sh/ to *out* (shout)	/p/-/l/ to *ant* (plant)

Remove-a-Sound

Reinforce rhyme while focusing on the deletion of initial sounds in words to form new words. Ask students to say:

- *hat* without the /h/ (at)
- *fin* without the /f/ (in)
- *tall* without the /t/ (all)
- *box* without the /b/ (ox)
- *will* without /w/ (ill)
- *peach* without the /p/ (each)
- *nice* without the /n/ (ice)
- *meat* without the /m/ (eat)
- *band* without the /b/ (and)

Continue with other words in the same manner.

Mixed-Up Tongue Twisters

Think of a simple tongue twister such as *ten tired toads*. Say the tongue twister for students, but replace the initial letter in each word with another letter, such a *p*, to create nonsense words: *pen pired poads*. Explain to students that you need their help to make sense of the tongue twister by having them replace /p/ with /t/ and say the new tongue twister. Use the same procedure for other tongue twisters.

- copper coffee cups
- nine new nails
- two ton tomatoes
- long lean legs

Then ask partners to do this activity together.

The Name Game

Occasionally when a new sound is introduced, students might enjoy substituting the first sound of their names for the name of a classmate. Students will have to stop and think when they call one another by name, including the teacher. For example, Paul would call Ms. Vega, Ms. Pega; Carmen becomes Parmen; Jason becomes Pason; and Kiyo becomes Piyo. Just make certain beforehand that all names will be agreeable.

Take Away

New words can be formed by deleting an initial phoneme from a word. Have students say the new word that is formed.

flake without the /f/
(lake)

bring without the /b/
(ring)

swing without the /s/
(wing)

swell without the /s/
(well)

shrink without the /sh/
(rink)

shred without the /sh/
(red)

spread without the /s/-/p/
(read)

gloom without the /g/
(loom)

fright without the /f/
(right)

snout without the /s/-/n/
(out)

score without the /s/
(core)

slip without the /s/
(lip)

bride without the /b/
(ride)

block without the /b/
(lock)

spoke without the /s/
(poke)

snail without the /s/
(nail)

Sound-Blending Activities

I'm Thinking of a Word

Play a guessing game with students. Tell students that you will give them clues to a word. Have them listen closely to blend the sounds to say the word.

- I'm thinking of something that has words—
/b/-/o͞o/-/k/. (book)

- I'm thinking of something that comes in bunches—
/g/-/r/-/ā/-/p/-/s/. (grapes)

- I'm thinking of something that shines in the night sky—
/s/-/t/-/är/-/z/. (stars)

- I'm thinking of something that moves very slowly—
/s/-/n/-/ā/-/l/. (snail)

What's in the Box?

Place various objects in a box or bag. Play a game with students by saying **In this box is a /c/-/r/-/ā/-/o/-/n/. What do you think is in the box?** (crayon) Continue with the other objects in the box, segmenting the phonemes for students to blend and say the word.

Sound-Segmenting Activities

Sound Game

Have **partners** play a word-guessing game, using a variety of pictures that represent different beginning sounds. One student says the name on the card, separating the beginning sound, as in **p-late**. The partner blends the sounds and guesses the word. After students are proficient with beginning sounds, you could have them segment all the sounds in a word when they give their clues, as in **d-o-g**.

Count the Sounds

Tell students that you are going to say a word. Have them listen and count the number of sounds they hear in that word. For example, say the word *task*. Have children repeat the word and tell how many sounds they hear. Students should reply *four*.

tone (3)	four (3)
great (4)	peak (3)
pinch (4)	sunny (4)
stick (4)	clouds (5)
flake (4)	feel (3)
rain (3)	paint (4)

Vocabulary Games

Vocabulary Game Boards

To give students additional vocabulary practice, use the Vocabulary Game Boards and copying masters provided in the Intervention Kit. Two different games can be played on each game board. Directions for each game are printed on the back of the board on which the game is played. There are a total of five game boards, which students can use to play ten different games. For best results, use the games to review vocabulary at the end of each theme, so that there are more words to play with.

Copying Masters

The copying masters that accompany the game boards provide some other materials that students will need to play the games. These include:

- spinners
- game pieces
- game cards

Illustrated directions on the copying masters show students how to create the game materials. They may need scissors, crayons or colored markers, and glue. Pencils and paper clips are used to construct spinners. When game markers are called for, provide students with buttons, counters, or some other small item.

Additional Materials

When the directions for a game call for **word cards**, use the vocabulary word cards from *Trophies*. In addition, some games require the use of a vocabulary list, definition cards that students can create, a dictionary, and commonly available items such as a paper bag.

Use the following charts to plan for and organize the vocabulary games.

Game Board I: Hopscotch

Games	Skills Practiced	Players	Additional Materials
Wordscotch	definitions	2	Wordscotch Copying Master *Trophies* word cards dictionary game markers
Syllable Hop-Along	number of syllables	2	Syllable Hop-Along Copying Master *Trophies* word cards dictionary game markers

Game Board 2: Tic-Tac-Toe

Games	Skills Practiced	Players	Additional Materials
Tic-Tac-Know	creating sentences	2	word cards with meaning on back (to be made by students) game markers
Riddle Me	definitions and number of syllables	4	word cards with meaning on back (to be made by students) paper bag vocabulary list game markers

Game Board 3: Do You Remember?

Games	Skills Practiced	Players	Additional Materials
Match a Pair	definitions	2	word cards with meaning on back (to be made by students) *Trophies* word cards
Syllable Match	number of syllables	2	*Trophies* word cards dictionary

Game Board 4: Safari

Games	Skills Practiced	Players	Additional Materials
Safari Spin	number of syllables	2	Safari Spin Copying Master *Trophies* word cards dictionary
Safari Wordwatch	definitions	2–4	Safari Wordwatch Copying Masters vocabulary list dictionary

Game Board 5: Word Castle

Games	Skills Practiced	Players	Additional Materials
Castle Construction	definitions	2	Castle Construction Copying Master *Trophies* word cards dictionary
Knight's Syllable Spin	number of syllables	2	Knight's Syllable Spin Copying Masters *Trophies* word cards dictionary

Vocabulary Activities

The six activities on the following pages provide additional opportunities for vocabulary practice and application. Two activities are offered for individual students, two for pairs of students, and two for small groups of three or four students. All require a minimum of preparation and call for materials that are readily available in the classroom.

Word Book

INDIVIDUAL ACTIVITY

MATERIALS
- paper
- markers
- stapler
- simple binding materials

As students progress through a theme, encourage them to identify new vocabulary that they find interesting or that they think will be useful to them. Have students create a page for each of the special words they choose. Encourage them to check the spelling of the word and to include the definition and other information they might find helpful, such as how the word is divided into syllables, how it is pronounced, whether it has a prefix or a suffix, synonyms and antonyms, and how the word may be related to other words they know. Students can also draw pictures and include captions and labels.

Upon completion of the theme, have students make a cover for the book. Staple the pages together or help students use simple materials to bind them. Encourage them to share their word books with classmates and to use them as a resource for their writing.

Draw a Smile

PARTNER ACTIVITY

MATERIALS
- list of vocabulary words from a complete theme
- two sheets of paper and markers or chalk and chalkboard
- dictionary

Pairs of students can play this game on paper or on the board. Players should be designated Player 1 and Player 2. Player 1 begins by choosing a vocabulary word from the list for Player 2 to define. If Player 2 defines the word correctly, he or she gets to draw one part of a smiling face. If Player 2 cannot define the word correctly, he or she cannot draw on that turn. Players take turns choosing words for each other to define and adding parts to their drawings each time they define a word correctly. Encourage students to use a dictionary to check definitions as necessary.

A completed drawing has five parts, to be drawn in this order: (1) head, (2) one eye, (3) the other eye, (4) nose, (5) smile. The first player to draw a complete smiling face wins the game.

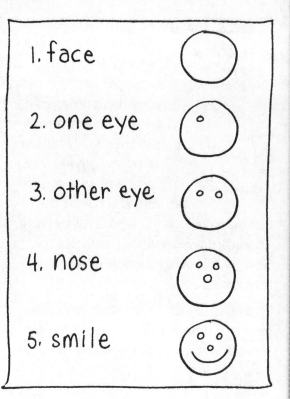

1. face

2. one eye

3. other eye

4. nose

5. smile

Make a Word Garden

SMALL GROUP ACTIVITY

MATERIALS
- bulletin board
- colored construction paper
- markers
- scissors
- masking tape
- pencil
- paper

Students can create a word garden by drawing and cutting out large flowers from construction paper. Encourage them to use their imaginations to create flowers in a variety of shapes and colors. Have students use markers to write a vocabulary word on each flower and then arrange the flowers to make a garden on the bulletin board.

Then have students create a key on a separate sheet of paper by making a small drawing of each of the large

flowers and writing the definition of the word that appears on the matching large flower. Students should display the key on the bulletin board with their garden.

What's the Score?

INDIVIDUAL ACTIVITY

MATERIALS
- list of vocabulary words from a theme or several lessons within a theme
- pencil and paper
- dictionary

Make a list of six to eight vocabulary words that may have given students some difficulty. Have students copy the words from the list and write a definition for each word from memory.

Then have them use a dictionary to check their definitions. Tell them to keep score by writing down the number of words they defined correctly.

Then have students copy the words from the list in reverse order, beginning at the bottom. Have them again write a definition for each word from memory, check the definitions in a dictionary, and count the words they defined correctly. Tell students to compare this score to their first score to see how much they improved.

Finger Puppets

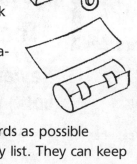

SMALL GROUP ACTIVITY

MATERIALS

- finger puppet pattern
- construction paper
- markers
- scissors
- tape
- list of vocabulary words from a theme

Give students a simple pattern that they can trace to make finger puppets. Have students use construction paper and markers to create puppets that represent favorite characters from a particular theme.

Have students work together to make up simple dramatizations using the finger puppets. Challenge students to use as many words as possible from the vocabulary list. They can keep track of the words they use by checking them off the list.

Guess My Word

PARTNER ACTIVITY

MATERIALS

- list of vocabulary words from a theme
- scrap paper
- pencils

Display the list of vocabulary words where both players can see it. Students take turns choosing a word from the list for each other to guess.

The student who is guessing may ask questions about the meaning of the word, how it is spelled, the number of syllables, or any other information they think may help them, as long as the questions can be answered with *yes* or *no*. Encourage students to jot down information that they find out about the word that can help narrow down the list. You may want to give examples of questions that players might ask and explain how they can use the information they obtain.

QUESTION: Does the word begin with a consonant?

INFORMATION: If the answer is *yes*, you can look at the words that begin with consonants and ask more questions to figure out which of those is the correct word. If the answer is *no*, you can rule out the words that begin with consonants and focus on those that begin with vowels.

QUESTION: Does the word have an *-ed* ending?

INFORMATION: If the answer is *no*, you can rule out all words with *-ed* endings. If the answer is yes, focus on the words with *-ed* endings. Ask more questions to figure out which of those words is the correct one.

BEFORE

Building
Background
and Vocabulary

Use with

"The Hot and Cold Summer"

Review Phonics: Short Vowels /a/*a*, /i/*i*, /o/*o*, /u/*u*; Long Vowels /ā/*a-e*, /ī/*i-e*, /ō/*o-e*, /oo/*u-e*

Identify the sounds. Have students repeat the following sentence aloud three times: *Nat and Nate had yams on a plate.* Ask students to identify the words that have the short and long *a* vowel sounds. (*Nat, had, yams*); (*Nate, plate*) Repeat for short *i* and long *i* words, short *o* and long *o* words, and short *u* and long *u* words, using these sentences: *Tim has time to shine the tin. Rob strode up the slope with his fishing rod. Chuck sits on a dune and hums a tune.*

Associate letters to sounds. Write on the board the sentence *Nat and Nate had yams on a plate.* Point out the short *a* vowel sound and the CVC pattern in *Nat, had,* and *yams*. Point out the long *a* vowel sound and the *a-e* pattern in *Nate* and *plate*. Use a similar procedure with the sentences above for words with the short *i* and long *i* vowel sounds, the short *o* and long *o* vowel sounds, and the short *u* and long *u* vowel sounds.

Word blending. Model how to blend the letters and sounds to read the word *plate*. Slide your hand under the whole word as you elongate the sounds: /plāāt/. Then say the word naturally—*plate*. Follow a similar procedure with the other words.

Apply the skill. *Vowel Substitution* Write the following words on the board, and have students read each aloud. Make the changes necessary to form the words in parentheses. Have students read each new word aloud.

sham (shame)   **pin** (pine)   **strip** (stripe)   **mop** (mope)   **plum** (plume)

INTERVENTION
PRACTICE
BOOK

page 4

Introduce Vocabulary

PRETEACH **lesson vocabulary.** Tell students that they are going to learn six new words that they will see when they read a story called "The Hot and Cold Summer." Teach each Vocabulary Word using the following process.

Use the following suggestions or similar ideas to give the meaning or context.

Write the word.
Say the word.
Track the word and have students repeat it.
Give the meaning or context.

authority   A person who is an authority has special knowledge about a subject.

souvenir   The spot of ketchup on my shirt is a souvenir of my lunch.

incredible   An incredible experience is one you don't forget: It would be incredible to fly in the space shuttle.

vow	When people get married, we say they take vows.
commotion	Recall with students some kind of commotion in school, such as the crowd of students on the first day of school.
exhausted	This word comes from Latin words meaning "to empty." When a person feels exhausted, he or she feels empty of all energy.

For vocabulary activities, see Vocabulary Games on pages 2–7.

Apply Vocabulary Strategies

Use context clues. Write on the board these sentences: *My uncle is an authority on fishing. Many people ask his advice about it.* Explain to students that they often can figure out what a word means by reading the surrounding sentences. Model using the strategy.

MODEL I don't know what the word *authority* means. I read the next sentence and see a clue—people ask an authority for advice.

Remind students to use this strategy as they read the selection.

RETEACH **lesson vocabulary.** Give students word cards for the Vocabulary Words. Read the following sentences aloud, saying "blank" for each blank. Students hold up the correct word card. Reread the sentences with the appropriate words.

1. Many people think Ann Landers is an (authority) on problems.
2. Matt kept the baseball from the playoffs as a (souvenir).
3. Tall tales are about (incredible) people and events.
4. Members of the club had to take a (vow) of secrecy.
5. The escaped elephant caused quite a (commotion) at the zoo.
6. After a long, hot soccer practice, I feel (exhausted).

FLUENCY BUILDER Use *Intervention Practice Book* page 3.
Read aloud each of the words in the first column and have students repeat it. Then have students work in pairs and take turns reading the words to each other. Follow the same procedure with each of the remaining columns. After each partner has had a turn reading aloud the words in each column, have them practice reading the entire list and time themselves.

INTERVENTION PRACTICE BOOK

page 3

USE SKILL CARD 1A

(Focus Skill) **Prefixes, Suffixes, and Roots**

PRETEACH **the skill.** Explain to students that many words include special parts called prefixes and suffixes. Often, knowing about them and about their roots can help students decode words that seem unfamiliar.

Have students look at **side A of Skill Card 1: Prefixes, Suffixes, and Roots.** Read the definitions of *prefix*, *suffix* and *root*, and have students read them with you. Point out that the root of the word is the part of the word with all the prefixes and suffixes removed.

Next, call attention to the boxes in the middle of the card. Have students refer to these boxes as a volunteer reads the first line in the chart at the bottom. Ask:

- **What is the prefix?** (*un-*) **What is the root word?** (*lock*)

- **When you add *un-* to *lock*, what word have you made?** (*unlock*)

- **What is the meaning of that word?** (to do the opposite of *lock*)

Continue in a similar manner with the remaining entries in the chart.

Remind students to look for prefixes, suffixes, and familiar roots when they meet new words in their reading.

Prepare to Read: "The Hot and Cold Summer"

Preview. Explain that the selection "The Hot and Cold Summer" is realistic fiction. Remind students that realistic fiction seems real but is made up by the author. Then preview the selection.

DISTANT VOYAGES
pages 22–40

- **Pages 22–27:** So far the pictures show the same girl and two boys. I wonder whether the three are friends. The boys seem to be ignoring the girl.

- **Pages 28–31:** The girl is holding a fancy cake. I wonder who or what "Bolivia" is. On the next two pages, the girl is looking out a window at the boys, but she doesn't look happy.

- **Pages 32–37:** Look at this beautiful bird! I wonder why the man needs a ladder. I think the bird has escaped, and people are trying to catch it.

Set purpose. Model setting a purpose for reading "The Hot and Cold Summer."

MODEL From what I have seen, I think the story is about a parrot that escapes. I want to read to find out whether the people capture it again.

Reread and Summarize

Have students reread and summarize "The Hot and Cold Summer" in sections, as described in the chart below.

Pages 22–25

Let's reread pages 22–25 to remind ourselves of what is happening.

Summary: Derek and Rory are unhappy. They have agreed to come to a cookout to meet Bolivia, but they don't want to go.

Pages 26–29

As we reread pages 26–29, let's recall how the boys manage not to talk to Bolivia at the cookout.

Summary: The boys keep their mouths full of food so they do not have to talk to Bolivia. She wants the boys to come to see Lucette.

Pages 30–31

When we reread pages 30–31, we'll remind ourselves that Derek and Rory are convinced that Lucette is Bolivia's little sister.

Summary: When Bolivia shouts that Lucette has escaped, the boys see a large green parrot. So, Lucette is a bird.

Pages 32–37

Let's reread pages 32–37 to find out how everyone tries to get Lucette, the parrot, to return.

Summary: Everyone tries to get Lucette, but nothing works. Finally, Bolivia remembers that Lucette likes country music. Derek turns his radio to a country station.

Pages 38–40

Reread pages 38–40 to find out how the story ends.

Summary: Mr. Dunn gets Lucette down from a tree. Derek asks Bolivia questions about Lucette.

FLUENCY BUILDER Be sure students have copies of *Intervention Practice Book* page 3. Call students' attention to the sentences at the bottom of the page. Explain that the slashes break the sentences into phrases to allow them to work on natural phrasing. Tell students that their goal is to read each phrase or unit smoothly. Model appropriate pace, expression, and phrasing as you read each sentence and have students read it after you. Then have partners practice by reading each sentence aloud three times.

INTERVENTION PRACTICE BOOK

page 3

Directed Reading: "A Fish Tale" pp. 6–12

Have a volunteer read the title of the story aloud. If necessary, explain that a "fish story" is a story that exaggerates, or stretches the truth. Have students view the illustration on page 6 and read page 6 to find out how Sam feels about Ingrid. Ask: **How does Sam feel about Ingrid?** (*He doesn't like her.*) **MAIN IDEA**

TAKE
FLIGHT
pp. 6–12

Page 6

Ask: **Why doesn't Sam like Ingrid?** (*because she is from a foreign country and she speaks differently*) **CAUSE/EFFECT**

Page 7

Have students read page 7 to find out how Sam and Travis treat Ingrid. Ask: **How do Sam and Travis treat Ingrid?** (*Possible response: They are rude. Sam tells her to hug a slug.*) **MAKE JUDGMENTS**

Page 8

Ask students to read page 8 to find out what Ingrid does to prove that she can fish. Ask: **What does Ingrid do to prove that she can fish?** (*She buys a big catfish from a store and pretends that she caught it.*) **IMPORTANT DETAILS**

Page 9

Ask students to read page 9 to find out whether Sam and Travis believe that she caught the fish. Ask: **Do Sam and Travis seem to believe that Ingrid caught the catfish?** (*Possible response: Sam seems doubtful, but Travis seems to believe her.*) **SPECULATE**

How can you tell that Travis's feelings about Ingrid are changing? (*Possible response: He seems impressed when she says she can cut up fish; he says they could go fishing sometime.*) **DRAW CONCLUSIONS**

Page 10

Why do you think Sam is mad when he sees Travis and Ingrid fishing? (*Possible response: He's jealous; he and Travis had made a vow to keep the pond to themselves.*) **CAUSE/EFFECT**

Page 11

Have a volunteer read aloud the first two paragraphs of page 11, and have students predict what the boys will think now that Ingrid tells the truth. Then have a volunteer finish the page to see whether their predictions are correct. Model using the Make and Confirm Predictions strategy:

> **MODEL** I predicted that because the boys didn't like Ingrid to start with, they'd be angry when they found out she had lied to them. But my prediction was not correct. I found out that since the boys had so much fun playing with Ingrid, they thought she was a good friend.
> **MAKE AND CONFIRM PREDICTIONS**

Then ask: **How do you know that Ingrid felt bad about lying to the boys?** (*Possible response: The last word in the second paragraph on page 11 is* ashamed. *I look at the root word,* shame, *and I know that it names a bad feeling. I look at the prefix,* a-, *which means "to make," and the ending,* -ed, *which shows the past form of a word. So, I know Ingrid felt ashamed, or felt bad.*) **PREFIXES, SUFFIXES, AND ROOTS**

Ask: **What does Ingrid plan to do at the end of the story?** (*tell the people at the* Lakefront News *the truth about the fish*) **SEQUENCE**

Summarize the selection. Have students retell the main events in three or four sentences.

Answers to *Think About It* Questions

1. Ingrid just moved to Kansas from Finland, and she wanted to be friends with Sam and Travis. **SUMMARY**

2. Possible response: By that time, they are pals with Ingrid. **INTERPRETATION**

3. Students' responses will vary but should briefly describe Ingrid and the big catfish and should be written in the third person. **WRITE A NEWS STORY**

AFTER

Skill Review
pages 44–45

USE SKILL CARD 1B

(Focus Skill) Prefixes, Suffixes, and Roots

RETEACH **the skill.** Have students look at **side B of Skill Card 1: Prefixes, Suffixes, and Roots.** Read the skill reminder with them. Then ask volunteers to read the paragraph and the directions aloud.

Model filling out the chart with the first word, *usually*. Say:

- Leave the first column blank because *usually* has no prefix.

- In the second column, write the root word, *usual*.

- In the next column, write the suffix in *usually*: *-ly*.

- In the last column write *usually* and its meaning: *in a usual way*.

Suggest that pairs of students complete the chart together.

Point out some words with prefixes and suffixes in "The Hot and Cold Summer." Students may explain their meanings or enter them in the chart. Examples in the selection include *proudly*, *directly*, *removed*, *forkful*, *refill*, *activity*, *neighborhood*, *endlessly*.

FLUENCY BUILDER Be sure students have copies of *Intervention Practice Book* page 3. Explain that students will practice the sentences on the bottom half of the page by reading them aloud on tape. Assign new partners. Have students take turns reading the sentences aloud to each other and then reading them on tape. After students listen to the tape, have them tell how they think they have improved their reading of the sentences. Then have them read the sentences aloud on tape a second time with improved pacing and tone.

INTERVENTION PRACTICE BOOK

page 3

Expressive Writing: Narrative Sentences

Build on prior knowledge. Point out to students that the stories "A Fish Tale" and "The Hot and Cold Summer" are narratives. They tell stories by explaining what happened first, next, and last. Tell students that they will write narrative sentences about something that really happened to the class. Display the following framework.

What was the event?
>   **What happened first?**
>   **What happened next?**
>   **What happened last?**

Construct the text. "Share the pen" with students in a collaborative writing effort. As students dictate words and sentences, write them on the board or on chart paper. Ask questions and offer suggestions as needed. Help students choose a topic, and work with them to craft an interesting topic sentence that tells what the narrative is about. Remind students that they should use the first-person point of view, which involves using pronouns like *I* and *we*.

Then ask students what happened first. Write one or two sentences students provide. Ask students what happened after that. Work with students to have them offer several more sentences that tell what happened next. Then guide students to tell how the story ends.

Revisit the text. Go back and reread the sentences together. Ask: **Is the order of the events clear? Which words help show the order of events?** (*Possible response: first, next, then, last*)

- Guide students to make sure they have told the events from the first-person point of view by using pronouns such as *our* and *us*.

- Ask: **How can you let a reader know that your class was really at the event?** (*Possible response: tell about the thoughts and feelings of classmates*) Make any needed corrections.

- With students, reread the sentences orally.

> **On Your Own**
>
> Have all the students write their own personal narrative about something that happened to them. Remind them to tell what happened at the beginning, in the middle, and at the end and to use pronouns such as *I* and *me*.

Connect Spelling and Phonics

RETEACH short vowels /a/*a*, /i/*i*, /o/*o*, /u/*u*; long vowels /ā/*a-e*, /ī/*i-e*, /ō/*o-e*, /ōō/*u-e*. Write *bat*, *ten*, *rib*, *mop*, and *run* on the board. Remind students that these words have short vowel sounds and follow a consonant-vowel-consonant pattern. Then write *cage*, *life*, *rode*, and *tune* on the board. Remind students that these words have long vowel sounds and follow the vowel-consonant-e pattern. Then dictate the following words, and ask students to write them. After each word is written, display the correct spelling so students can proofread their work. They should draw a line through a misspelled word and write the correct spelling beside it.

I. glad*	2. case*	3. gift*	4. five*
5. spot*	6. poles*	7. brush*	8. tune

*Word appears in "A Fish Tale."

Dictate the following sentence for students to write: *Dan and Dale spot five plumes of smoke.*

Build and Read Longer Words

Remind students that they have learned how to decode words with short vowel sounds in a consonant-vowel-consonant pattern and words with long vowel sounds in a vowel-consonant-e pattern.

Write the word *bravely* on the board. Remind students that they can sometimes figure out a long word by removing prefixes or suffixes. In this word, they can notice the *a*-consonant-e pattern and decide that *brave* has the long *a* vowel sound. Have students blend the root word and the suffix to read the word *bravely*. Invite students to build other long words, such as *rerun*, *replace*, *unmade*, *shameful*, *niceness*, *pridefully*, *foggy*, *unspoken*, and *unruly*.

INTERVENTION
ASSESSMENT
BOOK

FLUENCY BUILDER Ask students to choose a passage from "A Fish Tale" to read aloud to a partner. Have students choose one of these passages they found particularly interesting or another:

- Read page I0. (From *Travis and Ingrid* . . . through . . . *dripping wet*. Total: 88 words)

- Read page I1. (From *The next day was* . . . through . . . *fish tale!*" Total: 92 words)

Ask students to read the selected passage aloud to their partners three times. Have students rate their own readings on a scale from I to 4.

Encourage readers to note their improvement from one reading to the next by completing sentence frames such as *I know my reading has improved because* _____.
The listening partner can offer positive feedback.

SCALE
I Not good
2 Pretty good
3 Good
4 Great!

Review Vocabulary

To revisit the Vocabulary Words prior to the weekly assessments, use these sentence frames. Have students write the correct answers. Discuss why the answers are correct.

1. Your best friend calls to tell you some **incredible** news. You
   a. ask what happened.   b. are bored.

2. You hear a **commotion** inside the gym. You know that
   a. nobody is inside.   b. a class is playing a game.

3. If you met an **authority** on the latest video game, you might ask
   a. for tips on playing it.   b. how to make a phone call.

4. A **souvenir** of your vacation reminds you of
   a. where you went.   b. how much the trip cost.

5. You and your best friend **vow** to stay friends forever. You have
   a. played a trick on her.   b. made a serious promise.

6. You come home from a soccer game at night and feel **exhausted**. You want to
   a. go to bed.   b. go outside to play.

Correct responses: 1a, 2b, 3a, 4a, 5b, 6a

This is a good time to show the Vocabulary Words and definitions on page 9. Have students copy them to use for studying for the vocabulary test.

★ Focus Skill Review Prefixes, Suffixes, and Roots

To review prefixes, suffixes, and roots before the weekly assessment, distribute *Intervention Practice Book* page 6. Have volunteers read aloud the directions and the sentences. Then guide students to use the chart to list the prefixes and suffixes in the words they identify and to tell what the words mean.

INTERVENTION
PRACTICE
BOOK

page 6

Review Test Prep

Ask students to turn to page 45 of the *Pupil Edition*. Call attention to the tips for answering the test questions. Tell students that paying attention to these tips can help them answer not only the test questions on this page but also questions on other tests.

DISTANT
VOYAGES

page 45

INTERVENTION
ASSESSMENT
BOOK

✔

Have students follow along as you read aloud each test question and the tip that goes with it. Discuss how knowing that the prefix *pre-* means "before" can help students remember that the word *prefix* means a "word part that has been added before the root word."

Self-Selected Reading

Have students select their own books to read independently. They might choose books from the classroom library shelf, or you may wish to offer a group of appropriate books from which students can choose.

- *Lonely No More* (See page 45M of the *Teacher's Edition* for a lesson plan.)

- *In My Momma's Kitchen* by Jerdine Nolen. Lothrop, Lee & Shepard, 1999.

- *The Adventures of Ali Baba Bernstein* by Johanna Hurwitz. Avon, 1995.

You may also wish to choose additional books that are the same genre or by the same author, or that have the same kind of text structure as the selection.

After students have chosen their books, give each student a copy of My Reading Log, which can be found on page R38 in the back of the *Teacher's Edition*. Have students fill in the information at the top of the form. Then have them use the log to keep track of their reading and to record their responses to the literature.

Conduct student-teacher conferences. Arrange time for each student to confer with you individually about his or her self-selected reading. Have students bring their Reading Logs to share with you at the conference. Students might also like to choose a favorite passage to read aloud to you. Ask questions about the book designed to stimulate discussion. For example, you might ask what information the student learned from a nonfiction text, how the author structured the text, or how illustrations or diagrams helped students understand the topic.

FLUENCY PERFORMANCE Have students read aloud to you the passage from "A Fish Tale" that they selected and practiced with their partners previously. Keep track of the number of words a student reads correctly. Ask the student to rate his or her own performance on the 1–4 scale. If students are not happy with their oral reading, give them an opportunity to continue practicing and then to read the passage to you again.

See *Oral Reading Fluency Assessment* for monitoring progress.

Use with

"Sees Behind Trees"

Review Phonics: Short Vowel /e/e; Long Vowel /ē/ee, ea, ey

Identify the sounds. Have students repeat the following sentence aloud three times: *Nell's red vest got wet in the shed.* Ask: **Which words have the /e/ sound?** (*Nell's, red, vest, wet, shed*) Then repeat this sentence aloud three times: *The teams will meet at Green Valley Camp.* Ask: **Which words have the /ē/ sound?** (*teams, meet, Green, Valley*)

Associate letters to sounds. Write on the board the two sentences above. Underline the words with the /e/ vowel sound in the first sentence and the /ē/ vowel sound in the second sentence. Point out the letter pattern that stands for the short or long e vowel sound in each word. For the word *Valley*, point out that letter *y* acts as a vowel.

Word blending. Model how to blend and read the word *green*. Slide your hand under the whole word as you elongate the sounds: /ggrrēēnn/. Then say the word naturally—*green*. Repeat with *vest*, *teams*, and *valley*.

Apply the skill. *Letter Substitution* Write the following words on the board, and have students read each aloud. Make the changes necessary to form the words in parentheses. Have students read each new word aloud.

fed (feed)   **dell** (deal)   **fell** (feeble)   **kept** (key)

INTERVENTION
PRACTICE
BOOK
page 8

Introduce Vocabulary

PRETEACH **lesson vocabulary.** Tell students that they are going to learn six new words that they will see again when they read a story called "Sees Behind Trees." Teach each Vocabulary Word using the process in the box.

Use the following suggestions or similar ideas to give the meaning or context.

> Write the word.
> Say the word.
> Track the word and have students repeat it.
> Give the meaning or context.

tread	Students may be more familiar with the usage of this word to refer to the rubber on a tire. Point out that it can also be used to refer to a sound.
moss	People today use moss to grow some houseplants. People long ago burned moss as fuel or used it as stuffing for mattresses and chairs.
sternly	Point out the suffix *-ly* and the base word *stern*. Doing something sternly means doing it in a no-nonsense way.
compose	This is a multiple-meaning word. Relate its meaning to children being out at recess and then composing themselves to begin class again.

exaggerate	Point out the /j/ consonant sound of the double *g*. In the story of Pinocchio, the puppet's nose would grow longer when he would exaggerate, or stretch the truth.
quiver	Ask students to look at the illustration on page 58 of the *Pupil Edition*. The quiver held the arrows of the warriors.

For vocabulary activities, see Vocabulary Games on pp. 2–7.

For vocabulary activities, see Vocabulary Games on pp. 2–7.

AFTER

Building Background and Vocabulary

Apply Vocabulary Strategies

Use familiar patterns. Explain to students that they can sometimes figure out new words by looking for familiar spelling patterns. They can also use the patterns to pronounce the words.

Use the word *tread* as an example. Point out that it has the *ea* letter pattern that stands for the short e vowel sound.

> **MODEL** I recognize the letter combination *tr*, as in the word *tree*. I also know that the letter *e* in this new word stands for the short *e* vowel sound. So, I can put the sounds together to read /tred/.

Tell students to apply this strategy in their reading.

RETEACH lesson vocabulary. Be sure each student has a set of word cards for the Vocabulary Words. Read aloud the following sentences, and have students hold up the appropriate word card. Reread the sentences with the appropriate word choices.

1. She heard the __(tread)__ of footsteps as her dad came to tuck her in.
2. We added __(moss)__ to the soil in the garden.
3. The librarian looked __(sternly)__ at the children who were arguing.
4. After nearly having a car accident, the man had to __(compose)__ himself.
5. The boy liked to __(exaggerate)__ by saying that his cat was a tiger.
6. Walnut pulled arrows from his __(quiver)__ and shot at the moss.

Vocabulary Words

tread sound of a footstep

moss green or brown plant that grows in clumps on other plants

sternly with a strict manner; in a stubborn way

compose to settle down; to become calm

exaggerate to enlarge beyond truth; to stretch the truth

quiver portable case for carrying arrows

FLUENCY BUILDER Using *Intervention Practice Book* page 7, read each word in the first column aloud and have students repeat it. Then have partners read the words in the first column aloud to each other. Follow the same procedure with each of the remaining columns. Then ask partners to take turns reading the sentences below the lists.

INTERVENTION PRACTICE BOOK
page 7

⭐(Focus Skill) Narrative Elements

PRETEACH **the skill.** Tell students that narrative elements are part of most fiction stories. Explain that an author tells a story by using characters, setting, a problem, and the solution, or answer.

Have students look at **side A of Skill Card 2: Narrative Elements**. Read aloud the introductory sentence and the definitions. Read the story aloud as students read it silently. Then call attention to the chart, and explain that you will work with them to fill it in with information from the story.

- Ask: **Who are the characters in the story "Lost Fish"?** (*John, Mike, Mark*) Have students fill in the information. Then ask: **What is the setting, or the place?** (*in a boat on Mirror Lake, near the shore*)

- Point out that the conflict is the problem the characters have. Ask: **What problem do they have?** (*The stringer of fish that they caught sank into the lake.*) Explain that the rising action— seeing the stringer in the water—shows how the characters work to solve the problem.

- Tell students that the turning point—putting the oar in the water—is the event that shows how the problem will be solved. The falling action tells about solving the problem. Ask: **How is the problem solved?** (*They loop the stringer and pull it up.*)

Prepare to Read: "Sees Behind Trees"

Preview. Tell students that "Sees Behind Trees" is historical fiction. It takes place in the past and has characters and events that seem real for that time. Remind students to watch for the narrative elements of characters, setting, problem or conflict, and solution.

DISTANT VOYAGES

pages 48–62

- **Pages 48–51:** I see pictures of Native American people in the woods. These people must be the characters. The setting is the woods.

- **Pages 52–55:** The people look very serious, or solemn. I think they have a problem they need to solve. In one picture the boy has a blindfold. It might be part of the problem or part of the solution.

- **Pages 56–59:** The characters are walking through the woods together. I think they are going to a place to solve the boy's problem.

Set purpose. Model setting a purpose for reading "Sees Behind Trees."

MODEL I will read to see what problem the boy has and how he solves it. I also want to find out what the blindfold is used for.

Reread and Summarize

Have students reread and summarize "Sees Behind Trees" in sections, as described in the chart below.

Pages 48–52

Let's reread pages 48–52 to recall what was difficult for the boy to do and what was easy for him to do.

Summary: The boy has difficulty seeing the object and hitting it with the arrow, even after practicing. However, he can do other things well.

Pages 53–55

As we read pages 53–55 let's remember how the mother helped the boy "see" with his ears.

Summary: The mother and the boy go out to practice again, but this time she blindfolds him. He begins to notice the sounds and smells.

Pages 56–57

Reread pages 56–57 to remember how the boy felt and how his father tried to help him be more relaxed for the contest.

Summary: The boy does not want to embarrass his father, so he goes to it unhappily.

Pages 59–60

Let's read pages 59–60 to recall what contest came before the regular contest.

Summary: The weroance announces a contest for the boys to use their senses of smell and hearing.

Pages 61–62

As we read pages 61–62 let's find out why the boy did not have to enter the regular contest and what name he was given.

Summary: The blindfolded boy hears Gray Fire walking in the forest and laughing. He is given the name "Sees Behind Trees."

FLUENCY BUILDER Be sure students have copies of *Intervention Practice Book* page 7. Call attention to the sentences on the bottom half of the page. Model appropriate pace, expression, and phrasing as you read each sentence, and have students read it after you. Then have students practice by reading the sentences aloud to a partner.

INTERVENTION
PRACTICE
BOOK
page 7

Directed Reading: "The Quiver" pp. 14–21

Tell students the story they will read today is a fiction story. Remind them to look for the narrative elements in the story. Tell them to identify the characters, setting, problem or conflict, and the solution as they read "The Quiver."

TAKE FLIGHT
pp. 14–21

Page 14

Read aloud the title of the story. Ask: **Who do you think the boy in the picture is?** (*Will; the main character*) ⭐ **NARRATIVE ELEMENTS**

Direct students' attention to the quiver Will is holding and, if necessary, explain that a quiver is a portable case for arrows. Ask: **Now that Will is lost, what do you think he will do next?** (*Possible response: try to find his way back to the wagons*) To help students understand Will's problem, model using the Create Mental Images strategy:

> **MODEL** The last paragraph says that Will was exploring the area and soon realized he was lost. I can picture in my mind how someone might act when he or she is lost. I can "see" in my mind how easy it is to get lost when you are not paying attention. ⭐ **CREATE MENTAL IMAGE**

Page 15

Have students read page 15 to learn the advice Pa has given to Will and whether Will follows it. Ask: **What has Pa told Will to do if he ever gets lost? Does Will follow Pa's advice?** (*Possible response: Pa has told Will not to panic and to stay in one place; Will doesn't follow his advice.*) **IMPORTANT DETAILS**

Page 16

After students read page 16, have them look at the illustration. Ask: **What is the blurry image that Will notices?** (*Possible response: another boy who is looking for something*) **IMPORTANT DETAILS**

Ask: **Why do you think the other boy begins to weep?** (*Possible responses: He has lost something important; he also is lost and afraid.*) **DRAW CONCLUSIONS**

Page 17

Ask: **What does the author mean when she says that Will and the other boy have "seen" each other's feelings?** (*Possible response: They each know the other is sad because they have seen each other crying.*) **AUTHOR'S CRAFT/APPRECIATE LANGUAGE**

Page 18

After students read page 18, ask: **How does the other boy figure out that Will is lost?** (*Possible response: Will draws a picture of a wagon and a team of oxen in the mud.*) **CAUSE/EFFECT**

Ask: **What do the other boy's actions tell you about him?** (*Possible response: He cares about others and is helpful.*) **CHARACTERS' TRAITS**

Page 19

Have students read page 19 to find out whether the other boy is able to help Will find his family. Ask: **How is Will able to spot the wagons?** (*Possible response: Will sees the deep ruts of wagon wheels on the land. The ruts help him find the wagons.*) **DRAW CONCLUSIONS**

Directed Reading: "The Quiver" pp. 14–21

Have students read page 20 to find out how Will's ma and pa react to his return. Model using the Create Mental Images strategy:

> **MODEL** The story says that Will's ma and pa just hugged him and let him tell about his adventure. I can picture in my mind the three people hugging each other and smiling at each other. This helps me know that Will's ma and pa were not angry but were very glad to have Will back. (Focus Strategy) **CREATE MENTAL IMAGES**

Summarize the selection. Have students think about what happens to Will after he gets lost in the woods. Then help them summarize the story.

Answers to *Think About It* Questions

1. Will gives the lost quiver back to him. He helps Will find the wagons and his ma and pa. **SUMMARY**

2. Possible response: No, Will does not feel bad. Will is very sad, and the boy is sad and weeping, too. **INTERPRETATION**

3. Diary entries should recount Will's getting lost and his initial fright and then relief at meeting the other boy in the woods, and should be written from Will's point of view. **WRITE A DIARY ENTRY**

(Focus Skill) Narrative Elements

AFTER

Skill Review
pages 68–69

USE SKILL CARD 2B

RETEACH the skill. Have students look at **side B of Skill Card 2: Narrative Elements.** Read the skill reminder with them. Ask a student to read the narrative elements in the box. Ask students to read the story "Windy Recess" silently. Then ask a student to read the story aloud. Direct students to work in pairs to complete the chart.

When they are finished, ask students to identify the characters in the story. (*Nancy, Barb, Eric, Mr. Smith*) Then ask them to name the setting. (*the playground*) Ask students what the problem is and how it is solved. (*The ball is on the roof. Eric tells Mr. Smith about the ball and Mr. Smith gives them another ball.*)

FLUENCY BUILDER Distribute copies of *Intervention Practice Book* page 7. Assign students new partners, and have them practice reading the sentences at the bottom of the page. This time, tape-record their readings. Have students take turns reading the sentences aloud to each other and commenting on each other's performance. Each student should report on what the other student did well and make suggestions for improving the reading next time. Students then read the sentences again and report on their improvement.

Expressive Writing: Descriptive Sentences

Build on prior knowledge. Tell students that they are going to write descriptive sentences about a circus. Students should use words that appeal to the five senses: *sight, hearing, smell, touch,* and *taste.* Write the following on the board:

> popcorn
> cotton candy
> costumes and painted faces
> band playing
> peanut shells on the ground

Tell students to think of words that describe popcorn. (*Possible responses: fresh, popping, buttery, fluffy, white*) Write their suggestions next to *popcorn*. Repeat for the remaining ideas.

Construct the text. "Share the pen" with students in a collaborative writing effort. As students dictate phrases and sentences, write them on the board or on chart paper, guiding the process by asking questions and offering suggestions as needed. For example:

- The smell of buttery, fresh popcorn filled our noses.
- We bought fluffy bags of sweet pink cotton candy.
- Clowns with silly painted faces and polka-dotted costumes were juggling.
- Lively march music played by shiny brass horns seemed to make the air sparkle.
- Peanut shells crunched under our feet as we hurried to our seats.

Revisit the text. Read the sentences aloud with students. Ask: **How can we make the sentences more descriptive?** (*Possible response: add lively describing words*)

- Guide students to add other words that describe things, people, and actions. Point out that describing words that tell about things and people are adjectives and that those that describe actions are adverbs.
- Point out the use of the comma in descriptions like *buttery, fresh popcorn*.
- Have students read the revised sentences aloud.

On Your Own

Have students write a descriptive paragraph about some place they have visited or would like to visit. It could be a vacation place, a museum, a ball game, or a shopping mall. Remind students to use descriptive words that appeal to the senses.

Connect Spelling and Phonics

RETEACH **short vowel /e/e; long vowel /ē/ee, ea, ey.** Dictate the following words, and have students write them. Then display the correct spellings so students can proofread their work. They should draw a line through a misspelled word and write the correct spelling.

l. west*	2. telling*	3. deep*	4. trees*
5. team	6. speaking*	7. hockey	8. jockey

***Word appears in "The Quiver."**

Dictate the following sentence for students to write: *I went to greet the hockey team.*

Build and Read Longer Words

Write the word *getting* on the board. Point out to students that when the ending *-ing* is added to a word that has a short vowel sound, the final consonant is usually doubled. Also point out that two-syllable words that have a double consonant are usually divided into syllables between the doubled consonants. Draw a line between the *t*'s in *getting*, and say each syllable as you point to it. Then read the word naturally—*getting*. Repeat with the words *puddle, letting, wedding,* and *glasses.*

INTERVENTION
ASSESSMENT
BOOK

Write the word *sleeping* on the board. Tell students that they can sometimes figure out how to pronounce longer words by breaking them into syllables and looking for familiar patterns. Cover *-ing,* and have a volunteer say the root word *sleep.* Then cover *sleep* and have students say *-ing.* Point out that *ee* in *sleep* has the /ē/ sound. Have students blend the word parts to read the word *sleeping.* Follow the same procedure with these words: *fleeing, greeted, sealing, treatment, monkey.* Give students other long words with /ē/*ea, ee, ey.*

FLUENCY BUILDER Have students choose a passage from "The Quiver" to read aloud to a partner. Have students choose one of these passages or another they particularly enjoyed.

- Read pages 14–15. (*From Will was lost . . .* through *. . . We'll find you"?* Total: 116 words)
- Read pages 16–17. (*From A blurry image . . .* through *. . . to that boy.* Total: 91 words)
- Read pages 18–19. (*From The boy looked . . .* through *. . . see the wagons.* Total: 105 words)

Students read the selected passage aloud to their partners three times. Have the listener rate each reading on a scale of 1 to 4.

Review Vocabulary

To revisit Vocabulary Words prior to the weekly assessment, use these sentence frames. Read the statements to students, and ask them to write the correct answer. Go over the answers, and discuss why the answers are correct.

1. We heard the **tread** of footsteps in the hall, so we knew that
    a. mom was home.   b. no one was home.
2. Clumps of **moss** might grow
    a. on icebergs.   b. on the sides of trees.
3. Our teacher spoke **sternly** to us, so we knew she
    a. was happy with our actions.   b. was unhappy with our actions.
4. After **recess** the students composed themselves to
    a. return to their class.   b. play kickball.
5. It would be **exaggeration** to say that a basketball player is
    a. 7 feet tall.   b. 12 feet tall.
6. The **quiver** on Walnut's back carried
    a. his lunch.   b. his arrows.

Correct responses: 1a, 2b, 3b, 4a, 5b, 6b

You may want to display the Vocabulary Words and definitions on page 19 and have students copy them to use when they study for the vocabulary test.

 ## Review Narrative Elements

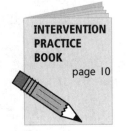

INTERVENTION PRACTICE BOOK

page 10

Before the weekly assessment on narrative elements, distribute *Intervention Practice Book* page 10, and have a student read aloud the box at the top of the page. Ask students to read the story silently, and then have a student read it aloud. Have students fill in the chart and then share their responses.

Review Test Prep

INTERVENTION ASSESSMENT BOOK

Direct students' attention to the tips on page 69 of the *Pupil Edition*. Tell students that paying attention to the tips can help them answer not only these test questions but also questions on other tests. Have students read the tips silently as you read them aloud. Have students read the story and answer each question. Remind them to use the tips when answering the questions.

Self-Selected Reading

Have students select their own books to read independently. They may choose books from the classroom library shelf, or you may wish to offer a group of appropriate books from which students can choose. Titles might include

- *Fire from Ice* (See page 69M of the *Teacher's Edition* for a lesson plan.)

- *Morning Girl* by Michael Dorris. Disney, 2000.

- *Anasazi* by Leonard Everett Fisher. Atheneum, 1997.

You may also wish to choose additional books that are the same genre, are by the same author, or that have the same kind of text structure as the selection.

After students have chosen their books, give each student a copy of My Reading Log, which can be found on page R38 in the back of the *Teacher's Edition*. Have students fill in the information at the top of the form. Then have them use the log to keep track of their reading and to record their responses to literature.

Conduct student-teacher conferences. Arrange time for each student to confer with you individually about his or her selected reading. Have students bring their Reading Logs to share with you. Students might also like to choose a favorite passage to read aloud to you. To give students more practice with summarizing and paraphrasing, ask them to read a short section and to summarize and then paraphrase it.

FLUENCY PERFORMANCE Have students read aloud to you the passage from "The Quiver" that they selected and practiced with their partners. Keep track of the number of words each student reads correctly. Ask students to rate their own performances on the 1–4 scale. If students are not happy with their oral reading, give them an opportunity to continue practicing and to reread the passage again.

See *Oral Reading Fluency Assessment* for monitoring progress.

Use with

"Yang the Third and Her Impossible Family"

Review Phonics: Vowel Variant /ôl/*al, all*

Identify the sound. Have students repeat this sentence: *June called to ask if she could get a malt.* Ask students which words have the /ôl/ sound heard in *halt*. (*called, malt*)

Associate letters to sounds. Write the above sentence on the board. Circle the words *called* and *malt*, and ask students how these words are alike. (*the /ôl/ sound; al or all*) Underline the letters *al* or *all* in each word. Tell students that in these words, the letters *al* and *all* stand for the /ôl/ sound. Write the words *fall*, *salt*, *tall*, and *false* on the board, and underline the *al* or *all* in each.

Word blending. Model how to blend the sounds and letters to read the word *fall*. Slide your hand under the letters as you elongate the sounds /ffôôll/. Then say the word naturally—*fall*. Follow a similar procedure with *salt*, *tall*, and *false*. Then write the words *talk* and *balk* on the board. Point out to students that words with *alk* have the same /ô/ sound, but the *l* is silent. Read *talk* and *balk*, and have students repeat them.

**INTERVENTION
PRACTICE
BOOK**

page 12

Apply the skill. *Consonant Substitution* Write the following words on the board. Make the changes necessary to form the words in parentheses. Have a student read aloud each new word.

hall (call)   **malt** (salt)   **walk** (talk)

Introduce Vocabulary

PRETEACH **lesson vocabulary.** Tell students they are going to learn six new words from "Yang the Third and Her Impossible Family." Teach each vocabulary word using this process.

Use these suggestions to give the context.

audition	This word is related to *audio* and comes from the Latin word *audire*, meaning "to hear."
sonata	This word comes from the Italian word *sonare*, "to sound."

> Write the word.
> Say the word.
> Track the word and have students repeat it.
> Give the meaning or context.

accompanist	*Companion* is related to this word. A *companion* is someone who goes along.
accompaniment	Use the previous word in context: *He had to practice with his* accompanist *before he performed his solo.*
grimaced	Use facial expressions to show students the difference between *grimace*, *smile*, and *frown*.
simultaneously	This word comes from the Latin word *simul* which means "at the same time."

AFTER

Building Background and Vocabulary

Apply Vocabulary Strategies

Decode multisyllabic words. Model decoding *audition* by breaking it into smaller parts.

> **MODEL** This is a word with several syllables. I see that it ends with -*tion*, which I can pronounce. The first two syllables are *au* and *di*. When I put the syllables together, I pronounce this word au-di-tion.

Tell students to use this strategy on *accompanist* on page 74.

Vocabulary Activity

Read aloud the following sentences. Ask students to hold up the word card that completes each sentence.

I. He was very nervous before his ___(audition)___ .

2. She sat and listened to the ___(sonata)___ on her new CD.

3. The ___(accompanist)___ for my solo made a mistake.

4. I practiced the ___(accompaniment)___ without the soloist for weeks.

5. He ___(grimaced)___ when they announced who the finalists were.

6. They ___(simultaneously)___ blurted out the same answer.

FLUENCY BUILDER Use *Intervention Practice Book* page 11. Read aloud each of the words in the first column and have students repeat it. Then have students work in pairs and take turns reading the words aloud to each other. Follow the same procedure with each of the remaining columns. Then have students read aloud the entire list.

INTERVENTION PRACTICE BOOK

page 11

(Focus Skill) Prefixes, Suffixes, and Roots

PRETEACH **the skill.** Explain to students that knowing the meanings of prefixes, suffixes, and roots will help them understand the meanings of unfamiliar words.

Have students look at **side A of Skill Card 3: Prefixes, Suffixes, and Roots.** Explain that each word part carries meaning. Discuss the prefixes, suffixes, and roots in the charts, and point out the example words. Ask students to name other words they know that contain prefixes, suffixes, and roots.

- Write the following words on the board:
  run, build, afraid, tie, eager, final, wish, and *rest.*

- Have students use the prefixes and suffixes in the charts to make new words. (rerun, rebuild, unafraid, untie, eagerly, finally, wishful, and restful)

Prepare to Read: "Yang the Third and Her Impossible Family"

Preview. Tell students that they are going to read a selection called "Yang the Third and Her Impossible Family." Explain that this is a realistic fiction story. Point out that this kind of story has characters and events that are like real people and events. Then preview the selection.

DISTANT VOYAGES
pages 72–84

- **Pages 72–73:** I see the title of the story, and an illustration of a girl and her cat. I think this is probably an illustration of Yang the Third, or Mary.

- **Pages 74–75:** I notice the music notes on the top of page 74. I think this story is about music. Perhaps Mary plays an instrument. There is some large text that says something about a brother who cares about her feelings. Maybe she has a special relationship with this brother.

- **Pages 80–81:** The illustrations on these pages show another girl playing her violin with a pianist accompanying her. There are people sitting and it seems to be someone's living room. I wonder why the girl looks so unhappy with her violin.

  MODEL From previewing these pages, I think this is a story about a girl who loves music. For some reason, her friend who plays the violin looks unhappy.

Tell students to set a purpose for their reading, based on their preview. Remind them that one purpose for reading a story may be to enjoy a story.

Reread and Summarize

Have students reread and summarize each section of "Yang the Third and Her Impossible Family" using the questions in the chart below.

Pages 74–75

Let's reread pages 74–75 to remember the two girls in the story and what is happening in their lives.

Summary: Holly is being pushed by her mother to do an audition. Mary is trying to get her mother, who is still very Chinese, to be more accepted by Americans.

Pages 76–79

As we reread pages 76–79, let's remember Yang's problem.

Summary: Mary knows that her mother could help Holly in her audition, but she also knows that Holly does not want to go to the tryout.

Pages 80–81

When we reread pages 80–81, notice how polite the Yang family tries to be and how that politeness is misunderstood.

Summary: Mrs. Hanson praises Mary's mother for her playing. Her mother follows the Chinese custom of refusing compliments.

Pages 82–84

On pages 82–84, let's find out what important lesson Mary learns.

Summary: Holly and her mother are upset because they think the Yangs don't want Holly to do well at the audition. When Mary tries to explain, she learns more about the complexity of English. She learns that it is not just her mother who makes embarrassing mistakes, but that she does as well. Holly and Mrs. Hanson also learn more about Chinese customs and become more understanding.

FLUENCY BUILDER Use *Intervention Practice Book* page 11. Call attention to the sentences at the bottom of the page. Model reading the sentences. Have students repeat after you, using the same pace, expression, and phrasing you used. Then have students practice reading aloud each sentence three times to a partner.

INTERVENTION
PRACTICE
BOOK

page 11

Directed Reading of "The Audition" pp. 22–28

Ask a volunteer to read the title of the story. Help students identify Jean and the pianist. Have them read page 22 to find out who else is at the audition. (*Chad, Jan, other kids*) Ask: **Why do you think Jean thinks, "Oh no!" when she sees Aldo and his cello?** (*Possible response: Jean also plays the cello, and she is afraid that Aldo might play better than she does.*) **INTERPRET CHARACTERS' MOTIVATIONS**

TAKE FLIGHT
pages 22–28

Page 22–23

Ask: **How does Jean feel about her ability to play the cello?** (*She doesn't think that she plays very well, but she still hopes she can win the audition.*) **DETERMINE CHARACTERS' EMOTIONS**

Pages 24–25

Read aloud pages 24 and 25. Then say,

> **MODEL** I'm not sure why Miss Small would tell the other band members to be patient and sit still. I ask myself, "Why might the band members be impatient and act nervously?" I know that auditions can make people nervous. Miss Small must think that some of the band members are anxious to audition. (Focus Strategy) **SELF-QUESTION**

Ask: **How do you think Aldo feels when his string breaks?** (*Possible responses: He feels angry, disappointed, and upset.*) **DETERMINE CHARACTERS' EMOTIONS**

Page 26–27

Ask: **What happens to Aldo after his string breaks?** (*Possible response: He has to stop playing because he doesn't have a spare string.*) **CAUSE-EFFECT**

Ask: **How does Jean feel when she first realizes that Aldo cannot finish his audition?** (*Possible response: She is glad because now she has a better chance of winning the audition.*) **DETERMINE CHARACTERS' EMOTIONS**

Jean stops to think about what has happened. What does this reaction tell you about her? (*Possible response: She wants what is best for the band.*) **DETERMINE CHARACTERS' TRAITS**

Ask: **Why do you think Jean feels she has won something, too?** (*Possible response: She knows she has done the right thing by not acting selfishly.*) **INTERPRET CHARACTERS' MOTIVATIONS**

Summarize the selection. Ask students to think about what happened first, next, and last at the audition. Then have them summarize the story. Then have them complete *Intervention Practice Book*, page 13.

Answers to *Think About It* Questions

1. A string on his cello has broken. He can't play the sonata. **SUMMARY**

2. Jean feels she has won the audition because Aldo can't play anymore. At the end, she feels she has won because she has helped Aldo. **INTERPRETATION**

3. Accept reasonable responses. Compositions should include dialogue in which Aldo thanks Jean for her help. **WRITE AN ENDING**

Page 28

AFTER

Skill Review
pages 88–89

USE SKILL CARD 3B

(Focus Skill) Prefixes, Suffixes, and Roots

Have students look at **side B of Skill Card 3: Prefixes, Suffixes, and Roots.** Read aloud the skill reminder. Ask a volunteer to read the paragraph aloud. Point out the underlined words in the paragraph and ask students what they notice about the words (They all contain a prefix, suffix, or a root.)

Have students write each underlined word in the first column of the chart. Then have them complete the chart by writing the prefix, suffix, or root for each word.

After students have completed their charts, call on volunteers to tell the meanings of the words, using the definitions of the prefixes, suffixes, and roots they learned on Side A of the Skill Card.

FLUENCY BUILDER Be sure students have copies of *Intervention Practice Book* page 11. Explain that they will practice the sentences on the bottom of the page by reading them aloud on tape. Have students choose new partners. Have students take turns reading the sentences aloud to each other and then reading them on tape. After students listen to the tape, have them tell how his or her reading has improved. Then have them record the sentences again.

INTERVENTION PRACTICE BOOK

page 11

Expressive Writing: Story

Build on prior knowledge. Tell students that you are going to work together to write a two-paragraph realistic fiction story.

Work with students to think of a character, setting, and a plot that includes a problem and a solution. Draw a story map on the board to help students organize the story.

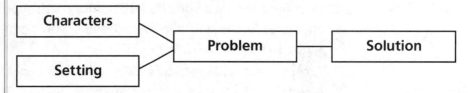

Construct the text. "Share the pen" with students. Use the suggestions below to guide students through the process. Ask for a volunteer to supply the next sentence.

- Write a sentence that introduces the character and the setting. Tell students to use the completed story map to guide them.

- Write down the next sentence suggested by the volunteer. Then ask for another volunteer to supply the next sentence. Remind the class that the story needs to have a problem, and somehow the character needs to resolve the problem.

- Guide students in bringing the story to a conclusion.

Revisit the Text. As students revise their story, remind them to make sure the problem and the solution are realistic. Ask them to review the story events to see if they are in a logical order. Have a volunteer read the story aloud.

On Your Own

Have students write a story in ten sentences. Tell them to make sure to include the story, characters, a setting, and a problem that is resolved at the end.

Connect Spelling and Phonics

RETEACH **vowel variant /ôl/ *al, all*.** Remind students that the /ôl/ sound can be spelled *all* or *al*. Have students number a sheet of paper from 1–8. Dictate the following words and have students write them on their papers. After the students write each word, display the correct spelling so students can proofread their work. Have them draw a line through a misspelled word and write the correct spelling beside it.

I. waltz*	2. halt*	3. walrus	4. wall*
5. hall*	6. small*	7. talking*	8. stalk

*Word appears in "The Audition."

Dictate the following sentence for students to write: *The tall bald man talked as he walked past the walnut tree.*

Build and Read Longer Words

Write the word *sidewalk* on the board. Tell students that when they see a longer word, they can check if it is made up of two shorter words. Cover *walk*, and have students read the word *side*. Then cover *side* and have them read the word *walk*. Have students blend the two word parts to form the longer word *sidewalk*. Repeat the procedure with *windfall*, *baseball*, *pitfall*, and *basketball*.

INTERVENTION
ASSESSMENT
BOOK

FLUENCY BUILDER Have students choose a passage from "The Audition" to read aloud to a partner. You may have students choose passages they found particularly interesting, or have them choose one of the following options:

- Pages 22–23. (Total words: 103)
- Pages 24–25. (Total words: 102)

Ask students to read the selection aloud to their partners three times. Have students rate their own readings on a scale of 1 to 4. Encourage students to rate their progress from readings they have previously completed.

Review Vocabulary

Before the weekly assessment, review the core vocabulary words. Then, read the statements to students and ask them to write the correct answers on their papers. Go over the answers and discuss why the answer is correct.

1. He had to go to his audition, meaning
   a. his tryout
   b. his rehearsal

2. She loved his new sonata, which is
   a. a musical composition of several movements.
   b. a dance routine using slow movements.

3. The accompanist for the solo is
   a. the person who introduces the soloist.
   b. the person who plays music to support the solo.

4. She was fully prepared to play the accompaniment, which is
   a. the solo sections of the sonata
   b. the music that supports the main part.

5. When she got a shot, she grimaced, which was how
   a. she expressed pain.
   b. she sang.

6. He decided to submit his poems to two magazines simultaneously. That means
   a. he submitted them at the same time.
   b. he submitted them one after the other.

Correct responses: 1a, **2**a, **3**b, **4**b, **5**a, **6**a.

Prefixes, Suffixes, and Roots

Review prefixes, suffixes, and roots before the weekly assessment by having students name some common affixes and roots. Then have them complete *Intervention Practice Book* page 14.

Review Test Prep

Ask students to turn to page 89 of the *Pupil Edition*. Point out the tips for answering the test questions. Tell students that these tips can help them answer not only the test questions on this page but also other test questions like them.

Have students follow along as you read each question. Help students understand that they should use the definition of the prefix or suffix to determine the meaning of each word. Tell students that it is important to read each test question carefully before answering it.

Self-Selected Reading

Encourage students to select their own books to read on their own. If students have difficulty selecting a book, suggest titles such as these:

- *Kwan's Big Performance* by Kimberly Jackson. See page 89K of the *Teacher's Edition* for a lesson plan for reading this book.

- *The Laziest Boy in the World,* by Lensey Namioka. Holiday House, 1998.

- *Max Found Two Sticks,* by Brian Pinkney. Aladdin Paperbacks, 1997.

In addition, you may want to suggest books that are the same genre or by the same author, or those that have the same kind of text structure as the selection.

Using "My Reading Log" Have students fill out the information at the top of their personal copy of "My Reading Log", found on page R38 in the back of the *Teacher's Edition*. Tell students to use the log to keep track of their reading and to record their responses to the literature.

Conduct student-teacher conferences. Arrange for an individual conference time with each student to discuss his or her self-selected reading. Tell students to bring their Reading Logs to share during the conference. You may also want to have the student choose a favorite passage to read aloud to you. Then ask questions designed to stimulate discussion.

FLUENCY PERFORMANCE Have students read aloud the passage from "The Audition" that they practiced. Keep track of the number of words the student reads correctly. Ask each student to rate his or her performance on the 1 to 4 scale. If students aren't happy with their oral reading, give them an opportunity for additional practice.

See *Oral Reading Fluency Assessment* for monitoring progress.

Use with

"Dear Mrs. Parks"

Review Phonics: *R*-controlled Vowel /är/*ar*

Identify the sound. Have students repeat the following sentence aloud three times: *You can see the stars sparkle from the dark backyard.* Ask students which words have the /är/ sound. (*stars, sparkle, dark, backyard*)

Associate letters to sound. Write on the board the sentence above. Circle *stars, sparkle, dark,* and *backyard,* and ask students how these words are alike. (*/är/ sound; the letters* ar). Tell students that in each of these words, the letters *ar* stand for the /är/ sound they hear in *car*.

Word blending. Model blending the sounds of the letters in *stars* to read the word. Point to *s* and say /s/. Point to *t* and say /t/. Draw your hand under *ar* and say /är/. Point to *s* and say /z/. Slide your hand under the entire word as you elongate the sounds: /sstärzz/. Then say the word naturally—*stars*. Repeat with *sparkle, dark,* and *backyard*.

Apply the skill. *Letter Substitution* Write the following words on the board, and have students read each aloud. Make the changes necessary to form the words in parentheses. Have students read each new word aloud. Try to give every student an opportunity to respond.

INTERVENTION
PRACTICE
BOOK

page 16

mat (mark)	**can** (card)	**dash** (dart)	**standing** (starting)
bat (bar)	**chat** (charm)	**past** (part)	**span** (spark)

Introduce Vocabulary

PRETEACH lesson vocabulary. Tell students they are going to learn seven new words they will see again when they read a story called "Dear Mrs. Parks." Teach each vocabulary word, using the process in the box.

Use the following suggestions or similar ideas to give the meaning or context.

> Write the word.
> Say the word.
> Track the word and have students repeat it.
> Give the meaning or context.

ridiculed   The actor was ridiculed for not knowing his lines.

dignity   The king and queen entered the room with much dignity.

counsel   The teacher will counsel the students as they write the class play.

potential   The race car was being driven slowly, but it had the potential to go very fast.

inspire   When the team was losing, the fans tried to inspire them to play well.

correspondence	The mail carrier brings correspondence to our home in the morning.
mentor	When Maria helped the new student learn about the school, she acted as a mentor.

For vocabulary activities see Vocabulary Games on pages 2–7.

Apply Vocabulary Strategies

Use word, sentence, and paragraph context. Explain that students can sometimes understand an unfamiliar word by looking for clues in other parts of a sentence or passage. Use these sentences to model the strategy: *On Friday evening the Lee family packed some suitcases. They were planning a weekend excursion to the mountains.*

> **MODEL** The word *excursion* is unfamiliar to me. The sentences mention suitcases, the weekend, and mountains. So, I think that an excursion must be a trip.

Tell students to use word, sentence, and paragraph context as they read.

RETEACH **lesson vocabulary.** Have students listen to the following sentences. Be sure each student has a set of word cards with the Vocabulary Words. Read the sentences and ask students to hold up the appropriate word card. Reread the sentences with the appropriate word choices.

1. The newspaper writer (ridiculed) the movie for being too silly.
2. The band marched with (dignity) , and everyone clapped.
3. The president needs good (counsel) when there is a serious problem.
4. The rocket had the (potential) to go to Mars, but it went only to the moon.
5. The teacher had the ability to (inspire) her students to do their best.
6. Our mailbox was filled with (correspondence) and junk mail.
7. Mrs. Jones was a (mentor) who helped new workers learn their jobs.

Vocabulary Words

ridiculed made fun of

dignity proud, calm, and controlled behavior

counsel to give advice and support

potential ability or power to do something in the future

inspire to make someone feel excited about something

correspondence letter writing

mentor a wise, caring adviser

FLUENCY BUILDER Distribute *Intervention Practice Book* page 15. Read each word aloud and have students repeat it. Then have students work in pairs and take turns reading the words to each other. Then ask partners to take turns reading each of the sentences below the lists of words.

INTERVENTION PRACTICE BOOK

page 15

 **Make Judgments**

PRETEACH the skill. Tell students that when authors write stories, they are communicating ideas and messages. Explain that when we read, we need to identify statements that support the message. Point out that when we find details that support the message, we can make valid judgments about the message.

USE SKILL CARD 4A

Have students look at **side A of Skill Card 4: Make Judgments.** Read the explanation about making a judgment. Have students examine the picture and describe what is happening.

Tell students to read the story silently as you read it aloud. Read the first statement.

- **Is the statement valid?** (*yes*) **What evidence makes it a valid judgment?** (*Although Father said it was too windy, Jason flew his kite.*)

- **Is the second statement valid? How do you know?** (*No; she scolded him.*) **Is the third statement valid? How do you know?** (*Yes; he may have crashed a kite on a windy day at one time.*)

Explain that in nonfiction, evidence that supports a valid judgment is reasonable, reliable, and based on facts.

Prepare to Read: "Dear Mrs. Parks"

Preview. Tell students they are going to read a selection called "Dear Mrs. Parks." Explain that this selection includes a number of letters in which Rosa Parks answers children's questions. Ask students to look for evidence to learn about Rosa Parks' character so they can make valid judgments about her. Then preview the selection.

DISTANT VOYAGES
pages 92–104

- **Pages 92–93:** I see a picture of a woman who must be Rosa Parks. Her picture seems to be on a postage stamp. Other pictures show other African Americans with her.

- **Pages 94–95:** I see two letters at the top of the pages. I notice people using a computer and a man and a boy sharing something. I see an old car and a new car, too.

- **Pages 96–97:** I see a letter and postmarks on these pages. Students in a class are raising their hands to answer a question or say something.

- **Pages 98–99:** There are two people in a bedroom or hospital room. Maybe one of them wrote one of the letters.

Set purpose. Model setting a purpose for reading "Dear Mrs. Parks."

MODEL I want to read to find out who wrote the leters and what the letters say. I also want to find out who Mrs. Parks is.

Reread and Summarize

Have students reread and summarize "Dear Mrs. Parks" in sections as described in the chart below.

Pages 92–93

Let's reread pages 92–93 to recall who is writing this story.

Summary: Rosa Parks is writing the story. The story will include letters from students and her replies to them.

Pages 94–97

Let's reread Mrs. Parks's letters on pages 94–97 and her responses.

Summary: Mrs. Parks tells Jimmy to always ask questions. She tells Richard that no one knows everything and to keep learning things. She tells Shata to keep working hard even though others make fun of her.

Pages 98–101

Let's reread pages 98-101 to see what Mrs. Parks learned from her grandmother.

Summary: Rosa Parks learned personal dignity from her grandmother, who taught her at home. She also learned that listening to older people can help others learn about the past and keep the past alive.

Pages 102–104

Reread pages 102–104 to learn how Mrs. Parks says things have changed over the years.

Summary: Rosa Parks says that many good things have happened in our country in the past but that people must keep working to make things better. She tells Larry that each person has the ability to make a difference in the world.

FLUENCY BUILDER Be sure students have copies of *Intervention Practice Book* page 15. Call attention to the sentences at the bottom of the page. Model appropriate pace, expression, and phrasing as you read each sentence, and have students read it after you. Then have students practice by reading the sentences aloud to a partner.

INTERVENTION
PRACTICE
BOOK

page 15

Directed Reading: "Lessons from Barbara Jordan" pp. 30–37

Take
Flight
pp. 30–37

Page 30

Ask a volunteer to read the title of the story. Explain that the illustration shows Jane Barr using a laptop computer to write an e-mail message. Make sure students understand that the words on the page are the message that Jane has written. Have them read page 30. Ask: **What does Jane ask?** (*She asks her grandmother what Barbara Jordan was like.*) **IMPORTANT DETAILS**

Why would Jane's grandmother know anything about Barbara Jordan? (*She met her once.*) **CAUSE/EFFECT**

Page 31

Have students review pages 30–31 to analyze the format of the letters. Model the Use Text Structure and Format strategy:

> **MODEL** I can read the names after the labels *FROM* and *TO* at the top of each message to know who has written it and who has received it. The other labels tell me the date and time it was sent and what the message is about. I can also read the greeting of each letter to see who it was written to. (Focus Strategy) **USE TEXT STRUCTURE AND FORMAT**

Have students read page 31 to find out what Grandma says in her reply to Jane's message. Ask: **Why was Grandma inspired by meeting Barbara Jordan?** (*Barbara Jordan was a smart woman who had dignity and confidence.*) **MAIN IDEA**

Page 32

Have students look at the picture on page 32. Ask: **Who do you think the picture is of?** (*Barbara Jordan*) Have them read page 32 to find out what Jane's mother tells her about Barbara Jordan. (*She sat in Congress.*) **IMPORTANT DETAILS**

Page 33

Have students read page 33 to find out how Barbara Jordan got her start. Ask: **Why was it unusual for Barbara Jordan to be in the Texas Senate?** (*At the time it was rare for African Americans to be in Texas's state senate.*) **IMPORTANT DETAILS**

How did Barbara Jordan's life change after she was elected to the U.S. Congress for the third time? (*Possible responses: She became sick; she moved back to Texas; she became a teacher.*) **SEQUENCE/SUMMARIZE**

Page 34

After students read page 34, ask: **Was Jane successful in gathering information about Barbara Jordan by using technology? Why or why not?** (*Possible response: She was very successful because she got facts in e-mails from her grandmother and she found pictures and other facts by using the World Wide Web.*) **STORY EVENTS**

Page 35

Have students read page 35 to find out how Grandma feels about Barbara Jordan's life and why she feels that way. (*She admires Barbara Jordan's life because Barbara Jordan inspired people to tell the truth, to keep their promises, and to help others.*) **SUMMARIZE CHARACTERS' EMOTIONS**

INTERVENTION PRACTICE BOOK

page 17

Ask: **What does Grandma hope Jane will do?** (*be like Barbara Jordan and make small sacrifices to help humanity*) **THEME**

Have students read page 36 to find out whether Jane's talk was a success. Ask: **Was Jane's talk a success? How do you know?** (*It was a success because the essay shows an A+, and she tells Grandma that the class liked the talk.*) (Focus Skill) **MAKE JUDGMENTS**

Summarize the selection. Have students write two sentences to summarize how Jane learned about Barbara Jordan.

Answers to *Think About It* Questions

1. Jane's grandmother once met Barbara Jordan, so she can tell Jane what Jordan was like. Jane needs more facts about Jordan's life, so she uses the Web. **SUMMARY**

2. Possible response: Barbara Jordan was smart, confident, and inspiring. **INTERPRETATION**

3. E-mails should follow the format used in the selection. They should express thanks and tell what the students learned from the visit. **WRITE AN E-MAIL**

AFTER

Skill Review
pages 112–113

USE SKILL CARD 4B

(Focus Skill) Make Judgments

RETEACH the skill. Have students look at **side B of Skill Card 4: Make Judgments.** Read the skill reminder to students.

Read the story "Safe Halloween" to students as they read it silently. Then ask a volunteer to read the story aloud. Direct students to the first set of three lines labeled Evidence, and ask a student to read the lines aloud. Then ask students to use the statements to write a valid judgment. (*Possible response: Joe and Tina are wearing safe costumes and are following safety rules.*) Follow the same procedure for the second set of lines labeled Evidence. (*Possible response: Phil is not visible or safe in his costume.*)

FLUENCY BUILDER Be sure students have copies of *Intervention Practice Book* page 15. Explain that students will practice the sentences at the bottom of the page by reading them aloud on tape. Assign new partners. Have students take turns reading the sentences aloud to each other. Tell students to comment on each other's performance. Students should report on what their partners did well and make suggestions to improve the reading next time. Students should then read the sentences again and report on whether they feel they improved.

INTERVENTION PRACTICE BOOK

page 15

Expressive Writing: Narrative Paragraph

Build on prior knowledge. Rosa Parks shared some of her letters from students and her responses. Explain that writing that tells about experiences is called narrative writing and that students will write a narrative paragraph about an experience. Ask students to brainstorm experiences they have had with birthday parties, either their own parties or parties for others. Write their ideas on the board.

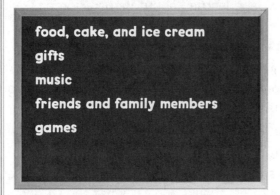

food, cake, and ice cream

gifts

music

friends and family members

games

Construct the text. "Share the pen" with students in a collaborative writing effort. As students dictate phrases and sentences about a birthday party, write them on the board or on chart paper. Guide the process by asking questions and offering suggestions. Begin by constructing a sentence about the main idea. Ask: **Let's write a sentence that tells what the event was.** Prompt students to dictate sentences in the first-person point of view. Ask: **How will a reader know the experience happened to you?** (*use pronouns such as I, me, we, and us*) Help students add details. Ask: **How can we make our sentences lively?** (*add descriptive words*)

Revisit the text. Go back and reread the paragraph together. Ask: **How can we make sure the reader knows the order of events?** (*add time-order words, such as* first, next, *and* last)

- Guide students to make sure the paragraph has a clear beginning, middle, and ending. Explain that time-order words help connect the sentences into a paragraph.

- Ask: **How would readers know how you felt about the event?** (*by telling thoughts and feelings about it*)

- Read the paragraph aloud with students.

On Your Own

Ask students to write a narrative paragraph about one of their birthday celebrations or another experience they had. Tell them to begin with a list of ideas. Remind them to use the first-person point of view and to make sure the paragraph has a clear beginning, middle, and ending.

Connect Spelling and Phonics

RETEACH **r-controlled vowel /är/ar.** Write the word *bark* on the board and point out the *ar* spelling. Then have students number a paper 1 to 8. Dictate the following words, and have students write them. After they write each word, display the correct spelling so that students can proofread their work. They should draw a line through a misspelled word and write the correct spelling beside it.

1. charm	2. sharp	3. start*	4. smart*
5. park	6. artist	7. startle	8. varnish

*Word appears in "Lessons from Barbara Jordan."

Dictate the following sentence: *Farmer Clark drove his car to the barn.*

Build and Read Longer Words

Explain that a syllable is a word part that can be said by itself and that every syllable has one vowel sound. Clap your hands once as you say *car*. Explain that this word has one syllable. Then clap your hands twice as you say *carpet*. Explain that this word has two syllables, *car* and *pet*. Then write *carpet* on the board. Have students identify two consonants next to each other. (*r, p*) Draw a line between *r* and *p*, and tell students that two-syllable words that have this pattern are usually divided between the two consonants that are next to each other. Frame *car* in *carpet*, and ask a volunteer to say it. Repeat with the remaining part, *pet*. Then draw your hand under the entire word as students read it.

Repeat with the words *market*, *tarnish*, and *starling*. Ask students to say each word and explain how they figured it out.

**INTERVENTION
ASSESSMENT
BOOK**

FLUENCY BUILDER Have students choose a passage from "Lessons from Barbara Jordan" to read aloud to a partner. You may have students choose passages that they found particularly interesting, or have them choose one of the following options.

- Read pages 30–31. (From *Grandma, I'm so . . .*through . . . *is lots of fun!* Total: 107 words)

- Read pages 32–33. (From *Grandma, Mom said . . .*through . . . *Love, Grandma.* Total: 106 words)

Ask students to read the passage aloud to their partners three times. Have students rate their own readings on a scale of 1 to 4. Encourage students to note their improvement from one reading to the next by completing the sentence *I know my reading has improved because* _____. Encourage listeners to offer positive feedback.

Review Vocabulary

Read the statements aloud, and ask students to write the correct answers on their papers. Go over the answers and discuss why the answers are correct.

1. After the actor received truckloads of **correspondence**, he
   a. hired people to help him read the letters.
   b. took a vacation.

2. The new policeman had a **mentor** who
   a. helped him learn the job.   b. gave him a week off.

3. I don't like to be **ridiculed** for
   a. being rude.   b. doing the right things.

4. With much **dignity**, Charlie accepted the award. He walked to the stage
   a. straight and calmly.   b. chewing gum and humming.

5. At the museum our teacher will **counsel** us about
   a. how to behave inside.   b. how to be as loud as possible.

6. When we say that people have different **potential**, we mean that they have
   a. different abilities and skills.   b. different colors of eyes.

7. Mr. Simms tried to **inspire** Zack to improve his math grades by giving him
   a. the answers.   b. a pep talk.

Correct responses: la, 2a, 3b, 4a, 5a, 6a, 7b

You may want to display the Vocabulary Words and definitions on page 39 and have students copy them to use when they study for the vocabulary test.

 ## Review Make Judgments

Before the weekly assessment, distribute *Intervention Practice Book* page 18. Remind students that valid judgments, or valid opinions, are based on evidence. Ask students to read the story silently. Then have a student read it aloud. Read the first question to students. Have them circle the letter of their response. Then ask students to finish the second question on their own. Call on volunteers to share their answers.

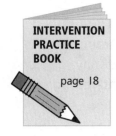

**INTERVENTION
PRACTICE
BOOK**

page 18

Review Test Prep

Ask students to turn to page 113 of the *Pupil Edition*. Call attention to the tips for answering the test questions. Tell students that paying attention to these tips can help them answer not only the test questions on this page but also other test questions like these.

**DISTANT
VOYAGES**

page
113

Have students read the first tip silently as you read it aloud. Direct students to look at the next tip. Have students read the story and answer each question. Remind them of the tips when answering.

**INTERVENTION
ASSESSMENT
BOOK**

Self-Selected Reading

Have students select their own books to read independently. They may choose books from the classroom library shelf, or you may wish to offer a group of appropriate books from which students can choose.

- *Dear Grandma* (See page 113K of the *Teacher's Edition* for a lesson plan.)
- *Grandmama's Joy* by Eloise Greenfield. Philomel, 1984.
- *If a Bus Could Talk: the Story of Rosa Parks* by Faith Ringgold. Simon and Schuster, 1999.

After students have chosen their books, give each student a copy of My Reading Log, which can be found on page R38 in the back of the *Teacher's Edition*. Have students fill in the information at the top of the form. Then have them use the log to keep track of their reading and to record their responses to literature.

Conduct student-teacher conferences. Arrange time for each student to confer with you individually about his or her selected reading. Have students bring their Reading Logs to share with you at the conference. Students might also like to choose a favorite passage to read aloud to you. To give students more practice with summarizing and paraphrasing, ask them to read a short section and to summarize and then paraphrase it.

FLUENCY PERFORMANCE Have students read aloud to you the passage from "Lessons from Barbara Jordan" that they selected and practiced with their partners. Keep track of the number of words students read correctly. Ask the student to rate his or her own performance on the 1–4 scale. If students are not happy with their oral reading, give them an opportunity to continue practicing and to read the passage to you again.

See *Oral Reading Fluency Assessment* for monitoring progress.

BEFORE

Building Background and Vocabulary

Use with

"Elena"

Review Phonics: Short Vowel /a/ *a*; Long Vowel /ā/ *ai, ay*

Identify the sounds. Have students repeat the following sentence aloud three times: *Pat wishes to catch the midday train.* Ask them to identify the words that have the /a/ sound they hear in *map.* (*Pat, catch*) Then have students repeat the sentence and name the words with the /ā/ sound they hear in *made.* (*midday, train*)

Associate letters to sounds. Write on the board the sentence above. Circle *Pat* and *catch.* Remind students that words that have a single vowel between consonants usually have a short vowel sound. Have students read each word aloud. Then underline *ay* in *midday.* Point out that the letters *ay* stand for the /ā/ sound. Underline *ai* in *train*, and tell students that the letters *ai* also can stand for the long *a* sound.

Word blending. Write *train* on the board, and then model how to blend and read it. Slide your hand under the whole word as you elongate all the sounds /trrāānn/. Then read the word naturally—*train.* Follow the same procedure with *snail, stay*, and *grab.*

Apply the skill. *Letter Substitution* Write the following words on the board, and have students read each aloud. Make the changes necessary to form the words in parentheses. Have students read each new word aloud.

INTERVENTION PRACTICE BOOK

page 20

hay (hat)	**bran** (brain)	**clay** (clap)	**stay** (stand)
man (main)	**pal** (pail)	**tray** (trap)	**clam** (claim)

Introduce Vocabulary

PRETEACH **lesson vocabulary.** Tell students that they are going to learn six new words that they will see again when they read a story called "Elena." Teach each vocabulary word using the following process.

Use the following suggestions or similar ideas to give the meaning or context.

> Write the word.
> Say the word.
> Track the word and have students repeat it.
> Give the meaning or context.

revolution	People who disagreed with the king protested and started a revolution against him.
determination	The players had much determination to win the game.
mocking	Baseball fans were mocking the player when he didn't catch the ball.

plunged	The bird plunged into the water and caught a fish.
ravine	Villagers built a bridge across the deep ravine.
condolences	When Grandmother died, many people gave us their condolences.

For vocabulary activities, see Vocabulary Games on pp. 2–7.

For vocabulary activities, see Vocabulary Games on pp. 2–7.

AFTER

Building Background and Vocabulary

Apply Vocabulary Strategies

Use words with multiple meanings. Tell students that many words have more than one meaning. Explain that they should look for context clues to help them know which meaning is being used. Model using context clues to distinguish meanings. Use these sentences: *During the revolution, the people protested in the city square. The Earth makes one revolution around the sun each year.*

MODEL In the first sentence, the words *people protested* help me know that *revolution* means "an overthrowing." In the second sentence, the words *Earth* and *sun* let me know that *revolution* means "a complete orbit."

Tell students to use this strategy as they read the selection.

RETEACH lesson vocabulary. Make sure each student has a set of word cards for the Vocabulary Words. Read aloud the following sentences. Ask students to hold up the appropriate word card. Then reread the sentence with the correct word choice.

1. After the people's __(revolution)__, the laws of the country changed.
2. His __(determination)__ to run well won him a gold medal in the race.
3. The circus clowns were __(mocking)__ each other for doing silly things.
4. The diver __(plunged)__ into the deep water in search of sponges.
5. Many wild animals lived in the deep __(ravine)__.
6. After Zack was hurt in a car accident, he received many __(condolences)__.

Vocabulary Words

revolution sudden change of government, often by overthrow

determination strength of purpose

mocking making fun of

plunged dived; fell rapidly

ravine a deep, narrow gap in the Earth

condolences expressions of sympathy or comfort

FLUENCY BUILDER Distribute *Intervention Practice Book* page 19. Read each word aloud and have students repeat it. Then have students work in pairs and take turns reading the words to each other.

INTERVENTION PRACTICE BOOK

page 19

BEFORE

Reading "Elena" *pages 116–129*

USE SKILL CARD 5A

Focus Skill Narrative Elements

PRETEACH the skill. Tell students that fiction stories have narrative elements. Remind them that the narrative elements include characters, setting, a series of events called the plot, and the theme. Remind them that the plot contains a problem, or conflict, and a solution.

Have students look at **side A of Skill Card 5: Narrative Elements.** Read aloud the opening sentence, and have volunteers read aloud the items in the box. Then direct students' attention to the illustration, and ask: **What is the setting in the picture? What kind of people are the characters? What predictions can you make about what will happen in the story?**

Then read the story aloud as students read it silently. Call on a different student to read each row of the chart, and discuss how each element helps the reader understand the story.

Prepare to Read: "Elena"

Preview. Tell students that they are going to read a selection called "Elena." Explain that this fiction story has narrative elements. Direct students to preview the story with you and identify some of the characters and settings in the story.

DISTANT VOYAGES pages 116–129

- **Pages 116–119:** I think this story takes place in a warm country, because I see palm trees in one picture. In the other picture I see men riding horses. I think the story happened in the past.
- **Pages 120–123:** In one picture a woman seems very sad. I wonder what happened to her. In the next picture the same woman is with some dangerous-looking soldiers. Judging by their clothing, I think they are in Mexico or Central America.
- **Pages 124–127:** It looks like a lot of people want to get on the train. They must be taking a long trip. In the next picture I see a woman standing near a girl who is reading. I think the girl must be Elena.

Set purpose. Model setting a purpose for reading "Elena."

MODEL From what I have seen, I think this selection takes place in Mexico. I wonder why the woman is upset and what the soldiers want at her house. I also want to know what happens to the girl.

Reread and Summarize

Have students reread and summarize "Elena" in sections.

Pages 116–121

Let's look again at the beginning of the story and the early events.

Summary: It is 1930 in Mexico, and Elena's father is accidentally killed on a trip out of town. Before he dies, he warns Elena's mother of danger in the countryside.

Pages 122–125

Reread pages 122–125 to see what happens in the middle of the story.

Summary: Elena's mother hides her son and her horses from the soldiers. When Pancho Villa and other soldiers come to her door, she sells him her last hat. The family decides it is too dangerous to stay, so they leave on a train north.

Pages 126–128

Let's reread pages 126–128 to find out what the family does in the United States.

The family goes first to San Francisco and then to Los Angeles. They settle in Santa Ana. The children begin to feel like Americans, but the mother still longs for Mexico. In time they learn that the soldiers have burned their village in Mexico. By taking family members to the United States, the mother has saved them.

FLUENCY BUILDER Be sure students have copies of *Intervention Practice Book* page 19, which you used for the Fluency Builder Activity. Call attention to the sentences at the bottom of the page. Model appropriate pacing, expression, and phrasing as you read each sentence, and have students read it after you. Then have students practice by reading the sentences aloud to a partner.

INTERVENTION
PRACTICE
BOOK

page 19

Directed Reading: "Painting My Homeland" pp. 38–45

Tell students that they will read a nonfiction selection about a real person. Remind them that this type of story is a biography and that they should identify characters, setting, problem, and solution in the story. Have them identify the theme as well.

TAKE FLIGHT pages 38–45

Page 38

Have a student read aloud the story title, and have everyone preview the story by looking at the illustrations and artwork of Diego Rivera. Have them predict what the selection is about. Then ask students to read page 38 to find out where Diego Rivera calls home and why he wants to return to his home. Ask: **Where is Diego Rivera from?** (*Mexico*) **IMPORTANT DETAILS**

Ask: **Why does Diego Rivera want to go back home to create paintings of Mexico?** (*Possible response: He feels he must paint pictures about his homeland; he feels a calling to return to Mexico.*) (Focus Skill) **NARRATIVE ELEMENTS/THEME**

Page 39

Have students read page 39 to see how Diego's friends feel about his return to Mexico. Ask: **How do his friends compare Italy and Mexico?** (*They tell him there are only farms and cattle in Mexico and that no one will be able to pay him for his work.*) **RECOGNIZE BIAS**

Ask: **How do they know Diego Rivera will leave no matter what they say?** (*They can see the determination in his eyes.*) **CHARACTERS' TRAITS**

Page 40

Have students look at Diego sketching on the wall. Read page 40 to students, and ask: **How is each of the characters described?** (*One is small and frail. Diego is big and has wild hair.*) **COMPARE AND CONTRAST**

Read the last paragraph again. Ask: **What does it mean when the author says that** *the wide, white walls called urgently to him*? (*He feels that his paintings belong on the walls.*) **UNDERSTAND FIGURATIVE LANGUAGE**

Page 41

Have students read page 41 and identify why Diego Rivera wants to start sketching before the paint is dry. Ask: **Why does Diego want to sketch his outline in the wet paint?** (*If he sketches in the wet paint, the marks will stay fresh and be easy to see.*) **CAUSE/EFFECT**

Ask: **When Diego says he will mail the sketches to the man, is he serious? Explain.** (*No; the wall is too big to send by mail.*) **DRAW CONCLUSIONS**

Page 42

Have students identify objects in the painting on page 42. Then read page 42 aloud to students. Ask: **How do you know Diego has deep feelings for the people and land of Mexico?** (*He paints not only beautiful scenes, but also scenes of revolution and sorrow.*) **CHARACTERS' EMOTIONS**

Ask students to read page 43 and think about what will happen now that Diego is nearly done with his wall. Model using the Read Ahead strategy.

> **MODEL** I read that Diego has let only one friend see his paintings but that he is nearly finished. The friend thinks the paintings are great. I wonder if other people will think the same thing. I will read ahead to find out. On page 44 I read that some people don't think his work is art but that others thank him for painting their homeland. (Focus Strategy) **READ AHEAD**

INTERVENTION PRACTICE BOOK

page 21

Look at the artwork by Diego Rivera on this page. Ask: **What is your reaction to the paintings?** (*Students' responses will vary.*) **IMPORTANT DETAILS/EXPRESS PERSONAL OPINIONS**

Summarize the selection. Ask students to think about the dedication and determination of Diego Rivera to paint the history of Mexico. Many people tried to discourage him, but he knew what he was called to do and he did it with determination. Today his art is famous for showing not only the struggles of people, but also their hopes for a better future.

Answers to *Think About It* Questions

1. Diego included the scenery of Mexico and showed people's struggles as well as their hopes. **IMPORTANT DETAILS**
2. The widow liked the painting because she loved her country and was proud of Mexico just as Diego Rivera was proud of it. **THEME**
3. Responses will vary. **MAKE JUDGMENTS**

AFTER

Skill Review
pages 134–135

USE SKILL CARD 5B

(Focus Skill) **Narrative Elements**

RETEACH the skill. Have students look at **side B of Skill Card 5: Narrative Elements**. Read the skill reminder to them. Ask students to read the passage silently. Then ask a volunteer to read it aloud. Have partners answer the questions below the story. When students are finished, ask them to share their answers.

FLUENCY BUILDER Be sure students have copies of *Intervention Practice Book* page 19. Explain that students will practice the sentences at the bottom of the page by reading them aloud on tape. Assign new partners. Have students take turns reading the sentences aloud to each other. Tell students to comment on each other's performance. Students should report on what other students did well and make suggestions to improve the reading next time. Students should then read the sentences again and report on whether they feel they improved.

INTERVENTION PRACTICE BOOK

page 19

Expressive Writing: Narrative Paragraph

Build on prior knowledge. Tell students that they are going to discuss and begin a paragraph about things they did to get ready for the first day of school. Display the following information:

To get ready for the first day of school:
bought supplies
checked the bus schedule
found out where my room is

Construct the text. "Share the pen" with students in a collaborative writing effort. As students dictate phrases and sentences, write them on the board or on chart paper. Guide the process by asking questions and offering suggestions as needed. Remind students that since they are writing about events that happened to them, they should use pronouns like *I*, *me*, *my*, and *mine*. Begin by writing a topic sentence such as the following on the board:

There were many things I needed to do to get ready for the first day of school.

Have students use a graphic organizer of their choice to jot down their own ideas. Then ask students to use the ideas on the board and their own ideas to dictate sentences.

Revisit the text. Go back and reread the sentences together. Ask: **How can we make sure our sentences flow together into a paragraph?** (Possible responses: use signal words, such as *first, then,* and *last;* get rid of any ideas that are not about the subject)

- Guide students to discuss how using a graphic organizer helped them record their ideas. Ask: **How did using a graphic organizer help you?** (*Possible response: It helped me remember all the things I wanted to say.*)

- Ask: **What words and phrases can we add to make the separate sentences flow together?** (*Possible responses: the first thing we did; after that; the next task; in the last store*)

- Ask: **How can we make sure our paragraph is focused on the topic?** (*Possible response: get rid of any sentences that do not stick to the subject*)

- Have students read aloud the completed paragraph.

On Your Own

Tell students that they should continue the paragraph, writing about all the tasks they did before the first day of school. Tell them that the last sentence should tell their feelings about all they did getting ready for school.

Connect Spelling and Phonics

RETEACH short vowel /a/*a*; long vowel /ā/*ai, ay*. Have students number a sheet of paper 1 through 8. Dictate words 1–2, and have students write them. After students write each word, display it so students can proofread their work. Then write *way* on the board, and tell students that in the next three words you will say, the letters *ay* stand for the long *a* sound. Dictate words 3–5, and have students proofread as before. After that, write *pain* on the board, and tell students that in the next three words you will say, the letters *ai* stand for the long *a* sound. Dictate words 6–8, and have students proofread as before.

1. plant*	2. man*	3. day*	4. display*
5. way	6. frail*	7. detain*	8. paint*

*Word appears in "Painting My Homeland."

Build and Read Longer Words

INTERVENTION ASSESSMENT BOOK

Review breaking words with VCCV (vowel-consonant-consonant-vowel) pattern. Write the word *cascade* on the board. Have students identify two consonants next to each other. (*s, c*) Remind students that two-syllable words that have this pattern are usually divided between the two consonants that are next to each other. Frame *cas* and ask a student to say it. Frame *cade* and ask a student to say it. Then slide your hand under the entire word as students say it aloud. Follow a similar procedure with the words *maintain, payday, happen,* and *mailbag.*

FLUENCY BUILDER Have students choose a passage from "Painting My Homeland" to read aloud to a partner. You may have students choose passages that they found particularly interesting or have them choose one of the following options.

- Read pages 38–39. (From *Diego Rivera. . .* through . . . *get paid?* Total: 105 words)

- Read pages 40–41. (From *Time passed . . .* through . . . *plunged into his job.* Total: 121 words)

- Read pages 42–43. (From *Diego stayed. . .* through . . . *at the walls.* Total: 125 words)

Have students read a selected passage aloud to their partners three times. Then have the listeners rate each reading on a scale of 1 to 4.

Encourage students to note their improvement from one reading to the next by completing the sentence *I know my reading has improved because* _____. Encourage the listening partner to offer positive feedback about improvements.

Review Vocabulary

To revisit the Vocabulary Words prior to the weekly assessments, use these sentence frames. Read each statement aloud, and have students write the letter of the answer. Go over the answers, and discuss why they are correct.

1. The Smith family received many **condolences** when
   a. they won a free vacation.　　　b. their house burned down.

2. The explorers reached a deep **ravine** and had difficulty
   a. finding food for dinner.　　　b. continuing their journey.

3. During the **revolution**, the soldiers frightened the people by
   a. taking over the government.　　b. buying new cars.

4. When the airplane was high enough, the sky diver **plunged**
   a. out of the door.　　　　　　b. into the pilot's seat.

5. Because of his **determination**, Christopher Columbus
   a. gave up.　　　　　　　　　b. sailed to the Americas.

6. When the other team began **mocking** us for striking out,
   a. the coach gave us a pep talk.　b. we began laughing.

   Correct responses: 1b, 2b, 3a, 4a, 5b, 6a

You may want to display the vocabulary words and definitions on page 49 and have students copy them to use when they study for the test.

Review Narrative Elements

INTERVENTION
PRACTICE
BOOK

page 22

Before the weekly assessment of narrative elements, distribute *Intervention Practice Book* page 22. Ask students to read the story silently. Then read the story aloud to them. Ask a student to read the first question below the story, and then have a student read the choices aloud. Have each student circle the choice for the correct answer. Then ask students to finish the second and third questions on their own. When students are finished, call on a volunteer to share answers.

Review Test Prep

INTERVENTION
ASSESSMENT
BOOK

Ask students to turn to page 135 of the *Pupil Edition*. Call attention to the tips for answering the test questions. Tell students that paying attention to these tips can help them answer not only the test questions on this page but also questions on other tests. Have students look at the first tip and read it silently as you read it aloud. Direct students to look at the next tip. Have students read the story and answer each question. Remind them to use the tips when answering the question.

**DISTANT
VOYAGES**

page 135

Self-Selected Reading

Have students select their own books to read independently. They may choose books from the classroom library shelf, or you may wish to offer a group of appropriate books from which students can choose.

- *Estrella Shining Brightly* (See page 135K of the *Teacher's Edition* for a lesson plan.)

- *How Many Days to America?* by Eve Bunting. Clarion, 1998.

- *How My Family Lives in America* by Susan Kuklin. Simon & Schuster, 1992.

You may also wish to choose additional books that are the same genre or are by the same author, or that have the same kind of text structure as the selection.

After students have chosen their books, give each student a copy of My Reading Log, which can be found on page R38 in the back of the *Teacher's Edition*. Have students fill in the information at the top of the form. Then have them use the log to keep track of their reading and to record their responses to literature.

Conduct student-teacher conferences. Arrange time for each student to confer with you individually about his or her selected reading. Have students bring their Reading Logs to share with you at the conference. Students might also like to choose a favorite passage to read aloud to you. To give students more practice with summarizing and paraphrasing, ask them to read a short section and to summarize and then paraphrase it.

FLUENCY PERFORMANCE Have students read aloud to you the passage from "Painting My Homeland" that they selected and practiced with their partners. Keep track of the number of words students read correctly. Ask the student to rate his or her own performance on the 1–4 scale. If students are not happy with their oral reading, give them an opportunity to continue practicing and to read the passage to you again.

See *Oral Reading Fluency Assessment* for monitoring progress.

BEFORE

Building
Background
and Vocabulary

Use with

"We'll Never Forget You, Roberto Clemente"

Review Phonics: Long Vowel /ō/ *oa*

Identify the sound. Have students repeat the following sentence aloud twice: *Bob could not get his boat to float.* Have them identify the words with the /o/ sound they hear in *flock.* (*Bob, not*) Then have them identify the words that have the /ō/ sound they hear in *goat.* (*boat, float*)

Associate letters to sound. Write on the board the sentence above. Underline the *o* in *not* and *Bob*, and remind students that words that have this pattern usually have a short vowel sound. Next, underline the letters *oa* in *boat.* Tell students that the letters *oa* stand for the long o vowel sound. Remind students that when two vowels come together between consonants, they usually stand for a long vowel sound.

Word blending. Model how to blend and read the word *croak.* Slide your hand under all the letters as you elongate the sounds: /krrōōk/. Then read the word naturally—*croak.* Repeat the procedure with *coach* and *throat.*

Apply the skill. *Letter Substitution* Write the following words on the board, and have students read each aloud. Make the changes necessary to form the word in parentheses. Have a student read each new word aloud.

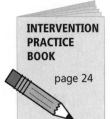

INTERVENTION
PRACTICE
BOOK

page 24

bond (boat)	**got** (goat)	**boss** (boast)	**rot** (roam)
sock (soak)	**top** (toad)	**clock** (cloak)	**toss** (toast)

Introduce Vocabulary

PRETEACH **lesson vocabulary.** Tell students they are going to learn six new words they will see again when they read a story called "We'll Never Forget You, Roberto Clemente." Teach each vocabulary word using the following process.

Use the following suggestions or similar ideas to give the meaning or context.

lineup	In the batting lineup, Sam was fourth to bat.
ace	Paul is an ace builder of model airplanes.
error	When the shortstop missed the ball, it was called an error.
artificial	The artificial flowers were colorful and almost looked real.
control tower	From high in the control tower, many planes could be seen.

> Write the word.
> Say the word.
> Track the word and have students repeat it.
> Give the meaning or context.

dedicated   The people dedicated a few
minutes of silence to those who
had died in the war.

**For vocabulary activities, see Vocabulary Games
on pages 2–7.**

For vocabulary activities, see Vocabulary Games on pages 2–7.

Vocabulary Words

lineup the players on a
team who take part in
a game

ace expert

error a mistake in a
baseball game

artificial made by
humans; not natural

control tower at an airport, a building from
which takeoffs and
landings are directed

dedicated set apart for
a special purpose

AFTER

Building
Background
and Vocabulary

Apply Vocabulary Strategies

Use shorter words. Write *baseball* and *lineup*
on the board. Explain that as students read,
they should look to see if words are made up
of two shorter words. Draw lines between
base and *ball* and between *line* and *up*.

MODEL **I can break these two words
into their word parts to figure them out. In
the words *base* and *line*, I see the familiar
pattern of one vowel between consonants.
So, I know they both have long vowel sounds: /bās/ and /līn/.**

Remind students to use this strategy as they read other words in the
selection, such as *well-known*, *teammate*, and *fastballs*.

RETEACH **lesson vocabulary.** Make sure each student has a set of
vocabulary cards. Have students listen as you read the following sentences.
Ask students to hold up the appropriate word card. Then reread the
sentence with the correct word choice.

1. Some of the baseball players were injured, so the coach changed
the ___(lineup)___ .

2. The team lost the game because they had made too many
___(errors)___ .

3. The ___(artificial)___ grass on the field looked almost real.

4. The new library was ___(dedicated)___ to a famous author.

5. During the fog, pilots relied on the ___(control tower)___ to help them
land.

6. To learn a sport like mountain climbing, hire an ___(ace)___ climber.

FLUENCY BUILDER Distribute *Intervention Practice Book*
page 23. Read each word in the first column and have
students repeat it. Then have students work in pairs
and take turns reading the words to each other. Follow
the same procedure with each of the remaining
columns. After partners have practiced reading aloud
the words in each column separately, have them
practice the entire list.

**INTERVENTION
PRACTICE
BOOK**

page 23

BEFORE

Reading "We'll
Never Forget You,
Roberto
Clemente"
pages 140–153

USE SKILL CARD 6A

(Focus Skill) Draw Conclusions

PRETEACH **the skill.** Tell students that sometimes, authors do not tell parts of a story directly. Instead they may give us ideas about what they mean. Explain that we can use the ideas and add them to what we already know about the topic to draw a conclusion.

Have students look at **side A of Skill Card 6: Draw Conclusions.** Read aloud the definition, and ask students to study the picture and describe what is happening. Tell students to read the story silently as you read it aloud. Have a student read the column headings in the chart. Then ask for a volunteer to read the information under each heading. Discuss how the information in the first two columns leads to the conclusions in the third column.

Prepare to Read: "We'll Never Forget You, Roberto Clemente"

Preview. Tell students that they are going to read a selection called "We'll Never Forget You, Roberto Clemente." Explain that this selection is a short biography about Roberto Clemente, a famous baseball player. Direct students to preview the story with you.

**DISTANT
VOYAGES**
pages
140–153

- **Pages 140–143:** I can see right away that this story will be about baseball or a baseball player. I see two flags, so maybe this player is from another country.

- **Pages 144–147:** I see a batter about to hit a ball and outfielders ready to catch it. I wonder what the sign that says "3,000" means.

- **Pages 148–151:** It looks like the baseball player is loading boxes labeled "Nicaragua." I wonder what is inside the boxes. On the next page a plane is taking off. Maybe he is taking the boxes in the plane to Nicaragua.

- **Pages 152–153:** The sign says "Adiós, amigo," which I think means "Good-bye, friend" in Spanish. I wonder if the baseball player went to Nicaragua and never came back.

Set purpose. Model setting a purpose for reading "We'll Never Forget You, Roberto Clemente."

MODEL I want to read this story to find out who Roberto Clemente is. I also wonder where he went on his trip and why he didn't come back.

Reread and Summarize

Have students reread and summarize "We'll Never Forget You, Roberto Clemente" in sections, as described in the chart below.

Pages 140–145

Reread the beginning of the selection to find out about Roberto Clemente's baseball experiences.

Summary: Roberto Clemente was a talented Puerto Rican baseball player who played for the Pirates. He was one of only a few players who had gotten 3,000 hits.

Pages 146–147

Reread pages 146–147 to find out how the earthquake in Nicaragua affected Roberto Clemente.

Summary: After a big earthquake hit Nicaragua in 1972, Roberto Clemente worked with many other people to help Nicaraguans get food, water, and medical supplies. He also wanted to know if a certain boy was all right.

Pages 148–151

Reread these pages to find out if Roberto made it to Nicaragua with the supplies.

Summary: Roberto Clemente gathered some supplies himself and found someone to fly him to Nicaragua. Not long after the plane took off, the plane exploded and crashed into the ocean. Roberto's body was never found.

Pages 152–153

Look back at pages 152–153 to read how Roberto's friends honored him.

Summary: Roberto Clemente's friends honored him by putting up a lighted sign, showing a message on a scoreboard, and dedicating a statue to him. His family honored him by building a sports city for poor children in Puerto Rico.

FLUENCY BUILDER Reuse *Intervention Practice Book* page 23, and call attention to the sentences at the bottom of the page. Model appropriate pace, expression, and phrasing as you read each sentence, and have students read it after you. Then have students practice by reading the sentences aloud to a partner.

INTERVENTION PRACTICE BOOK

page 23

Directed Reading: "The Pirate Hero" pp. 46–52

Tell students that today they will read another biography about a famous baseball player who helped others in many ways. Ask students to recall what they know about baseball and what they know about helping people in need. Read aloud the title of the story. Then have students view the illustration on page 46.

TAKE FLIGHT
pages 46–52

Ask: **What is the setting shown in the illustration?** (*a baseball game*) Point out Roberto Clemente. Explain that Roberto Clemente was a real baseball player.

Page 46

Have students read page 46. Ask: **What is important about the baseball game shown in the illustration?** (*The team that wins this set of games will be the best team in baseball.*) Ask: **What is Roberto Clemente's vow?** (*He promises himself that he will play hard for the Pirates.*) **MAIN IDEA**

Page 47

Have students read page 47. Ask: **Do the Pirates win the first two games?** (*no*) Ask: **How would you describe Roberto Clemente? Why?** (*Possible response: He is confident. He believes his team will win even though others say it cannot.*) **CHARACTERS' TRAITS**

Ask: **At this point, who do you think will win the set of games? Why?** (*Possible response: the Orioles, because they have won all the games so far*) **MAKE PREDICTIONS**

Page 48

Have students read page 48 to decide who was the man with number 21 on his uniform. Ask: **Who wore number 21? How did you decide this?** (*Possible response: Roberto Clemente; I already know that Clemente was a leader of his team. I used the information on page 46 and the picture on that page to decide that number 21 was Roberto Clemente.*) (Focus Skill) **DRAW CONCLUSIONS**

Page 49

Have students read page 49 to check their predictions about who won the set of games. Model using the Adjust Reading Rate strategy:

> **MODEL** This page has information about the last two games in the set. I will read more slowly to make sure I understand who won the final two. As I read, I see that the Orioles won game 6, so the two teams were tied. Then I read that the Pirates won the last one, so the Pirates were the overall winners. (Focus Strategy) **ADJUST READING RATE**

Page 50

Ask: **Why was Roberto Clemente considered to be a hero outside of baseball?** (*He liked to help people in need.*) **THEME**

Have students view the illustration on page 51. Ask: **What does the illustration show?** (*a statue of Roberto Clemente*) Then have students read page 51. Ask: **Who had the statue made?** (*the people of Pittsburgh*) Ask: **Why do you think the people of Pittsburgh did this?** (*Possible response: They wanted to honor Clemente and keep his memory alive so others could learn from his life.*) **CHARACTERS' MOTIVATIONS**

Summarize the selection. Ask students to think about what made Roberto Clemente a hero. Then have them summarize the selection.

Answers to *Think About It* Questions

1. He helped the Pirates by playing hard and by hitting a home run in the last game of the series. He helped other people by getting money for someone who needed artificial legs and by taking things to people who needed help. **SUMMARY**

2. Possible response: Clemente didn't boast because his good baseball playing was his way of keeping his promise to play hard. The fans liked Clemente even more for not boasting. **INTERPRETATION**

3. Webs and paragraphs should indicate an understanding of Clemente as a hard worker, a good hitter, a man who didn't boast, and a man who helped others. **WORD WEB/WRITE A PARAGRAPH**

INTERVENTION PRACTICE BOOK

page 36

AFTER

Skill Review *pages 160–161*

USE SKILL CARD 6B

(Focus Skill) Draw Conclusions

RETEACH **the skill.** Have students look at **side B of Skill Card 6: Draw Conclusions.** Ask a student to read the skill reminder aloud.

Read the story to students as they read it silently. Ask students to number a sheet of paper 1 to 3, and read the first question to students. Then read the next question, and remind them to look in the story for the answer. Read the last question, and ask students to draw a conclusion about the dog's behavior. Call on students to share their answers.

FLUENCY BUILDER Distribute *Intervention Practice Book* page 23. Explain that students will practice the sentences on the bottom half of the page by reading them aloud on tape. Assign new partners. Have students take turns reading the sentences aloud to each other. Tell students to comment on each other's performance. Students should report on what their partners did well and make suggestions to improve the reading next time. Students should then read the sentences again and report on whether they feel they improved.

INTERVENTION PRACTICE BOOK

page 23

Expository Writing: Detail Sentences

Build on prior knowledge. Tell students that they are going to write some sentences that give details about a topic. Display the following information:

> I love the sights, sounds, and smells of summer baseball games.

Construct the text. Discuss with students various observations about summer baseball games. Tell them to think especially of words that appeal to the senses of sight, smell, hearing, taste, and touch. Then "share the pen" with students in a collaborative writing effort. As students dictate phrases and sentences, write them on the board or on chart paper. Guide the process by asking questions and offering suggestions. For example:

1. The sky is just beginning to turn pink and orange as the umpire shouts, "Batter up."
2. I feel sand between my toes as I walk to the bleachers.
3. Puffs of dust come out of the catcher's mitt.
4. I smell salty hot dogs and buttery popcorn.
5. My skin feels damp, and I have to swat mosquitoes.

Revisit the text. Go back and reread the sentences together. Ask: **How can we make our sentences more vivid?** (*Possible response: add lively describing words, such as* red, powdery dust *and* oily catcher's mitt.)

- Guide students to decide whether any of the details are not about the subject. Make any appropriate changes so the topic is focused.

- Ask: **How can we use punctuation to make the sentences seem exciting?** (*Possible response: use exclamation points with sentences that show strong feeling, such as with* "Batter up!")

- Read the sentences aloud with students.

On Your Own

Tell students that they will write sentences to describe something they know well. They should use details that tell how things look, smell, feel, taste, and sound. Suggest topics such as baking cookies, swimming in a pool, or playing in the snow.

Connect Spelling and Phonics

RETEACH **long vowel /ō/oa.** Tell students that in every word you will say, the long o vowel sound is spelled *oa*. Then dictate the following words, and have students write them. After they write each word, display the correct spelling so students can proofread their work. Have them draw a line through a misspelled word and write the correct spelling beside it.

1. boat	2. boast*	3. toasted	4. roam
5. throat	6. groan	7. moaning	8. coal

*Word appears in "The Pirate Hero."

Dictate the following sentence for students to write: *We made toast over hot coals.*

Build and Read Longer Words

Write the word *tugboat* on the board. Remind students that when they see a long word, they should decide if it is made up of two shorter words. Ask students which part of the word sounds like /tug/ and which part sounds like /boat/. Have students blend the word parts together to form the longer word *tugboat*. Repeat the procedure with *crewmate*, *coachman*, and *roadside*.

INTERVENTION ASSESSMENT BOOK

FLUENCY BUILDER Have students choose a passage from "The Pirate Hero" to read aloud to a partner. You may have students choose passages that they found particularly interesting or have them choose one of the following options.

- Read pages 46–47. (From *When Roberto . . .* through . . . *game 2 as well.* Total: 117 words)

- Read pages 48–49. (From *For the next . . .* through . . . *still won the game.* Total: 120 words)

- Read pages 50–51. (From *Clemente was a . . .* through . . . *it going down.* Total: 121 words)

Have students read a selected passage aloud to their partners three times. Then have listeners rate the readings on a scale of 1 to 4.

Encourage students to note their improvement from one reading to the next by completing the sentence *I know my reading has improved because* _____. Encourage listeners to offer positive feedback about improvements.

Review Vocabulary

To revisit the Vocabulary Words before the weekly assessment, use these sentence frames. Read each statement aloud, and have students write the answers. Go over the answers, and discuss why they are correct.

1. When the second baseman made an **error**,
   a. the other team scored.   b. the game was called off.

2. The **lineup** for the game was changed because
   a. laundry was hanging on it.   b. Albert, the catcher, was sick.

3. After the **ace** carpenter built the new garage,
   a. the rain leaked into it.   b. it lasted for many years.

4. **Artificial** flowers look pretty, but
   a. they don't smell like real ones.   b. you have to water them.

5. In the airport's **control tower**, workers
   a. guided the planes to land safely. b. built airplanes.

6. In many cities, statues are **dedicated** to
   a. people who fought for freedom.   b. people who broke the laws.

   Correct responses: 1a, 2b, 3b, 4a, 5a, 6a

You may want to display the Vocabulary Words and definitions on page 59 and have students copy them to use when they study for the test.

 ## Review Draw Conclusions

INTERVENTION
PRACTICE
BOOK

page 26

Before the weekly assessment on drawing conclusions, distribute *Intervention Practice Book* page 26. Ask students to read the story silently. Then have one of the students read it aloud. Then read the first question to students, and ask them to read the four choices and circle the letter of the correct answer. Ask students to finish the second question on their own. When students are finished, call on volunteers to share their answers.

Review Test Prep

INTERVENTION
ASSESSMENT
BOOK

Ask students to turn to page 161 of the *Pupil Edition*. Call attention to the tips for answering the test questions. Tell students that paying attention to these tips can help them answer not only the test questions on this page but also the questions on other tests. Have students read the tips silently as you read them aloud. Have students read the story and answer each question. Remind them to use the tips when answering the questions.

DISTANT
VOYAGES
page 161

Self-Selected Reading

Have students select their own books to read independently. They may choose books from the classroom library shelf, or you may wish to offer a group of appropriate books from which students can choose.

- *The 3,000th Hit* (See page 16 IK of the *Teacher's Edition* for a lesson plan.)
- *The Hit-Away Kid* by Matt Christopher. Little, Brown, 1990
- *Teammates* by Peter Golenbock. Harcourt, 1990.

You may also wish to choose additional books that are the same genre or are by the same author, or that have the same kind of text structure as the selection.

After students have chosen their books, give each student a copy of My Reading Log, which can be found on page R38 in the back of the *Teacher's Edition*. Have students fill in the information at the top of the form. Then have them use the log to keep track of their reading and to record their responses to literature.

Conduct student-teacher conferences. Arrange time for each student to confer with you individually about his or her selected reading. Have students bring their Reading Logs to share with you at the conference. Students might also like to choose a favorite passage to read aloud to you. To give students more practice with summarizing and paraphrasing, ask them to read a short section and to summarize and then paraphrase it.

FLUENCY PERFORMANCE Have students read aloud to you the passage from "The Pirate Hero" that they selected and practiced with their partners. Keep track of the number of words students read correctly. Ask the student to rate his or her own performance on the 1–4 scale. If students are not happy with their oral reading, give them an opportunity to continue practicing and to read the passage to you again.

See *Oral Reading Fluency Assessment* for monitoring progress.

BEFORE

**Building
Background
and Vocabulary**

Use with

"Folktales from Asia"

Review Phonics: Long Vowel /ō/ow

Identify the sound. Have students repeat the following sentence aloud twice: *The crow has flown where the wind has blown.* Ask students to identify words with the /ō/ sound they hear in *grow.* (*crow, flown, blown*)

Associate letters to sound. Write the sentence *The crow has flown where the wind has blown* on the board. Underline the letters *ow* in *crow.* Tell students that the letters *ow* can stand for the long *o* vowel sound. Ask students to identify the other words in this sentence in which the letters *ow* stand for the long *o* vowel sound. (*flown, blown*) Read the entire sentence aloud as you point to each word.

Word blending. Model how to blend and read the word *blown.* Point to *b* and say /b/. Point to *l* and say /l/. Draw your hand under *ow* and say /ō/ . Point to *n* and say /n/. Slide your hand under the whole word as you elongate the sounds: /bllōōnn/. Then read the word naturally—*blown.*

Apply the skill. *Letter Substitution* Write the following words on the board and have students read each aloud. Make the changes necessary to form the words in parentheses. Have a volunteer read aloud each new word. Try to give each student an opportunity to respond.

**INTERVENTION
PRACTICE
BOOK**

page 28

top (tow)	**moss** (mow)	**flock** (flow)	**lot** (low)
box (bowl)	**on** (own)	**sock** (sow)	**throng** (throw)

Introduce Vocabulary

PRETEACH **lesson vocabulary.** Tell students that they are going to learn six new words that they will see again when they read a story called "Folktales from Asia." Teach each vocabulary word using the following process.

Use the following suggestions or similar ideas to give the meaning or context.

> Write the word.
> Say the word.
> Track the word and have students repeat it.
> Give the meaning or context.

diligence   *Diligent* comes from the Latin word *diligere*, which means "to esteem or love."

plodded   The old horse went at a very slow, plodding pace.

bountiful   This word and a related word, *bounty*, come from the Latin word *bonitas*, meaning "goodness."

destiny   The young man went into the army dreaming of his destiny to become a great general.

assured	*Assured* comes from the Latin word *assecurare*, meaning "to make sure."
entrusted	Mother entrusted the important task to me because she knew I would be able to do it.

For vocabulary activities, see Vocabulary Games on pages 2–7.

For vocabulary activities, see Vocabulary Games on pages 2–7.

Vocabulary Words

diligence willingness or ability to work steadily

plodded walked heavily; trudged

bountiful plentiful; existing in a great quantity

destiny outcome that is bound to come; fate

assured made certain; guaranteed

entrusted made responsible for something

AFTER

Building Background and Vocabulary

Apply Vocabulary Strategies

Decode multisyllabic words. Write the word *entrusted* on the board. Point out to students that they can decode a word that is unfamiliar by breaking it up into familiar parts and saying each part separately.

MODEL I will break this long word into parts and say each part by itself. I break this word into *en-*, *trust*, and *-ed*. I know how to say each of those, so I will put the parts back together and say it until it sounds familiar to me.

RETEACH lesson vocabulary. Be sure each student has a set of vocabulary cards. Read aloud the following sentences, saying "blank" for each blank. Then ask students to hold up the appropriate word card. Reread the sentence with the correct choice.

1. His _(diligence)_ paid off when he was given a scholarship.
2. The settlers _(plodded)_ through the desert.
3. We had good summer weather, so the harvest was _(bountiful)_.
4. The actress hoped that her _(destiny)_ was the stage.
5. The first people in line were _(assured)_ of getting good seats.
6. The teacher _(entrusted)_ her with carrying the money.

FLUENCY BUILDER Use *Intervention Practice Book* page 27. Read aloud each of the words in the first column and have students repeat it. Then have students work in pairs and take turns reading the words to each other. Follow the same procedure with each of the remaining columns. Then have students practice reading the entire list and time themselves.

INTERVENTION PRACTICE BOOK

page 27

USE SKILL CARD 7A

(Focus Skill) **Summarize and Paraphrase**

PRETEACH **the skill.** Tell students that they regularly use these skills without even knowing it. For example, if your sister asks you what your mother said, you retell your mother's message but use your own words. If someone asks what happened in a movie, you sum up the most important parts in a few sentences.

Have students look at **side A of Skill Card 7: Summarize and Paraphrase.** Ask a volunteer to read the first two lines aloud. Have other volunteeers read aloud the text in the Summarize and the Paraphrase boxes. Then read the story aloud. Ask:

- **How is the summary different from the paraphrase?** (*Possible response: summary: use main ideas only; short; paraphrase: retell entire story; use your own words*)

- **How do you decide what to include in the summary?** (*Possible response: Look for the main ideas; ignore the details.*)

- **What are some synonyms that are used in the paraphrase?** (*Possible responses:* called *instead of* dialed; unsafe *instead of* dangerous; sketch *instead of* draw)

Prepare to Read: "Folktales from Asia"

Preview. Tell students that they are going to read "Folktales from Asia." Explain that this is a set of three stories that were told by storytellers long before they were written down.

DISTANT VOYAGES
pages 164–178

- **Pages 164–168:** I read the title and know that Asia has a number of countries in it. This story is from China, so maybe there are other stories from other Asian countries, too.
I see pictures of the moon and the sun. I think this story tells how the moon and the sun came to be.

- **Pages 169–171:** I was right—this next story is from Thailand. The title asks "Who Is Best?" so I think the three men in the picture are all trying to be the best at something.

- **Pages 172–175:** The third story is from China. On one set of pages, a man is holding up his fist. He looks determined to do something. On the next page a man is cooking some fish. I wonder what this has to do with the story.

- **Pages 176–178:** On these three pages, I see the man with wood, a large pot of food, and a horse. I wonder how these pictures connect with the idea of virtue.

Set purpose. Model setting a purpose for reading "Folktales from Asia."

MODEL **I want to find out more about Asia. I will read these folktales to understand the cultures of these countries in Asia.**

Reread and Summarize

Have students reread and summarize "Folktales from Asia" in sections, as described in the chart below.

Pages 164–165

Let's look again at pages 164–165 to remember the introduction to these folktales.

Summary: Folktales serve to show us how we are all alike even though we are from different places.

Pages 166–168

Let's recall what happens when the moon becomes jealous of the sun.

Summary: Second daughter is jealous of how bright first daughter, the sun, is. Second daughter becomes very bright, but people don't know when to plant and when to sleep. So, their mother persuades second daughter to cover her face with ashes and glow lightly.

Pages 169–171

Let's reread pages 169–171 to find out which man is best.

Summary: Three men work hard for seven days. They are fed for six days. On the seventh day, two of the men find the hidden food and eat it. The third man then finds gold in the pot. They argue about who among them is best until the landowner decides all three are equal.

Pages 172–178

Let's reread this folktale to find out what Virtue learns in town.

Summary: Virtue goes to town to get a job but finds only a job as a cook. One day when the workers are late, Virtue eats all the food. To repay the workers, he does their work the next day. Seeing that one man can do the work of twenty, the foreman plans to fire everyone but Virtue. But Virtue persuades him to let the twenty men cook while he works.

FLUENCY BUILDER Reuse *Intervention Practice Book* page 27. Call attention to the sentences at the bottom of the page. State that the goal is to have each student read each phrase smoothly. Model the appropriate pace, expression, and phrasing as you read aloud each of the sentences. Then have students practice reading aloud each sentence two or three times to a partner.

INTERVENTION
PRACTICE
BOOK

page 27

Directed Reading: "The Rain and the Snow" pp. 54–61

Page 54

Ask a volunteer to read aloud the title of the story. Then read page 54 aloud to students and have them listen for information on the two main characters. Ask: **Tell me, in your own words, what Rain says to Snow.** (*Possible response: "You have to go away, Snow, because no one needs you."*) ⭐ **SUMMARIZE AND PARAPHRASE**

TAKE FLIGHT pp. 54–61

Page 55

Ask students to read page 55 to see what happens with this argument. Ask: **How do Snow and Rain solve their argument?** (*Possible response: They ask Sun to decide.*) **IMPORTANT DETAILS**

Page 56

Have students read page 56 to see how the trip went. Ask: **What do Rain and Snow say to Sun?** (*Rain explains the argument, and both Rain and Snow say the other isn't important. They ask for a decision from Sun.*) **IMPORTANT DETAILS**

Ask: **Why do you think Sun is slow to answer?** (*Possible response: Sun is wise and wants to think about it.*) **SPECULATE**

Page 57

Ask a volunteer to read aloud page 57. Ask: **What does Sun ask them to do?** (*Possible response: Sun asks them to demonstrate their value.*) ⭐ **SUMMARIZE AND PARAPHRASE**

Page 58

Read page 58 aloud. Ask: **How does Rain seem to act after his demonstration?** (*Possible response: proud and impatient*) **CHARACTERS' EMOTIONS**

Ask: **What happens because of Snow's demonstration? Why?** (*People can't get anywhere because the snow is too deep.*) **CAUSE/EFFECT**

Page 59

Read page 59 aloud, and ask students to notice the people's reactions. Ask: **What happens after the big snow?** (*Possible response: People play in the snow and have fun.*) **IMPORTANT DETAILS**

Page 60

Have a volunteer read page 60 aloud, and ask students to think about what the sun is doing. Model the strategy Use Context to Confirm Meaning:

> **MODEL** The story says *Sun glowed at the rain* and *Sun glowed at the snow*. This is an unusual way to use *glowed*, so I will use the meanings of other words and phrases to make sure I understand what it means. The story says that when the Sun glowed, the rain stopped and the snow melted. I know that in real life, the heat from the sun dries rain and melts snow. So, I think that *glowed* means "shone hot and bright." ⭐ **USE CONTEXT TO CONFIRM MEANING**

Ask: **What do you think Rain and Snow learn from Sun?** (*Possible response: They learn that they are both important and are there to serve people.*) **EXPRESS PERSONAL OPINIONS/MAKE JUDGMENTS**

Summarize the selection. Ask students to think about what happened before, during, and at the end of this story. Then have students write three or four sentences to summarize this selection.

Page 61

INTERVENTION PRACTICE BOOK

page 29

Answers to *Think About It* Questions

1. Sun has each of them demonstrate their value. Sun shows what she can do and sends them away to do their work. **SUMMARY**

2. Possible response: Sun is probably annoyed that they are quarreling but is patient and tries to help them understand their roles. **INTERPRETATION**

3. Responses will vary but should include quotation marks with dialogue written in the first person and in present tense. **WRITE DIALOGUE**

AFTER

Skill Review
pages 182–183

USE SKILL CARD 7B

(Focus Skill) Summarize and Paraphrase

RETEACH the skill. Have students look at **side B of Skill Card 7: Summarize and Paraphrase.** Ask students to read aloud together the skill reminder.

Then read to students the paragraph about the foreign trip. Ask them to read along silently and to pay attention to details.

Have students copy onto their papers the beginning of the summary from the card. Tell them to complete the summary by retelling only the main points in story order. (*Possible summary: On her first trip overseas, Sara carefully packed all the things she needed, including her passport.*)

Then ask students to use their own paper to complete the paraphrase provided on the card or to come up with their own. Remind students to retell all of the details in their own words. Ask volunteers to share their responses with the class.

FLUENCY BUILDER Reuse *Intervention Practice Book* page 27. Explain that each student will practice the sentences at the bottom of the page by reading them aloud on tape. Assign new partners, and have students take turns reading the sentences aloud to each other and then reading them on tape. After listening to the tape, have each person tell how he or she has improved the sentences. Then have them tape themselves again, focusing on improved pacing and tone.

INTERVENTION PRACTICE BOOK

page 27

Expository Writing: How-to Sentences

Build on prior knowledge. Tell students that they will talk about and write sentences that tell the first step in doing something they know well. Display the following information:

> I put my shoes on before I go outside.
>
> I help my mother shop for food.
>
> I clean my mouse's cage every week.
>
> I want to put my baseball cards in order.

Construct the text. Talk with students about these activities or others they know well. Ask them to think about the first step for doing each thing. "Share the pen" with students in a collaborative writing effort. As students dictate sentences, write them on the board or on chart paper. Guide the process by asking questions and offering suggestions. For example:

- First, I need to find where I left my shoes.

- The first step is to make a list of the things we want to eat.

- To begin, I get some old newspapers and spread them on the floor.

- Before I start, I decide what order I want the cards to be in.

Revisit the text. Go back over the sentences with students, and ask: **How did you know what step to write about?** (*Possible response: I pictured in my mind what I do to start the activity, and I wrote about that thing.*)

- Guide students to review various phrases that mean "first," such as *to begin with, before anything else,* and *at the start.* Ask students to name others they can think of.

- Ask: **Suppose you want to tell the very next step. What are some words and phrases you could use to begin that sentence?** (*Possible responses: Next, Then, After that, The second thing*)

- Reread the sentences aloud with students.

On Your Own

Have students choose three activities they know about, such as hobbies, sports, or crafts. Ask them to write a sentence for each activity in which they tell the first step. Encourage students to use a different word or phrase meaning "first" in each sentence.

INTERVENTION
ASSESSMENT
BOOK

Connect Spelling and Phonics

RETEACH long vowel /ō/*ow.* Write *grow* on the board. Explain that you will say eight words in which the /ō/ vowel sound is spelled *ow.* Dictate words 1 through 8, and have students write them. After they write each word, display it so that students can proofread their work.

1. show*	2. bellow*	3. throw	4. followed*
5. slow*	6. flow*	7. willow*	8. growing*

*Word appears in "The Rain and the Snow."

Dictate the following sentence, and have students write it: *Let that fellow show us he can throw a fast ball.*

Build and Read Longer Words

Write the word *slowpoke* on the board. Remind students that when they come to a longer word, they should look to see if it is made up of two smaller words. Ask students which part of the word sounds like *slow* and which part sounds like *poke.* Draw your hand under the entire word as students read it aloud. Then write these words on the board: *blowfish, crowbar,* and *snowball.* Have students read the words and tell how they figured them out.

FLUENCY BUILDER Have students choose a passage from "The Rain and the Snow" to read aloud to a partner. You may have students choose passages they found particularly interesting or have them choose one of the following options:

- Read pages 55–56. (From *Rain said to* . . . through . . . *Snow said.* Total: 105 words)

- Read pages 59–60. (From *Do you see* . . . through . . . *your destiny.* Total: 106 words)

Ask students to read their passages aloud to their partners three times. Have students rate their own readings on a scale of 1–4. Encourage students to note their improvement from one reading to the next by completing the sentence *I know my reading has improved because* _____. Encourage the listener to offer positive feedback.

Review Vocabulary

To revisit the Vocabulary Words prior to the weekly assessments, use these sentence frames. Have volunteers read the sentence stems and choices. Then students write the correct answers. Go over the answers and discuss why they are correct.

1. The king **entrusted** the princess with the jewels. This means that he
   a. took them away.   b. gave them to her.

2. She **plodded** home from soccer in the rain. She
   a. ran like a horse.   b. walked very slowly.

3. Because she had taken tennis lessons, she was **assured** a place on the team. This means that
   a. she was guaranteed a spot.   b. she had to compete for a spot.

4. When he heard the word *bountiful*, he always thought of
   a. pirates.   b. an abundance of things.

5. The new author felt that writing was her **destiny**, or
   a. her fate.   b. her problem.

6. **Diligence** was something he was known for. He
   a. took naps at work.   b. worked hard and steadily.

Correct responses: 1b, 2b, 3a, 4b, 5a, 6b

This is a good time to show the vocabulary words and definitions on page 69. Have students copy them to use for studying for the vocabulary test.

INTERVENTION
PRACTICE
BOOK

page 30

Review Summarize and Paraphrase

To review summarizing and paraphrasing before the weekly assessment, use *Intervention Practice Book* page 30. Guide students to fill in the first two blanks. Direct their attention to the next section. Have them write a summary and again list the differences between a summary and a paraphrase.

Review Test Prep

INTERVENTION
ASSESSMENT
BOOK

Ask students to turn to *Pupil Edition* page 183, and call attention to the tips. Tell students that paying attention to the tips can help them do well on tests. Remind students to follow directions closely for question 2, which asks for a paraphrase, not a summary. Make sure they understand that a paraphrase will be about as long as the two sentences but will be in their own words.

DISTANT
VOYAGES

page 183

Self-Selected Reading

Encourage students to select their own books to read on their own. They may choose books from your classroom library shelf, or you may select a group of appropriate books from which your students can choose.

- *Colorful Characters in American Tall Tales*. (See page 183M of the *Teacher's Edition* for a lesson plan.)

- *A Is for Asia* by Cynthia Chin-Lee. Orchard, 1997.

- *Grandfather's Journey* by Allen Say. Houghton-Mifflin, 1987.

After students have chosen their books, give each student a copy of My Reading Log, found on page R38 in the back of the *Teacher's Edition*. Have each student fill in the information at the top of the form. Then have students use the log to keep track of their reading and to record their responses to the literature.

Conduct student-teacher conferences. Arrange for an individual conference time with each student when you can discuss his or her self-selected reading. Have students bring their Reading Logs to share during the conference. You may also want to have the student choose a favorite passage to read aloud to you. Then ask questions designed to stimulate discussion. For example, you might question what information the student learned from a non-fiction text, how the author structured the text, or how the artwork helped the student understand the topic.

FLUENCY PERFORMANCE Have students read aloud to you the passage from "The Rain and the Snow" they selected and practiced previously with their partners. Keep track of the number of words each student reads correctly. Ask each student to rate his or her performance on the 1–4 scale. If students aren't happy with their oral reading, give them an opportunity to practice some more and then to reread the passage to you.

See *Oral Reading Fluency Assessment* for monitoring progress.

LESSON 8

BEFORE
Building Background and Vocabulary

Use with

"Iditarod Dream"

Review Phonics: *R*-controlled Vowel /ôr/*or, oor*

Identify the sound. Have students repeat the following tongue twister aloud three times: *Did a torch scorch the floor of the porch?* Ask them to identify the words that have the same /ôr/ sound. (*torch, scorch, floor, porch*)

Associate letters to sound. Write the following sentence on the board: *Did a torch scorch the floor of the porch?* Underline the letters *or* in *torch, scorch,* and *porch* and the letters *oor* in *floor.* Tell students that these letters often stand for the /ôr/ sound they hear in *scorch* and *floor.*

Word blending. Model how to blend the letters and sounds to read *scorch.* Touch *s* and say /s/. Touch *c* and say /k/. Draw your hand under *or* and say /ôr/. Touch *ch* and say /ch/. Slide your hand under the whole word as you elongate the sounds: /sskôôrrch/. Then say the word naturally—*scorch.* Follow a similar process for *torch* and *floor.*

Apply the skill. *Letter Substitution* Write the following words on the board, and have students read each aloud. Make the changes necessary to form the words in parentheses. Ask a volunteer to read aloud each new word.

man (morn)	**flock** (floor)	**ban** (born)
dock (door)	**pot** (port)	**spot** (sport)

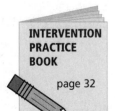

INTERVENTION PRACTICE BOOK

page 32

Introduce Vocabulary

PRETEACH **lesson vocabulary.** Tell students they are going to learn five new words that they will see again when they read a story called "Iditarod Dream." Teach each Vocabulary Word using the following process.

Use the following suggestions or similar ideas to give the meaning or context.

> Write the word.
> Say the word.
> Track the word and have students repeat it.
> Give the meaning or context.

headquarters Point out that this word can be considered either singular or plural.

positions Mention that this comes from the Latin word *positio,* which means "to place."

handlers The lion handlers were very careful with the big cats.

pace My mother goes at a slow pace when she walks my little sister to school.

tangle Let's fish from the boat so we won't tangle our fishing lines in the weeds.

For vocabulary activities, see Vocabulary Games on pp. 2–7.

For vocabulary activities, see Vocabulary Games on pp. 2–7.

Vocabulary Words

headquarters the place from which activities are directed

positions places occupied by people or things

handlers people who manage, control, or operate

pace rate of speed

tangle a confused mass; a snarl

AFTER

Building Background and Vocabulary

Apply Vocabulary Strategies

Use affixes and root words. Point to the word *headquarters* after you write it on the board. Remind students that they can sometimes figure out the meaning of an unfamiliar word by breaking it into its parts. In this case there are two roots put together.

MODEL I see two parts to this word—*head* and *quarters.* I know the word *head* has a number of meanings. One meaning can be "leader." One meaning of *quarters* is "areas of buildings." I think a *headquarters* is where the leadership of an organization meets.

Remind students to use this strategy when they encounter other unfamiliar words in their reading.

RETEACH lesson vocabulary. Be sure each student has a set of vocabulary cards. Read aloud the following sentences, saying "blank" for each blank. Have students hold up the correct word card. Then reread the sentences with the correct words.

1. We went to police __(headquarters)__ to report the robbery.
2. The horses took their __(positions)__ for the start of the parade.
3. The clowns said they wouldn't want to be tiger __(handlers)__.
4. The director motioned to slow down the __(pace)__ of the music.
5. The fishing lines were in a __(tangle)__.

FLUENCY BUILDER Use *Intervention Practice Book* page 31. Read aloud each of the words in the first column, and have students repeat it. Then have partners read the words to each other. Repeat for the remaining columns. After each partner has had a turn reading aloud the words in each column, have them practice reading the entire list while timing themselves.

INTERVENTION PRACTICE BOOK

page 31

★ Focus Skill · Draw Conclusions

PRETEACH **the skill.** Have students look at **side A of Skill Card 8: Draw Conclusions**. Read aloud the explanation as students follow along.

Then have students cover the bottom two illustrations and captions and look at the top illustration. Read the text aloud. Ask:

- **What has happened? What do you think will happen next?** (Possible response: A girl is going to ride a bike she doesn't know how to ride; she will get on the bike.)

- Have students look at the second illustration and read the second caption. Ask: **What is happening? What do story events and your own experience lead you to think will happen next?** (Possible response: She is rolling fast down a hill; she will lose control and fall.)

- Now ask students to look at the third illustration and read the caption. Ask: **How did you know this would be the conclusion?** (Responses will vary.)

Explain that as we read, we notice details and events in stories. We put the information together with our own experiences to draw conclusions about what will happen later in a story. Explain that sometimes, even good readers draw conclusions that turn out to be incorrect.

Prepare to Read: "Iditarod Dream"

Preview. Tell students that they are going to read a selection called "Iditarod Dream." Explain that this nonfiction selection gives true information about the topic and uses photographs to help tell the story. Then preview the selection.

DISTANT VOYAGES
pages 186–196

- **Pages 186–187:** I see a photograph of a man on a dogsled, so I think this selection will be about dogsledding.

- **Pages 188–189:** I see photos of a boy, a husky dog and a pack on a sled. I think the story will be about a dogsled trip.

- **Pages 190–191:** Now the boy and the sled are being pulled by the dogs. He has a number on his chest, so I think his trip is a race. I wonder how well he will do in the race.

Set purpose. Model setting a purpose for reading "Iditarod Dream."

MODEL I think this story tells of a boy who is in a sled race. I will read to find out how well he does in the race.

Reread and Summarize

Have students reread and summarize "Iditarod Dream" in sections, as described in the chart below.

Pages 186–187

Let's look again at pages 186–187 to remember setting and characters in this selection.

Summary: This story is about Dusty, who is competing in the junior competition of the dogsled race called the Iditarod.

Pages 188–189

As we read pages 188–189 again, let's recall Dusty's experience waiting for the race to start.

Summary: This is Dusty's second race. He has a good team and is ready. He checks over his sled and makes sure he has food for his dogs.

Pages 190–191

As we reread pages 190–191, let us notice how the race starts.

Summary: Dusty and his dogs have a good start, but they smash into a tree and get tangled up twice because of snowmobiles.

Pages 192–193

Let's reread pages 192–193 to remember how Dusty reaches the midpoint of the race, where they will stay overnight.

Summary: Dusty gets the dogs untangled and avoids a moose, which could be dangerous. Soon things are going smoothly. He knows he is in the lead and he makes it to the halfway point in seven hours.

Pages 194–196

Reread pages 194–196 to recall the last half of the race.

Summary: Dusty feeds and takes care of the dogs for the night. He and his team start again the next day before it is light, and he and the dogs win the race.

FLUENCY BUILDER Reuse *Intervention Practice Book* page 31. Call attention to the sentences at the bottom of the page. State that the goal is to have each student read each phrase smoothly. Model the appropriate pace, expression, and phrasing as you read aloud each of the sentences. Then have partners practice reading aloud each sentence two or three times.

INTERVENTION
PRACTICE
BOOK

page 31

Directed Reading: "Race for Life on the Iditarod Trail," pp. 62–68

TAKE FLIGHT
pp. 62–68

Pages 62–63

Read aloud the title of the story. Direct students' attention to the wintry surroundings in the illustration.

Explain that the story tells about a real event that happened in 1925 in the small town of Nome, Alaska, which is very far from other towns. Have them read page 62 to find out what is happening. Ask: **What is Dr. Welch worried about?** (*Possible response: He is worried that the children will die from diphtheria.*) **IMPORTANT DETAILS**

Ask: **What problem must be solved in this story?** (*Possible response: Medicine must be brought quickly more than 1,000 miles in stormy winter weather.*) **IMPORTANT DETAILS**

Pages 64–65

Ask students to read page 65 to find out what plans were made to save the people of Nome from being wiped out. (*Twenty dogsled champions would follow the mail route, the Iditarod Trail, to take the medicine to Nome.*) **IMPORTANT DETAILS**

Ask: **How long does it take to travel the Iditarod Trail?** (*Possible response: It can take up to two weeks, but champion mushers plan to do it in less than a week by dogsledding nonstop.*) **DRAW CONCLUSIONS**

Ask: **Will the medicine reach Nome in time to save the town?** (*Responses will vary.*) **MAKE PREDICTIONS**

Pages 66–67

Have students read page 66 to find out if the huskies can really make it to Nome. Model using the strategy Read Ahead:

> **MODEL** As I began reading page 66, I read "The huskies can't keep pace." So, I wonder if the medicine ever got to Nome. I will read ahead to see if the huskies are able to make it. **READ AHEAD**

Ask: **What are some of the obstacles that the mushers must overcome on the trail?** (*Possible responses: They must untangle knotted dog lines and travel alone without extra dog handlers; snowstorms make the trip more difficult.*) **IMPORTANT DETAILS**

Then have them read to see whether they predicted correctly. Ask: **Was the story problem solved? How do you know?** (*Possible response: The problem was solved because the medicine arrived in Nome in time to save the people.*) **CONFIRM PREDICTIONS**

Summarize the selection. Ask students to think about the story problem and how it was solved. Then have students write three sentences to summarize the beginning, middle, and ending of the story.

INTERVENTION
PRACTICE
BOOK

page 33

Answers to *Think About It* Questions

1. The medicine was needed quickly to stop the diphtheria and save lives. There was too much wind and snow for boats and planes to make the trip. **SUMMARY**

2. Possible response: They wanted to help the people of Nome, and they wanted to show that their dogs could do the job. **INTERPRETATION**

3. Responses will vary but should be written in the first person and should describe both the hardships Gunnar Kaasen overcame and his accomplishments. **WRITE A COMPOSITION**

AFTER

Skill Review
pages 200–201

USE SKILL CARD 8B

(Focus Skill) Draw Conclusions

RETEACH the skill. Have students look at **side B of Skill Card 8: Draw Conclusions**. Read the skill reminder aloud to them. Ask the students why drawing conclusions helps readers understand stories. (*It helps the reader stay interested in the story and pay closer attention to it.*) Have a student read aloud the paragraph. Ask students to use their own paper to complete the sentence starters on the skill card. (*Possible response for the first item: Shamika is a good singer, and Zoe and Suzanne are good dancers; possible response for the third item: Shamika will get a singing part, and Zoe and Suzanne will get dancing parts.*)

FLUENCY BUILDER Reuse *Intervention Practice Book* page 31. Explain that students will practice the sentences at the bottom of the page by reading them aloud on tape. Assign new partners, and have them take turns reading the sentences aloud to each other and then reading them on tape. After students listen to the tape, have them tell how they have improved their readings. Then have them tape themselves again, focusing on improved pacing and tone.

INTERVENTION PRACTICE BOOK

page 31

Expository Writing: Sentences That Summarize

Build on prior knowledge. Tell students that they will practice summarizing by writing a sentence for each page of text in "Race for Life on the Iditarod Trail." Tell students that as they summarize, they should look for the main nouns and verbs on the pages and ignore the describing words.

Construct the text. "Share the pen" with students in a collaborative writing effort. As students dictate, write the words, phrases, and sentences on the board or on chart paper. Guide the process by making suggestions as needed. For example:

- **Page 62:** People in Nome, Alaska, have diphtheria, but the nearest medicine is 1,000 miles away.

- **Page 65:** Dogsledding champions will take the medicine from Anchorage 674 miles to the Iditarod Trail. Then they will take the medicine over the trail to Nome.

- **Page 66:** A snowstorm makes the trip hard, but finally Gunnar Kaasen delivers the medicine.

Revisit the text. Go back and reread the sentences with students. Ask them to review the main nouns and verbs they have used to make sure they have included only the most important ideas.

- Remind students to check the spellings of names of people and places when writing about a nonfiction selection.

- Ask: **How should the names of special places begin?** (*with capital letters*)

- Read the sentences aloud with students.

On Your Own

Ask students to write a one- or two-sentence summary of each page of a selection they have previously read. Remind them to look for the main nouns and verbs as they decide which ideas to include.

Connect Spelling and Phonics

RETEACH *r*-controlled vowel /ôr/*or, oor.* Write *fort* on the board, and tell students that in the first seven words you say, the /ôr/ sound is spelled *or* as in *fort*. Dictate words 1–7, and have students write them. After they write each word, display the correct spelling so students can proofread their work. Next, write *door* on the board, and tell students that in the last word, the /ôr/ sound is spelled *oor* as in *door*. Dictate word 8, and have students proofread as before.

1. nor	2. corks	3. snowstorm*	4. forest
5. torn	6. morning*	7. transporting*	8. floor

***Word appears in "Race for Life on the Iditarod Trail."**

Dictate the following sentence, and have students write it: *We closed the doors when the morning storm hit.*

Build and Read Longer Words

**INTERVENTION
ASSESSMENT
BOOK**

Write the words *forward, transporting, forgetful,* and *doorstep* on the board. Ask volunteers to identify two consonants that are next to each other in the middle of the word *forward.* (*r, w*) Remind students that words that have this pattern are usually divided into syllables between the two consonants. Frame *for* and have students read it. Next frame *ward,* and ask students to read it. Then ask them to read the whole word aloud. Repeat the process for the remaining words.

FLUENCY BUILDER Have students choose a passage from "Race for Life on the Iditarod Trail" to read aloud to a partner. You may have students choose passages they found particularly interesting, or have them choose one of the following options:

- Read page 65. (From *Some people . . .* through *. . . to the next.* Total: 105 words.)

- Read page 66. (From *Then a snowstorm . . .* through *. . . they make it?* Total: 94 words.)

Ask students to read the selection aloud to their partners three times. Have students rate their own readings on a scale of 1 to 4.

Encourage students to note their improvement from one reading to the next by completing the sentence *I know my reading has improved because _____.* Encourage listeners to offer positive feedback about improvements.

Review Vocabulary

Read the questions to students and ask them to write the correct answers on their papers. Go over the answers and discuss why the answer is correct.

To revisit the Vocabulary Words prior to the weekly assessment, use these sentence frames. Read the statements to students, and have them write the answers. Review the answers, and discuss why they are correct.

1. From the army's **headquarters** the battles were
   a. fought.   b. planned.
2. The runners got into their starting **positions** to
   a. cross the finish line.   b. begin the race.
3. The **handlers** at the animal shelter
   a. worked with the animals   b. did paperwork.
4. I worked at too fast a **pace**, so I
   a. got tired quickly.   b. finished slowly.
5. Her hair was a **tangle** of curls after
   a. combing it.   b. sleeping all night.

Correct responses: lb, 2b, 3a, 4a, 5b

This is a good time to show the Vocabulary Words and definitions on page 79. Have students copy them to use for studying for the vocabulary test.

★ (Focus Skill) Review Draw Conclusions

To review drawing conclusions before the weekly assessment, use *Intervention Practice Book* page 34. Have a student read the first sentence aloud and suggest answers.

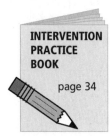

INTERVENTION
PRACTICE
BOOK

page 34

Direct students' attention to the rest of the page. Ask students to list six or seven important details of the selection. The first one is done for them.

Next, direct their attention to their conclusions. Help students conclude that the champions will work harder than anyone thought possible, even with very bad weather.

Review Test Prep

INTERVENTION
ASSESSMENT
BOOK

Ask students to turn to page 201 of the *Pupil Edition*. Point out the Tips for answering the test questions. Tell students that paying attention to these tips can help them answer these and other test questions. Remind students that when they are asked to draw conclusions, they must look to information from the selection and to their personal experiences.

DISTANT
VOYAGES
page 201

Self-Selected Reading

Encourage students to select their own books to read on their own. They may choose books from your classroom library shelf, or you may select a group of appropriate books from which students can choose.

- *Heroes in the Flames.* (See page 20 IM of the *Teacher's Edition* for a lesson plan.)

- *The Big Bike Race* by Lucy Jane Bledsoe. Avon, 1997.

- *Akiak* by Robert J. Blake. Philomel, 1997.

After students have chosen their books, give each student a copy of My Reading Log, found on page R38 in the back of the *Teacher's Edition*. Have each student fill in the information at the top of the form. Then have students use the log to keep track of their reading and to record their responses to the literature.

Conduct student-teacher conferences. Arrange for an individual conference time with each student to discuss his or her self-selected reading. Have students bring their Reading Logs to share during the conference. You may also want to have students choose a favorite passage to read aloud to you. Then ask questions designed to stimulate discussion. For example, you might ask what information the student learned from a nonfiction text, how the author structured the text, or how the artwork helped the student understand the topic.

FLUENCY PERFORMANCE Have students read aloud to you the passage from "Race for Life on the Iditarod Trail" they have selected and practiced previously with their partners. Keep track of the number of words each student reads correctly. Ask each student to rate his or her performance on the 1–4 scale. If students aren't happy with their oral reading, give them an opportunity to practice some more and to reread the passage to you.

See *Oral Reading Fluency Assessment* for monitoring progress.

Use with

"Woodsong"

Review Phonics: *R*-controlled Vowel /ôr/ *ore, oar, our*

Identify the sound. Have students repeat the following question aloud three times. *Do you sell oars at your store?* Have students identify the words that have the /ôr/ sound. (*oars, your, store*)

Associate letters to sound. Write this question on the board: *Do you sell oars at your store?* Underline the letters *oar, our,* and *ore* in the words. Tell students that when these groups of letters appear together in words, the letters usually stand for the /ôr/ sound in *store*.

Word blending. Write *shore, court,* and *board* on the board. Model blending letters and sounds to read *shore*. Touch *sh* and say /sh/. Draw your hand under *ore* and say /ôr/. Slide your hand under the whole word as you elongate the sounds: /shôôrr/. Then read the word naturally—*shore*. Follow a similar process for the words *court* and *board*.

Apply the skill. *Letter Substitution* Model making words with the /ôr/ sound. Write the following words on the board and have students read each aloud. Make the changes necessary to form the words in parentheses. Have a student read each new word aloud. Try to give each student an opportunity to respond.

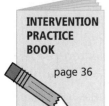

INTERVENTION
PRACTICE
BOOK

page 36

ignite (ignore)	**pot** (pour)	**rob** (roar)	**top** (tore)
hard (hoard)	**cob** (core)	**bear** (boar)	**got** (gourd)

Introduce Vocabulary

PRETEACH **lesson vocabulary.** Tell students they are going to learn seven new words that they will see again when they read a story called "Woodsong." Teach each Vocabulary Word using the following process.

Use the following sentences to give the meaning or context.

> Write the word.
> Say the word.
> Track the word and have students repeat it.
> Give the meaning or context.

resembled   When I was looking at old family pictures, I noticed how much my dad resembled my grandfather when Grandpa was younger.

bulk   The very large man had so much bulk that he was unable to fit into the small car.

pointedly   Since I was wearing my new shoes, Mom told me pointedly not to walk through the mud puddle.

harness	The farmer took the harness off the horse and began to brush him.
retired	Mrs. Lee had worked for the same company for 35 years before she retired.
disengage	My dog wanted me to disengage the hook to her leash so she could chase the cat.
snort	The big bull gave a mighty snort and began running toward the cowboy.

For vocabulary activities, see Vocabulary Games on pp. 2–7.

AFTER

Building Background and Vocabulary

Apply Vocabulary Strategies

Use prefixes and suffixes. Write *pointedly* and *disengage* on the board. Tell students that learning the meanings of prefixes and suffixes will help them understand many unfamiliar words.

MODEL In the word *pointedly* I see the suffix *–ly,* which I know means "in a way that is." I know that an arrow is pointed, so *pointedly* means "in a way that is sharp or aimed." In the word *disengage,* the suffix *dis-* means "opposite of." I know that *engage* can mean "to attach," so I know that *disengage* means "the opposite of *attach.*"

Tell students to use this strategy as they read.

RETEACH **lesson vocabulary.** Be sure each student has a set of vocabulary cards. Read aloud the following sentences, substituting "blank" for each Vocabulary Word. Ask students to hold up the correct word card. Reread the sentence with the appropriate word.

1. All of the boys in his family (resembled) each other.
2. My grandfather (retired) from working two years ago.
3. I had a bad cold, and my cough sounded like a (snort).
4. The blind woman had a Seeing Eye dog on a (harness).
5. If you (disengage) the gears of a car, it won't go forward.
6. The (bulk) of his camping gear would barely fit in his van.
7. Our teacher told us (pointedly) that no cheating was allowed.

FLUENCY BUILDER Use *Intervention Practice Book* page 35. Read aloud each of the words in the first column, and have students repeat it. Then have partners read each word aloud to each other. Repeat for the other two columns. After partners have practiced each column, have them practice the entire list.

INTERVENTION PRACTICE BOOK

page 35

(Focus Skill) Summarize and Paraphrase

PRETEACH the skill. Tell students that these two skills are very important for learning. Explain that being able to summarize shows that you understand a story and know what is most important. Being able to paraphrase shows that you can retell a story in your own words.

Have students look at **side A of Skill Card 9: Summarize and Paraphrase.** Have students read the explanations aloud and look at the illustrations. Ask volunteers to read the dialogue aloud. Ask:

- **What is happening in the first three panels?** (Possible response: The teacher is explaining how to do an assignment.)

- **Why is it important to understand the teacher's instructions?** (Possible response: to do the assignment correctly)

Ask a student to read aloud the text for the lower illustration. Then ask:

- **Has this girl told her friend everything the teacher said that was important?** (Possible response: Yes, but she used fewer words.) **Is this a summary or a paraphrase?** (summary)

Then ask volunteers to retell the instructions in their own words. Explain that they are paraphrasing if they try to include everything the teacher said.

Prepare to Read: "Woodsong"

Preview. Tell students that they are going to read a selection called "Woodsong." Explain to them that this is a personal narrative, which is a real story that has happened to a person. Then preview the selection.

- **Pages 204–207:** I see a picture of a large dog on page 205 and a team of dogs pulling a sled on pages 206–207. I think this story will be about a sled dog team or a man who uses a sled dog team.

DISTANT VOYAGES

pages
204–214

- **Pages 208–211:** The first picture shows a man dressed in very warm clothes. He probably is the person driving the sled. I wonder if he lives in Alaska or in northern Canada. I want to know what he is holding. On the following page he has a big wood-burning stove on the sled. Maybe he needs it to heat his cabin.

- **Pages 212–214:** Here again I see the dog with the stick in his mouth. I would like to know why the stick is important to the story. I know this is a true story, and I wonder what the dog uses it for.

Set purpose. Model setting a purpose for reading "Woodsong."

MODEL From my preview, I can tell that this story is about a man who uses a sled dog. I want to read to find out why this dog is special to the man and why the dog keeps a stick in its mouth.

Reread and Summarize

Have students reread and summarize "Woodsong" in sections, as described in the chart below.

Pages 204–206

Let's reread pages 204–206 to remember what the author tells us in the beginning of the story.

Summary: The author is writing a story to tell what he has learned from a hardworking yet playful sled dog named Storm.

Pages 207–209

Let's reread pages 207–209 to recall the joke Storm plays on his owner.

Summary: When the man stops to work on a dog's harness, Storm takes the man's hat and buries it in the snow. The man finds the hat by accident.

Pages 210–211

Reread pages 210–211 to find out what happens when the man tries to get a wood stove home on his sled.

Summary: Storm stares as the man loads a heavy stove onto the sled. Storm growls at the stove but begins pulling the sled anyway. At every break in the trip, Storm growls at the large stove.

Pages 212–214

Let's reread pages 212–214 to recall how Storm and the man find a way to communicate with each other.

Summary: During one trip Storm breaks a stick from a tree branch and runs with it in his mouth. Anytime Storm thinks the man is pushing the team too hard, he drops the stick and won't take it back from the man. In this way he teaches the man a lesson.

FLUENCY BUILDER Reuse *Intervention Practice Book* page 35. Bring to students' attention the sentences at the bottom of the page. State that the goal is to have each student read each phrase smoothly. Model the appropriate pace, expression, and phrasing as you read aloud each of the sentences. Then have students practice reading aloud each sentence two or three times to a partner.

INTERVENTION
PRACTICE
BOOK

page 35

Directed Reading "Fishing for Four" pp. 70–77

TAKE FLIGHT
pages 70–77

Page 70

Ask a volunteer to read aloud the title. Have the students look at the illustration on page 70, and help them identify the four people in the boat: Dad, Elinore (age 4), Suze, and the speaker. Ask students to predict what they think the story will be about. (*Responses will vary.*) Read page 70 to students. Ask: **Where are the people going in the rowboat?** (*Possible response: They are going to their big boat.*) **IMPORTANT DETAILS**

Why do you think they are going out to the bigger boat? (*Possible response: They need a bigger boat to go farther out to sea.*) **SPECULATE**

Page 71

Have students read page 71 to find out why the children are going fishing with their father. **What kind of work does the father do?** (*Possible response: He fishes for crabs.*) **IMPORTANT DETAILS**

Page 72

Ask a volunteer to read page 72 aloud while the students listen to find out where the family goes in the big boat. **Where does Dad take the boat?** (*Possible response: He steers the boat far offshore.*) **IMPORTANT DETAILS**

Page 73

Have students read page 73 to find out how much bait they need to catch today. **How many fish does Dad want them to catch?** (*Possible response: He estimates that they need to catch enough fish to fill four bushel baskets, or one basket each.*) **IMPORTANT DETAILS**

How would you summarize this page in one sentence? (*Possible response: The family begins fishing for bait.*) (Focus Skill) **SUMMARIZE AND PARAPHRASE**

Page 74

Have students read page 74. Ask: **What does the speaker mean by saying that the fish had "retired from swimming"?** (*Possible response: Because it was caught, the fish wouldn't be swimming any more.*) **AUTHOR'S CRAFT/APPRECIATE LANGUAGE**

What would be another way for that character to say that the fish had "retired from swimming"? (*Possible responses: The fish's life was over; the fish had to throw in the towel.*) (Focus Skill) **SUMMARIZE AND PARAPHRASE**

Page 75

Have volunteers read aloud the dialogue on page 75 while students listen to find out who appears to be winning the contest. Ask: **Who do you think is winning at this point?** (*Responses will vary.*) **SPECULATE**

Page 76

Ask a volunteer to read page 76 aloud to make sure they understand who wins the contest. Model using the Reread to Clarify strategy:

> MODEL When I read page 76, I don't quite understand what the author means by "A bunch of fish had met their match, and so had Suze and I." So, I reread the page. The author says Elinore's basket was full and overflowing, and she was grinning. I realize that Elinore, the four-year-old, has caught the most fish.

Ask: **Why is the ending of the story a surprise?** (*Possible response: The youngest child has caught the most fish, and she isn't even competing.*) **INTERPRET STORY EVENTS**

INTERVENTION
PRACTICE
BOOK

page 37

Page 77

Summarize the selection. Ask students to think about what happened first, next, and last on the fishing trip. Then have the students summarize the story in three sentences.

Answers to *Think About It* Questions

I. Possible response: The dad's job is fishing, and they go fishing to catch crab bait. **SUMMARY**

2. Possible response: The other girls are surprised and happy that Elinore got the most fish. I think this is true because they aren't angry when they see how many fish she has. **INTERPRETATION**

3. Responses will vary but should indicate friendly competition among all three sisters. **WRITE A CONVERSATION**

AFTER

Skill Review
pages 222–223

USE SKILL CARD 9B

(Focus Skill) Summarize and Paraphrase

RETEACH **the skill.** Have students look at **side B of Skill Card 9: Summarize and Paraphrase**. Read the skill reminder aloud, and have volunteers read the story aloud. Ask students to read the story silently.

Model the beginning of a paraphrase of the story: *Kim couldn't wait to get home from school.*

Assign writing partners to work on their own paraphrases. Ask volunteers to read their paraphrases aloud, and discuss the similarities and differences in them. Then ask students to write their own one- or two-sentence summaries.

FLUENCY BUILDER Use *Intervention Practice Book* page 35. Explain that each student will practice the sentences at the bottom of the page by reading them aloud on tape. Assign new partners. Have students take turns reading the sentences aloud to each other and then reading them on tape. After students listen to the tape, have them tell how they have improved. Then have them tape their readings again, focusing on improved pacing and tone.

INTERVENTION
PRACTICE
BOOK

page 35

Expository Writing: How-to Sentences

Build on prior knowledge. Tell students that they will talk and write a set of steps for how to make a mobile. Display the following information:

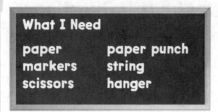

What I Need

paper	paper punch
markers	string
scissors	hanger

Construct the text. Ask students to think about how they would use the supplies to make a mobile. "Share the pen" with students in a collaborative writing effort. As students dictate sentences, write them on the board. Guide the process by asking questions and offering suggestions as needed. For example:

1. Use the markers to draw pictures.
2. Cut out the pictures.
3. Use the paper punch to make a hole in each picture.
4. Tie a string through the hole of each picture.
5. Tie the other end of each string to the hanger.
6. Hang up the mobile.

Revisit the text. Go back and read the list of steps together. Ask: **Why is it important to list the steps in order?** (Possible responses: Otherwise, the mobile might not turn out right.)

- Guide students to see that the steps don't flow together in a paragraph. Ask: **To turn the sentences into a paragraph, what words or phrases might we add?** (Possible responses: time-order words such as *first, next, then,* and *last*; transition phrases such as *after that* and *the next step*; combine two or more sentences)

- Work with students to construct a sentence that could begin a paragraph that explains the steps, such as *Here are the steps to follow to make a mobile.* Then add a transition word or phrase to the first step to continue the paragraph. For example: *The first step is to use markers to draw pictures on paper.*

- Have students read the numbered steps aloud and then the first two sentences of your paragraph.

On Your Own

Have students write the first two sentences of the paragraph you began above. Then ask them to finish constructing the paragraph. Remind them to add time-order words and phrases to make the sentences flow smoothly in a paragraph.

Connect Spelling and Phonics

RETEACH *r-controlled vowel /ôr/ore, oar, our.* Write *core* on the board, and tell students that in the first four words you will say, the /ôr/ sound is spelled *ore* as in *core.* Dictate words 1–4, and have students write them. After each word, display the correct spelling so students can proofread their work. Continue this procedure by writing *soar* or *four* on the board and dictating words 5–8.

1. bore*	2. chore*	3. more*	4. adore*
5. board*	6. oars*	7. four*	8. poured*

*Word appears in "Fishing for Four."

Dictate the following sentence for students to write: *There are four more oars in the shed.*

Build and Read Longer Words

INTERVENTION
ASSESSMENT
BOOK

Write the word *bore* on the board and have a volunteer read it aloud. Then write *boring* below it. Tell students that when the ending *-ing* is added to a word with the *ore* pattern, the final *e* is dropped. Follow a similar procedure with *snore/snoring* and *store/storing.* Write *score, adore, ignore,* and *implore* on the board, and have students add the *-ing* ending to each word, dropping the *e.*

Explain that these words can also be used to make longer words. Return to the word *bore,* and write *boredom* next to it. Ask a student to read the word. Follow the same pattern with *ignore/ignoring, adore/adorable, oar/oarlock,* and *corn/cornflake.*

FLUENCY BUILDER Have students choose a passage from "Fishing for Four" to read aloud to a partner. You may have students choose passages they found very interesting. Or you can assign them a particular passage, such as:

- Read pages 72–73. (From *Dad steered . . .* through . . . *flopping on the deck.* Total: 91 words)

- Read pages 75–76. (From *I got three . . .* through . . . *Suze and I.* Total: 98 words)

Ask students to read the selection aloud to their partners three times. Have students rate their own readings on a scale of 1 to 4.

Encourage students to note their improvement from one reading to the next by completing the sentence *I know my reading has improved because* _____. Encourage listeners to offer positive feedback.

Review Vocabulary

To revisit Vocabulary Words prior to the weekly assessment, read the following sentences aloud. Ask students to identify the correct choice and explain why it makes sense.

1. They said she **resembled** her aunt. This means that she
   a. looked like her aunt   b. liked her aunt

2. He was **retired** from the military, which means he
   a. had been promoted   b. was no longer in the military

3. The animal gave a loud **snort** and then ran away. A snort is
   a. a special dance
   b. a sound coming from air pushed through the nostrils

4. They found an old **harness** in the barn, which had been
   a. used to hitch the horse to the cart
   b. used at barn dances

5. When she moved, she started to **disengage** from her old friendships. This means
   a. she started to write a lot of letters
   b. she grew less connected

6. The herbs were sold in **bulk**, or
   a. in large lots   b. in wooden containers

7. She was told most pointedly that she was too young for the club. She was told
   a. with great emphasis   b. very quietly

   Correct responses: la, 2b, 3b, 4a, 5b, 6a, 7a

This is a good time to show the Vocabulary Words and definitions on page 89. Have students copy them to use for studying for the vocabulary test.

 Review Summarize and Paraphrase

INTERVENTION PRACTICE BOOK

page 38

To review summarizing and paraphrasing before the weekly assessment, use *Intervention Practice Book* page 38. Call attention to the title. Ask a volunteer to fill in the first two blanks, defining the words. Then have other students read each sentence aloud.

Ask students to read the story in the *Intervention Practice Book*. Ask volunteers to read aloud each paragraph. Then read summary statements aloud, and have students answer the questions. (Possible response: It is a summary. It is short and includes just the main points.)

Review Test Prep

INTERVENTION ASSESSMENT BOOK

Ask students to turn to page 223 of the *Pupil Edition*. Point out the tips for answering the test questions. Tell students that paying attention to these tips can help them answer these and other test questions.

DISTANT VOYAGES

page 223

Have students follow along as you read aloud each test question and the tip that goes with it. Remind them that a summary is a brief retelling.

Self-Selected Reading

Encourage students to select their own books to read independently. They may choose books from the classroom library shelf or you may select a group of appropriate books from which your students can choose.

- *Friends in Need.* (See page 223K of the *Teacher's Edition* for a lesson plan.)

- *Mush! Across Alaska in the World's Longest Sled-Dog Race* by Patricia Seibert. Millbrook, 1992.

- *Walk with a Wolf* by Janni Howker. Candlewick, 1998.

After each student has chosen his or her book, give the student a copy of My Reading Log, found on page R38 in the back of the *Teacher's Edition*. Have each student fill in the information at the top of the form. Then have students use the log to keep track of their reading and to record their responses to the literature.

Conduct student-teacher conferences. Arrange for an individual conference time with each of your students when you can discuss his or her self-selected reading. Have students bring their Reading Logs to share during the conference. You may also want to have each student choose a favorite passage to read aloud to you. Then ask questions designed to stimulate discussion. For example, you might question what information the student learned from a nonfiction text, how the author structured the text, or how the artwork helped the student understand the topic.

FLUENCY PERFORMANCE Have students read aloud to you the passages from "Fishing for Four" they have selected and practiced previously with their partners. Keep track of the number of words each student reads correctly. Ask each student to rate his or her performance on the 1–4 scale. If students aren't happy with their oral reading, give them an opportunity to practice some more and then to reread the passage to you.

See *Oral Reading Fluency Assessment* for monitoring progress.

LESSON 10

BEFORE
Building Background and Vocabulary

Use with

"Island of the Blue Dolphins"

Review Phonics: R-Controlled Vowel /ûr/ *ear, er, ir,* or *ur*

Identify the sound. Have students repeat the following sentences: *If I twirl around, the Earth seems to turn beneath my feet. My world is perfect.* Ask students to identify the words that have the same vowel sound as in *curl.* (*twirl, Earth, turning*)

Associate letters to sound. Write the sentence from above on the board. Underline the letters that stand for the /ûr/ sound: tw<u>ir</u>l, <u>Ear</u>th, t<u>ur</u>n, w<u>or</u>ld, p<u>er</u>fect. Tell students that the underlined letters all can stand for the /ûr/ sound they hear in *burn.*

Word blending. Model how to blend and read *pearl.* Slide your hand under the word elongating the sounds: /ppûrll/. Then say it naturally— *pearl.*

INTERVENTION PRACTICE BOOK

page 40

Apply the skill. *Letter Substitution* Write the following words on the board, and have students read each word aloud. Make the changes necessary to form the words in parentheses. Have students read each new word aloud. Try to give all students an opportunity to respond.

peas (pearl)   **still** (stir)   **lean** (learn)   **lunch** (lurch)

bark (bird)   **blunt** (blur)   **marry** (mercy)   **wood** (word)

Introduce Vocabulary

PRETEACH lesson vocabulary. Tell students that they are going to learn seven new words that they will see again when they read a story called "Island of the Blue Dolphins." Teach each Vocabulary Word using the following process.

Use the following suggestions or similar ideas to give the meaning or context.

> Write the word.
> Say the word.
> Track the word and have students repeat it.
> Give the meaning or context.

overcome	The people in the burning house were overcome by smoke.
forlorn	When I forgot to feed the dog, he looked forlorn.
pitched	The ship was pitched about on the stormy sea.
vainer	The vainer one of my two pet birds spends hours looking at itself in its mirror.
gorged	At the party the children gorged themselves on pizza, cake, and ice cream.

| abalone | We gathered abalone and added them to the fish stew. |
| lair | During the cold winter, the black bear sleeps in its lair. |

For vocabulary activities, see Vocabulary Games on pp. 2–7.

AFTER

Building Background and Vocabulary

Apply Vocabulary Strategies

Use words with multiple meanings. Explain to students that many words have a number of meanings. We can usually decide the meaning by using context, or other words.

MODEL I know that one of the story words is *overcome*. I have seen this word used in different ways. For example, I have heard people say they can overcome their problems. I have also heard people talk about being overcome with happiness. I will look at how the word is used in the story to decide its meaning.

Remind students to use this strategy in all their reading.

RETEACH lesson vocabulary. Be sure each student has a set of word cards. Have students listen to the following sentences. Read each sentence aloud, and ask students to hold up the appropriate word card. Reread the sentence with the appropriate word choice.

1. When we picked up our dog at the kennel, he gave us a __(forlorn)__ look.
2. On Thanksgiving we __(gorged)__ ourselves on turkey.
3. The wolves rested in their __(lair)__ to avoid the hot sun.
4. Our canoe __(pitched)__ about in the rapids of the river.
5. Some people use __(abalone)__ shells for decorations.
6. The tall movie star was __(vainer)__ than the short one.
7. At the movie I was __(overcome)__ by the sad story.

FLUENCY BUILDER Distribute *Intervention Practice Book* page 39. Read each word in the first column, and have students repeat it. Then have students work in pairs and take turns reading the words to each other. Follow the same procedure with each of the remaining columns. Then have partners practice the entire list.

INTERVENTION PRACTICE BOOK

page 39

USE SKILL CARD 10A

★ (Focus Skill) Narrative Elements

PRETEACH the skill. Tell students that fiction stories have the narrative elements of characters, setting, plot, and theme. The parts of the plot include the conflict, or problem, and its solution.

Have students look at **side A of Skill Card 10: Narrative Elements.** Read aloud the definition at the top of the page, and ask volunteers to read aloud the explanations in the box. Then ask students to look at the illustration and suggest the setting and possible characters in the story. Have students read "Winter Struggle" silently as you read it aloud.

Direct students' attention to the chart. Read aloud and discuss each element.

Ask: **How do you decide the theme of a story?** (Possible response: I think about what the character or characters learn by solving the problem.)

Ask: **Sometimes, the solution to the conflict is called the resolution. What is the resolution to the conflict in this story?** (Possible response: Wings of Eagle gets food from the People of the River.)

Prepare to Read: "Island of the Blue Dolphins"

Preview. Tell students they are going to read a selection called "Island of the Blue Dolphins." Explain that this is a fiction story and has characters, a setting, a plot with a problem and a solution, and a theme. Guide students to identify these narrative elements in the story.

> **DISTANT VOYAGES**
> pages 226–236

- **Pages 226–227:** On these pages I see water and land. I think the water must be the ocean, because there is a large ship. I think the land is an island, since *Island* is in the title. This place must be the setting.

- **Pages 228–229:** This looks like the same setting, except that the viewer is on land. I see men with boats on the shore who are waving to others who are running toward them. I think that the plot, or series of events, will tell about these people.

- **Pages 230–231:** There are two women on the ship, and one is pointing to someone on shore. I wonder if the problem in the story is the storm on the sea or the person who was left on the island.

- **Pages 232–233:** This is the same girl as in the other pictures, so I am sure she is a main character. She is swimming in the water. Maybe part of the conflict is that she returns to the shore.

Set purpose. Model setting a purpose for reading "Island of the Blue Dolphins."

> **MODEL** I think this is an adventure story. I want to read to enjoy the adventure and to find out what happens to the characters.

Reread and Summarize

Have students reread and summarize "Island of the Blue Dolphins"
in sections, as described in the chart below.

Pages 228–229

**Let's reread pages 228–229 to recall why the tribe has to leave the
island.**

Summary: The tribe has been attacked by hunters and must find a
safer place to live. The people take things they value and run toward
the boats that will take them to the ship. The ship cannot stay long
because of the storm.

Pages 230–231

Let's reread these pages to recall how Karana searches for Ramo.

Summary: Karana searches the ship for her brother, Ramo, but doesn't
find him. As the ship turns away from the island, Karana sees her
brother running along the cliff on the island.

Pages 232–233

**Reread these pages to learn the problem in the story and to find out
how Karana solves it.**

Summary: Karana does not want to be separated from her brother, so
she jumps out of the ship and into the ocean, and swims to shore.

Pages 234–236

**Reread the ending of the story to find out what happens when
Karana and Ramo return to the village.**

Summary: When Karana and Ramo return to the village, they find that
wild dogs have eaten all the food. Karana and Ramo gather more
food, but they are alone on the island with the wild dogs. They know
the ship will not come back for a long, long time.

FLUENCY BUILDER Be sure students have copies
of *Intervention Practice Book* page 39. Call attention to
the sentences at the bottom of the page. Model appropriate pace, expression, and phrasing as you read each
sentence, and have students read it after you. Then
have students practice by reading the sentences aloud
to a partner.

INTERVENTION
PRACTICE
BOOK

page 39

Directed Reading "Raindrop in the Sun": pp. 78–85

Page 78

Read aloud the title of the story. Have students look at the picture on pages 78–79 and then read page 78. Ask: **What is the man telling the girl that makes her angry?** (*He is telling her that girls can't gather abalones with the men.*) Ask: **What reason does Moro give for not letting girls gather abalones?** (*They aren't strong enough.*) **IMPORTANT DETAILS**

Ask: **What words would you use to describe Lani?** (*Possible responses: confident; has strong feelings and opinions*) **CHARACTERS' TRAITS**

Page 79

Read aloud page 79. Ask: **Why does Kalo say he'll hide Lani in his canoe?** (*Possible responses: He believes she could help bring home more abalones; he thinks the rule against letting girls go is unfair.*) **CAUSE/EFFECT**

Page 80

Have students read page 80. Ask: **Does Lani hide in Kalo's canoe?** (*yes*) Ask: **Why do you think Lani's mother lets her go?** (*Possible response: She also disagrees with the rule.*) **CHARACTERS' MOTIVATIONS**

Page 81

After students read page 81, ask: **What animals do Lani and Kalo see on the rocks?** (*seals*) **IMPORTANT DETAILS**

Page 82

Have students read page 82. Ask: **Are Kalo and Lani successful at gathering abalones?** (*yes*) Ask: **What problem happens in the story? How do you think it will be solved?** (*Possible response: A storm comes, and a wave flips the men's canoes over. I think Kalo and Lani will rescue the men.*) ✲(Focus Skill) **NARRATIVE ELEMENTS**

Page 83

Have students read page 83 to find out how Kalo and Lani rescue the men. Model using the Summarize strategy:

> **MODEL** On this page I find that Kalo and Lani rescue the men in the storm. I look at all the details and sum up the most important ideas. I summarize by saying that Lani turns the canoes right side up, Kalo pulls Moro and the other men from the water, and they all paddle for shore. (Focus Strategy) **SUMMARIZE**

Ask: **Why does Kalo tell Lani to throw the abalones overboard?** (*Possible response: to make the boat lighter and faster so they can get to the others quickly*) **IMPORTANT DETAILS**

Page 84

Have students read page 84. Ask: **What happens to Kalo and Lani once the group returns to shore?** (*Lani gives Mama the abalone shell that she saved.*) Ask: **Why does Moro give the pearl to Lani as a trophy?** (*Possible responses: The pearl is special; Lani has shown unusual bravery and strength in helping rescue the men.*) **CHARACTERS' MOTIVATIONS**

INTERVENTION PRACTICE BOOK

page 41

Summarize the selection. Ask students to tell why "Raindrop in the Sun" is or is not a good title for this story. Then help them summarize the selection in three sentences.

Answers to *Think About It* Questions

1. Possible responses: Moro says that a girl can't paddle a canoe and can't be strong enough to gather abalones. **SUMMARY**

2. Possible responses: Kalo takes his sister because he agrees that she is strong enough and can help him. When the storm comes up, he may be wishing that they were safe at home. **INTERPRETATION**

3. Conversations will vary but may indicate that some men are still reluctant to take girls along. Lani and the other girls may remind the men of the rescue as evidence that girls are strong and quick enough to go along. **WRITE DIALOGUE**

AFTER

Skill Review
pages 242–243

USE SKILL CARD 10B

(Focus Skill) Narrative Elements

Have students look at **side B of Skill Card 10: Narrative Elements.** Read the skill reminder at the top of the page. Have students read a "Hot, Dry Summer" silently, and then call on a volunteer to read it aloud.

Guide students to understand that this story is related to the one on side A of the skill card but that the time of year has changed. Remind students to decide whether the same character is the main character in both stories. Tell students to look for the elements of plot—the conflict and the solution. Explain that the theme, or message, will be similar to that on side A but will be a little different because of the new events. (Possible theme: Life can be easier for people who share their things and ideas.)

Direct students' attention to the chart at the bottom of the page. Tell students to work in pairs to fill in the information in the chart. When students are finished, have them share answers with the group.

FLUENCY BUILDER Distribute copies of *Intervention Practice Book* page 39. Assign new partners, and have them practice reading the sentences at the bottom of the page. This time their readings should be taped. Have students take turns reading the sentences aloud to each other. Tell students to comment on each other's performance. Each student should report on what the partner did well and make suggestions to improve the reading next time. Students should then read the sentences again and tell whether they feel they improved.

INTERVENTION PRACTICE BOOK

page 39

Timed or Tested Writing: Paragraph That Explains

Build on prior knowledge. Tell students that they will write a paragraph that explains why a family would choose a vacation in the mountains. Display the following information:

cool mountain air
hiking
fishing
toasted marshmallows
quiet

Construct the text. Discuss the ideas you have written as things to enjoy during a mountain vacation. "Share the pen" with students in a collaborative writing effort. As students dictate phrases and sentences, write them on the board or on chart paper. Guide the process by asking questions and making suggestions. Begin by constructing a sentence that gives the main idea. Then elicit sentences that explain the reasons. For example:

> One of the best vacations I know of is a trip to the mountains. The air in the mountains is cool. There are trails to hike on and streams to fish in. It's fun to eat the fish we catch. It's fun to toast marshmallows. Best of all, the mountains are quiet because there is no city traffic.

Revisit the text. Go back and reread the paragraph with students. Ask: **Why do we use a main idea sentence first in the explanation?** (Possible response: It lets the reader know what the paragraph is mostly about.)

- Ask: **How did making a prewriting list help us write the explanation?** (Possible response: It helped us think of reasons; it helped us remember to include all the reasons in the explanation.)

- Guide students to combine two related ideas into one sentence. Ask: **How could we combine the ideas about eating fish and eating marshmallows into one sentence? Why would we do this?** (Possible response: We could write one sentence saying *It's fun to eat the fish for dinner and toast marshmallows for dessert.* The ideas are related.)

- Read the completed paragraph aloud with students.

On Your Own

Direct students to think of a place they have visited or would like to visit. Ask them to write a list of ideas that explain why they would like this place. They should begin by writing a sentence telling about the overall idea and then add other sentences explaining the reasons.

Connecting Spelling and Phonics

RETEACH *r*-controlled vowel /ûr/*ear, ur, ir.* Write the word *dirt* on the board, and tell students that in the first two words you will say, the /ûr/ sound is spelled *ir* as in *dirt*. After students write each word, write it on the board so they can proofread their work. Repeat the procedure, using *her, burn, world,* and *earn* for words 3–10.

I. girl*	2. bird	3. perched*	4. derby	5. fur*
6. turned*	7. work*	8. worry*	9. pearl*	I0. early

*Word appears in "Raindrop in the Sun."

Build and Read Longer Words

INTERVENTION
ASSESSMENT
BOOK

Write the words *turnip, earnest, working, herbal,* and *stirrup* on the board. Ask students to underline the letters in each word that stand for the /ûr/ sound. (*ur; ear; ir; or; er*) Point out that when words that have these spelling patterns are broken into syllables, the letters always stay together. Frame the syllables of each word (*tur-nip; ear-nest; stir-rup; wor-king; her-bal*), and guide students to pronounce it. Draw your hand under the entire word, and have students pronounce it. Repeat with the words *purpose, Thursday; searchlight, earliest; birthday, thirteen; worldwide; merchant; alerted.*

FLUENCY BUILDER Have students choose a passage from "Raindrop in the Sun" to read aloud to a partner. You may have students choose passages that they found particularly interesting or have them choose one of the following options.

- Read pages 78–79. (From *Moro said . . .* through . . . *looked forlorn.* Total: I04 words)

- Read pages 80–81. (From *Lani looked . . .* through . . . *gorged on fish.* Total: I10 words)

- Read pages 82–83. (From *Kalo would . . .* through . . . *us too slow.* Total: I08 words)

Have students read a selected passage aloud to their partners three times. Then have the students rate each reading on a scale from I to 4.

Encourage students to note their improvement from one reading to the next by completing the sentence *I know my reading has improved because* _____. Encourage listeners to offer positive feedback about improvements.

Review Vocabulary

Read the statements to students, and ask them to write the correct answers. Go over the answers, and discuss why they are correct.

I. The lonely girl at the train station looked **forlorn** because

   a. she had no ride home.   b. it was a holiday.

2. When the earthquake destroyed the city, the people were **over-come** with

   a. happiness.   b. grief and sadness.

3. The high waves **pitched** the canoe up and down, and the canoe began

   a. to sink.   b. to float.

4. Safe inside the fox's **lair** were her

   a. babies.   b. enemies.

5. People collected **abalone**, a shellfish, to use as

   a. pencils.   b. food.

6. The hungry snake **gorged** itself on

   a. a small rock.   b. a small pig.

7. The **vainer** of the two boxers entered the boxing ring and shouted,

   a. "I can beat anybody!"   b. "I might not win!"

   Correct responses: la, 2b, 3a, 4a, 5b, 6b, 7a

You may want to display the Vocabulary Words and definitions on page 99 and have students copy them to use when they study for the vocabulary test.

★ Focus Skill Narrative Elements

INTERVENTION PRACTICE BOOK

page 42

Before the weekly assessment on narrative elements, distribute *Intervention Practice Book* page 42. Ask students to read the story silently. Then have a student read it aloud. Have students answer the questions below the story.

Review Test Prep

Ask students to turn to page 243 of the *Pupil Edition*. Call attention to the tips for answering the test questions. Tell students that paying attention to these tips can help them answer not only the test questions on this page but also questions on other tests.

DISTANT VOYAGES

page 243

INTERVENTION ASSESSMENT BOOK

Have students follow along as you read aloud the first question, its answer choices, and the tip. Guide students to understand that even though choice A, "on a boat," is mentioned in the story, most of the story is about events that happen in choice B, "in the sea." Direct students to use the tip to help them choose the answer. Repeat for the second question and tip.

Self-Selected Reading

Have students select their own books to read independently. They may choose books from the classroom library shelf or you may wish to offer a group of appropriate books from which students can choose.

- *Shipwrecked.* (See page 243M of the *Teacher's Edition* for a lesson plan.)
- *Birdie's Lighthouse* by Deborah Hopkinson. Atheneum, 1997.
- *Neptune Adventures: Danger on Crab Island* by Susan Saunders. Avon, 1998.

After students have chosen their books, give each student a copy of My Reading Log, which can be found on page R38 in the back of the *Teacher's Edition*. Have students fill in the information at the top of the form. Then have them use the log to keep track of their reading and to record their responses to literature.

Conduct student-teacher conferences. Arrange time for each student to confer with you individually about his or her selected reading. Have students bring their Reading Logs to share with you at the conference. Students might also like to choose a favorite passage to read aloud to you. To give students more practice with summarizing and paraphrasing, ask them to read a short section and to summarize and then paraphrase it.

FLUENCY PERFORMANCE Have students read aloud to you the passage from "Raindrop in the Sun" that they selected and practiced with their partners. Keep track of the number of words students read correctly. Ask each student to rate his or her own performance on the 1–4 scale. If students are not happy with their oral reading, give them an opportunity to continue practicing and to read the passage to you again.

See *Oral Reading Fluency Assessment* for monitoring progress.

Use with

"Everglades"

Review Phonics: Long Vowels /ā/a; /ē/e, y; /ī/i, y; /ō/o; /o͞o/u

Identify the sounds. Ask students to repeat the following sentence aloud two times: *This baby tuna will be a giant fish by October.* Ask students to identify a word other than *a* that has the /ā/ sound. (*baby*) Then have them identify two words that have the /ē/ sound they hear in *even.* (*be, baby*) Ask students to identify the words that have the /ī/ sound (*giant, by*), a word that has the /ō/ sound (*October*), and a word that has the /o͞o/ sound. (*tuna*)

Associate letters to sounds. Write the sentence from above on the board. Underline the letters that stand for the long vowel sounds as follows: b<u>a</u>b<u>y</u>, t<u>u</u>na, b<u>e</u>, g<u>i</u>ant, b<u>y</u>, Oct<u>o</u>ber. Tell students that in some words, a single vowel can stand for a long vowel sound. Read aloud each word and have students repeat the word. Then ask: **Which word has the long e vowel sound you hear in we?** (*be, baby*) **Which words have the long u vowel sound we hear in tuba?** (*tuna*) **Which word has the long a vowel sound heard in label?** (*baby*) **Which words have the long i vowel sound we hear in nice?** (*giant, by*)

Word blending. Write the word *volcano* on the board. Model how to blend and read it. Slide your hand under the word as you elongate the sounds: /vvoollkkāānno͞o/. Slide your hand under the whole word as you read it naturally—*volcano.*

INTERVENTION PRACTICE BOOK

page 44

Apply the skill. *Letter Substitution* Write the following words on the board and have students read each aloud. Make the changes necessary to form the words in parentheses. Have a volunteer read aloud each new word.

oven (over)   **fin** (find)   **lad** (lady)   **shell** (she)   **hot** (host)

Introduce Vocabulary

PRETEACH **lesson vocabulary.** Tell students that they are going to learn six new words that they will see again when they read a story called "Everglades." Teach each Vocabulary Word using the following process.

Use the following suggestions or similar ideas to give the meaning or context.

eons	The sun and moon have been around for eons.
scurried	When the fox came, the rabbits scurried into their hole.

> Write the word.
> Say the word.
> Track the word and have students repeat it.
> Give the meaning or context.

pondered	Mom and Dad pondered letting me have a sleepover.
multitude	If a huge number of people are in a place, we say there is a multitude of people.
peninsula	Part of Florida is a large peninsula since it sticks out into the ocean and has water on all sides but one.
plenitude	Grandma serves a plenitude of good food on Thanksgiving.

For vocabulary activities, see Vocabulary Games on pp. 2–7.

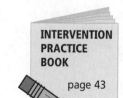

Vocabulary Words

eons many decades or centuries

scurried moved quickly

pondered thought very deeply

multitude a great number of persons or things

peninsula land almost surrounded by water

plenitude abundance; hugeness

AFTER
Building Background and Vocabulary

Apply Vocabulary Strategies

Use reference sources. Write the word *eons* on the board. Explain that students can use a dictionary to find unfamiliar words.

> **MODEL** **This word looks unfamiliar to me, so I will use a dictionary. I know to look for the singular form, *eon*. All of the definitions have to do with periods of time, so eons must be periods of time.**

Remind students to use the dictionary as needed when they read.

RETEACH **lesson vocabulary.** Give students vocabulary cards, and read aloud these sentences. Say "blank" for each blank. Ask students to hold up the correct card. Reread the sentence with the correct word.

1. We learned about previous ___(eons)___ when dinosaurs lived.
2. He watched as the ants ___(scurried)___ across the sidewalk.
3. We knew that Dad had ___(pondered)___ his decision.
4. The ___(multitude)___ of fans at the concert was overwhelming.
5. From the ___(peninsula)___ we could fish on the ocean or in the bay.
6. The ___(plenitude)___ of help from our neighbors was welcome.

FLUENCY BUILDER Use *Intervention Practice Book* page 43. Read aloud each word in the first column and have students repeat it. Then have partners read the words to each other. Repeat for the remaining columns. Then have partners practice reading the entire list and time themselves.

INTERVENTION PRACTICE BOOK

page 43

USE SKILL CARD 11A

(Focus Skill) Prefixes, Suffixes, and Roots

PRETEACH **the skill.** Tell students that good readers can figure out many unfamiliar words by figuring out the meanings of word parts.

Have students look at **side A of Skill Card 11: Prefixes, Suffixes, and Roots.** Ask a volunteer to read the first sentence aloud. Then have students read aloud, together, the next three sentences. Then read the last sentence to them.

Point out the word *indivisible*, and ask students where they have heard this word. (Possible response: in the Pledge of Allegiance) Say: **Let's take the word apart so we can understand it. What is the root?** (*divis*) **What does this mean?** ("divide") Ask students to identify the prefix (*in-*), the suffix (*-ible*), and their meanings. Guide them to put the meanings of the three parts together to form the meaning of the whole word. Then read aloud and discuss sentence 1.

Follow the same procedure with the remaining words in the chart and the sentences. Explain that readers can often figure out longer words by dividing them into word parts such as prefixes, suffixes, and roots. Remind students that they can use a dictionary for help.

Prepare to Read: "Everglades"

Preview. Tell students that they are going to read a selection called "Everglades." Explain that this is informational fiction, which gives information, but the people and events may not be real.

DISTANT VOYAGES
pages 248–267

- **Pages 248–249:** I see a picture of a water bird and people fishing in the background. The title says "Everglades," so I think this swampy place must be the Everglades.

- **Pages 250–253:** Again I see this swampy place. In one picture a man is taking children on a trip in a small boat. I think he is telling them about the Everglades.

- **Pages 254–257:** These scenes are much the same, except that I see insects, birds, and other animals. Maybe the people in the boat are looking at the animals.

- **Pages 258–261:** I see pictures of a lizard, a panther, and another water bird. There must be a lot of living things in the Everglades.

Set purpose. Model setting a purpose for reading "Everglades."

MODEL From my preview, I think the man is guiding students on a tour of the Everglades. I want to read about what he teaches them about the Everglades.

Reread and Summarize

Have students reread and summarize "Everglades" in sections, as described in the chart below.

> ### Pages 248–251
> **Let's look again at pages 248–251 to remember the start of the story of the Everglades.**
>
> Summary: A storyteller takes children on a boat ride and tells them the story of the Everglades of Florida.
>
> ### Pages 252–255
> **As we read pages 252–255 again, let's recall the story that is told of how the Everglades came to be.**
>
> Summary: The water that spilled out of Lake Okeechobee formed a huge, shallow river called the Everglades. It had many grasses and other plants, and fish, turtles, and alligators had plenty to eat.
>
> ### Pages 256–259
> **Let's notice what other things lived in the Everglades.**
>
> Summary: The Everglades was also full of birds, snakes, frogs, deer, panthers, and other animals. The Calusa people lived there, too.
>
> ### Pages 260–263
> **Let's reread these pages to see how things changed.**
>
> Summary: Explorers arrived and pushed some Native Americans deep into the Everglades. The explorers hunted many animals and plants.
>
> ### Pages 264–267
> **Let's reread to find out what has happened because of the changes.**
>
> Summary: Farms and towns were built, and many plants and animals died. The children hope to change the Everglades back to the way it once was.

FLUENCY BUILDER Reuse *Intervention Practice Book* page 43. Call attention to the sentences at the bottom of the page. State that the goal is to have each student read each phrase smoothly. Model the appropriate pace, expression, and phrasing as you read aloud each of the sentences. Then have students practice reading aloud each sentence two or three times to a partner.

INTERVENTION
PRACTICE
BOOK

page 43

Directed Reading: "The Gift of the Manatee" pp. 86–92

TAKE FLIGHT
pages 86–92

Page 86

Ask a student to read aloud the title of the story. Ask students to listen to find out what a manatee is. Have a volunteer read page 86 while other students listen. Ask: **What do you think Jason thinks about his gift?** (*Possible response: He is confused and doesn't know what it is.*) **IMPORTANT DETAILS**

Ask: **What does Jason learn from his grandfather about manatees?** (*They are called "sea cows" and they live in warm, shallow rivers and bays in Florida.*) **IMPORTANT DETAILS**

Page 87

Ask students to read page 87 to find out why the manatees have a problem. Ask: **What is happening to the manatees?** (*Possible response: There are not many left.*) **IMPORTANT DETAILS**

Pages 88–89

Have students read page 88 to discover where the manatees came from. Ask: **Where did manatees once live?** (*on land*) **NOTE DETAILS**

Page 90

Have a volunteer read page 90 aloud as students think about where else manatees live. Model using the Create Mental Images strategy:

> **MODEL** I make a picture in my mind of a world map to see where manatees live. I know that Africa is a huge continent east of South America. I know that the Amazon River is in South America. And I know that the Caribbean Sea is between North and South America. Making a picture in my mind of these places helps me understand the story. (*Focus Strategy*) **CREATE MENTAL IMAGES**

Ask: **How can you use the root of the word *multitudes* to know how many manatees there once were?** (*Possible response: The root* multi *means "many" or "much," so there once were many manatees.*) (*Focus Skill*) **PREFIXES, SUFFIXES, AND ROOTS**

Page 91

Read page 91 aloud. Ask students to listen to find out how Jason responds. Ask: **What does receiving the gift make Jason want to do?** (*to help save the manatee*) **IMPORTANT DETAILS**

How do you think the author feels about this problem? (*Possible response: She is very concerned about the environment and the future of the manatee.*) **AUTHOR'S PURPOSE AND PERSPECTIVE**

INTERVENTION
PRACTICE
BOOK

page 45

Summarize the selection. Ask students to think about the questions Jason asks and what he learns about manatees. Then have students write three or four sentences to summarize this selection.

Answers to *Think About It* Questions

1. The manatees' homes and environments are being disrupted and taken away. **SUMMARY**

2. Possible response: Grandpa cares about nature and shows it by trying to get Jason concerned as well. **INTERPRETATION**

3. Responses will vary but should state the problem and tell what can be done and how individuals can help. **WRITE A WEBSITE ENTRY**

AFTER

Skill Review
pages 272–273

USE SKILL CARD 11B

(Focus Skill) Prefixes, Suffixes, and Roots

RETEACH the skill. Have students look at **side B of Skill Card 11: Prefixes, Suffixes, and Roots.** Ask students to read the sentences aloud.

Draw students' attention to the chart, and read the entries aloud to them. Have partners select three of the roots to find words for. Direct students to make their lists on their own papers. Possible response:

cent	dict	grat
centennial	dictionary	congratulations
centipede	predict	ingratitude
percent	dictator	grateful

Assign a number of words to each team of students. Have them draw lines through the roots and then use a dictionary to look up the meaning of each prefix and suffix. (Possible response for *centennial*: ~~cent~~ennial; *ennial* means "year" or "yearly") When teams finish, have students share their findings with the class.

FLUENCY BUILDER Reuse *Intervention Practice Book* page 43. Explain that each student will practice the sentences at the bottom of the page by reading them aloud on tape. Assign new partners, and have them take turns reading the sentences aloud to each other and then reading them on tape. After students listen to the tape, have them tell how they have improved their reading. Then have them tape themselves again, focusing on improved pacing and tone.

INTERVENTION PRACTICE BOOK

page 43

Persuasive Writing: Review

Build on prior knowledge. Tell students that they will write sentences that would persuade readers that "The Gift of the Manatee" is a good selection to read. Display the following information:

> The topic: "The Gift of the Manatee" is a good selection.
>
> The audience: other students
>
> The purpose: to persuade them to read the selection

Construct the text. "Share the pen" with students in a collaborative writing effort. As students dictate sentences and phrases for the review, write them on the board or on chart paper. Guide the process by asking questions and making suggestions.

- Ask: **How can we use our topic and purpose to write a main idea sentence?** (Possible response: Combine the ideas to write *"The Gift of the Manatee" is a good selection that you should read*.)

- Ask: **How can we support our opinion that the selection is good?** (Possible responses: page through the selection and take notes about the things we like; then tell about those things.) Write sentences as students construct them.

Revisit the text:

- Go back and reread the sentences with students. Ask: **Are these reasons in the best order? If not, what should we do?** (Possible responses: Put the most important reason either first or last; follow story order.)

- Ask: **Are there any places where we should use pronouns instead of nouns? If we have used any possessive nouns that use apostrophes, are the apostrophes used correctly?** Have students guide you to make any necessary corrections.

- Ask: **Did we say who would enjoy this selection? Did we say how students could use the information in this book?** (Responses will vary.)

- Have students read the completed sentences aloud.

On Your Own

Ask students to write sentences that could be part of a book review or a movie review. They should try to persuade the reader that he or she should or should not read the book or see the movie. Have students jot down the topic, audience, and purpose before they begin writing. Ask volunteers to read their reviews aloud.

Connect Spelling and Phonics

RETEACH long vowels /ā/*a*; /ē/*e, y*; /ī/*i, y*; /ō/*o*; /oo/*u*. Have students number their papers 1 through 8. Dictate the following words and have students write them. After they write each word, display the correct spelling so students can proofread their work.

1. migrate*   2. she   3. hurry   4. fry
5. dying*   6. open*   7. both*   8. tuba

*Word appears in "The Gift of the Manatee."

Dictate the following sentences, and have students write them: *Omar was carrying the gigantic tuba. That's why he bumped into the table.*

Build and Read Longer Words

INTERVENTION ASSESSMENT BOOK

Tell students that in some words with more than one syllable, a vowel between two consonants can have a long vowel sound. Write the word *flavor* on the board. Explain that when students come across such a word, they should try breaking it after a vowel. Frame the syllable *fla*, and have students repeat it after you. Do the same for the syllable *vor*. Then slide your hand under the entire word as students read it aloud. Follow a similar procedure with *prevent, labeled, provide, museum*, and *chosen*.

FLUENCY BUILDER Have students choose a passage from "The Gift of the Manatee" to read aloud to a partner. You may have students choose passages they found particularly interesting or you can assign them a particular passage, such as:

- Read pages 86–87. (Starting with *"Happy Birthday!"*. . . through . . . *will they live?* Total: 120 words)

- Read pages 87–88. (Starting with *Jason turned the* . . . through . . . *help them swim.* Total: 120 words)

Ask students to read the selection aloud to their partners three times. Have students rate their own readings on a scale of 1 to 4. Encourage students to note their improvement from one reading to the next by completing the sentence *I know my reading has improved because* _____. Encourage the listening partner to offer positive feedback about improvements.

SEE INTERVENTION PRACTICE BOOK
page 43

Review Vocabulary

Read the sentence beginnings and choices to students, and ask them to write the correct answers on their papers. Go over the answers and discuss why the answers are correct.

1. The teacher says that dinosaurs lived **eons** ago. Eons are
   a. days of the week.   b. long periods of time.

2. The rat **scurried** down the alley. This means that it
   a. waddled.   b. moved quickly.

3. Dad **pondered** his decision to take a new job. He
   a. thought deeply about it.   b. thought nothing of it.

4. She had a **multitude** of different sandwiches to choose from. So,
   a. she had two choices.   b. she had many choices.

5. Florida is a **peninsula**. It is a state that is
   a. almost surrounded by water.   b. in the mountains.

6. They found a **plenitude** of fresh fruit in the market. That is,
   a. there was much fruit.   b. there was little fruit.

Correct responses: 1b, 2b, 3a, 4b, 5a, 6a

This is a good time to show the Vocabulary Words and definitions on page 109. Have students copy them to study for the vocabulary test.

INTERVENTION
PRACTICE
BOOK

page 46

Prefixes, Suffixes, and Roots

To review prefixes, suffixes, and roots before the weekly assessment, use Intervention Practice Book page 46. Guide students to complete the first four items. For the next section, guide students to identify the first root and its meaning, tell the prefix and suffix and their meanings, and say how the prefixes and suffixes change the root's meaning. Students should use dictionaries to complete the page.

Review Test Prep

INTERVENTION
ASSESSMENT
BOOK

Ask students to turn to page 273 of the *Pupil Edition.* Point out the tips for answering the test questions. Tell students that these tips can help them answer these and other test questions.

DISTANT
VOYAGES
page 273

Have students follow along as you read aloud each test question and the tip that goes with it. Mention that just the wording of the first question indicates the answer. Since *cautious* means "careful," adding the prefix *in-* changes it to mean "not careful," or *careless.*

Self-Selected Reading

Encourage students to select books to read on their own. They may choose books from your classroom library shelf or you may select a group of appropriate books from which your students can choose.

- *Exploring the Everglades.* (See page 273M of the *Teacher's Edition* for a lesson plan.)

- *Trees and Plants of the Rain Forest* by Saviour Pirotta. Steck-Vaughn, 1999.

- *Everglades: Buffalo Tiger and the River of Grass* by Peter Lourie. Boyds Mills, 1994.

After students have chosen their books, give each student a copy of My Reading Log, found on page R38 in the back of the *Teacher's Edition.* Have each student fill in the information at the top of the form. Then have students use the log to keep track of their reading and to record their responses to the literature.

Conduct student-teacher conferences. Arrange for an individual conference time with each student when you can discuss his or her self-selected reading. Have students bring their Reading Logs to share during the conference. You may also want to have the student choose a favorite passage to read aloud to you. Then ask questions designed to stimulate discussion. For example, you might question what information the student learned from a nonfiction text, how the author structured the text, or how the artwork helped the student understand the topic.

FLUENCY PERFORMANCE Have students read aloud to you the passages from "The Gift of the Manatee" they have selected and practiced previously with their partners. Keep track of the number of words each student reads correctly. Ask each student to rate his or her performance on the 1–4 scale. If students aren't happy with their oral reading, give them an opportunity to practice some more and then to reread the passage to you.

See *Oral Reading Fluency Assessment* for monitoring progress.

Use with

"Summer of Fire"

Review Phonics: Vowel Diphthongs /ou/*ou, ow*

Identify the sound. Have students repeat the following sentence aloud three times: *We heard the hound howl all around town.* Have students identify the words with the same /ou/ sound. (*hound, howl, around, town*)

Associate letters to sound. Write on the board the sentence above. Underline the letters *ou* in *hound* and *around*. Tell students that the vowel combination *ou* usually stands for the /ou/ sound in *sound*. Then underline the letters *ow* in *howl* and *town*. Point out that the letters *ow* can also stand for the /ou/ sound.

Word blending. Model how to blend and read the word *shout*. Point to each letter and say its sound. Slide your hand under the whole word as you elongate sounds /sshoutt/. Then say the word naturally—*shout*. Repeat the procedure with *crowd, growl,* and *down.*

Apply the skill. *Letter Substitution* Write the following words on the board, and have students read each aloud. Make the changes necessary to form the words in parentheses. Ask a volunteer to read aloud each new word.

clean (clown)   **sand** (sound)   **pond** (pound)   **rind** (round)

Introduce Vocabulary

PRETEACH **lesson vocabulary.** Tell students they are going to learn seven new words that they will see again when they read a selection called "Summer of Fire." Teach each vocabulary word using the following process.

Use the following suggestions or similar ideas to give the meaning or context.

geyser	Have students picture water or steam shooting up from a spot in the ground.
veered	Pantomime veering in a car.
canopy	Have three students stand side-by-side and hold a large towel or sheet over their heads to demonstrate the meaning of *canopy*.
tinder	Tell students that very dry grass, twigs, or leaves could be used as tinder.

> Write the word.
> Say the word.
> Track the word and have students repeat it.
> Give the meaning or context.

INTERVENTION PRACTICE BOOK

page 48

dwindled	Put a pile of paper clips on a desk. Remove one at a time, pointing out how the pile is slowly becoming smaller.
embers	Have students picture a campfire that has almost gone out.
policy	Tell students that a *policy* is a plan or a certain way of taking action or behaving. Help students name a good school policy.

For vocabulary activities, see Vocabulary Games on pages 2–7.

AFTER
Building
Background
and Vocabulary

Apply Vocabulary Strategies

Use reference sources. Write *geyser* on the board. Tell students that when they encounter an unfamiliar word they can use reference sources to find out the meaning. Model the strategy.

> **MODEL** I don't know the meaning of this word. I can't even figure out the meaning of the word from the context, so I will look up *geyser* in the dictionary. I find that it means "a natural spring that gushes with hot water or steam."

Have students use this strategy as they encounter other unfamiliar words.

RETEACH lesson vocabulary. Have each student make a set of word cards for the Vocabulary Words. Read aloud the definition or a synonym for each word, and have students hold up the correct card. Discuss why each response is correct.

Vocabulary Words

geyser a natural spring that shoots up a fountain of hot water or steam

veered shifted or changed direction

canopy any covering overhead, such as a tree

tinder anything dry that will easily catch fire on contact with a spark

dwindled became steadily smaller or less; shrank

embers something no longer in flames but still glowing

policy a plan or method of action or conduct

 FLUENCY BUILDER Have students look at *Intervention Practice Book* page 47. Read aloud each word in the first column and have students repeat it. Then have pairs of students read the words aloud to each other. Tell students to follow the same procedure with each of the remaining columns. After each partner has had a turn reading aloud the words in each column, have them read aloud the entire list.

INTERVENTION
PRACTICE
BOOK

page 47

★ (Focus Skill) **Graphic Aids**

PRETEACH the skill. Tell students that authors often present information in a graphic form. Explain that knowing how to interpret graphic aids can help them understand difficult or complex information.

Have students look at **side A of Skill Card 12: Graphic Aids.** Have a volunteer read the explanation of graphic aids.

Have students read the information in the chart. Tell them that it is easier and faster to get this information in a graphic form than if it were written out in a paragraph.

Prepare to Read: "Summer of Fire"

Preview. Tell students that they are going to read a nonfiction selection called "Summer of Fire." Explain that nonfiction gives information about a topic. It often includes graphic aids. Then preview the selection.

DISTANT VOYAGES
pages 276–287

- **Pages 276–277:** I see the title "Summer of Fire" and the author's name. I also see a photograph of some animals and what looks like a large fire in the background.

- **Pages 278–279:** I see lightning. Maybe these pages are about how lightning can cause forest fires.

- **Pages 280–281:** I see a map of Yellowstone fires. The large photo on these pages makes me feel almost as if I am in the middle of the fire.

- **Pages 282–283:** I see a photo of some fire fighters and another large photo of a forest fire. Maybe this section will tell me what firefighters do when a fire gets that big.

- **Pages 284–285:** The fire fighter on page 285 looks tired. I think I may read something about how long and hard fire fighters work.

- **Pages 285–286:** These photos show a burning tree and a deer. I think this must mean that many living things survived the fire.

Set purpose. Remind students that they can set a purpose for their reading based on their preview. Tell them that a common purpose for reading nonfiction is to get information on a specific topic. Guide students in creating a purpose for reading "Summer of Fire."

MODEL From previewing these pages, I think I will read to gain information about forest fires, how they are fought, and what happens to the forest after the fire is over.

Reread and Summarize

Have students reread and summarize "Summer of Fire" in sections, as described in the chart below.

Pages 278–279

Let's reread pages 278–279 to recall how the author introduces the topic of forest fires.

Summary: The summer of 1988 was very dry. There were many forest fires, and some of them were started by lightning strikes.

Pages 280–281

As we reread pages 280–281, let's recall the park policy for forest fires.

Summary: The park did not fight fires unless they threatened life or property, but there was no rain that summer. The park had to change its policy and start fighting more fires.

Pages 282–283

As we reread pages 282–283, let's find out why the fires could not be put out.

Summary: Fire fighters tried to stop the fires but they kept burning because there was no rain, and strong winds created bigger fires.

Pages 284–285

Let's reread pages 284–285 to recall how the fires were finally put out.

Summary: It began to rain and then snow. Fire fighters had protected most of the park from the fires.

Page 286

Let's reread page 286 and recall the conclusion to this selection.

Summary: The forest was not ruined. Fires have always renewed the landscape.

FLUENCY BUILDER Reuse *Intervention Practice Book* page 47. Call attention to the sentences on the bottom half of the page. Model reading aloud each of the sentences. Have students repeat after you, imitating your expression, phrasing and pace. Then have students practice reading aloud each sentence three times to a partner.

INTERVENTION
PRACTICE
BOOK

page 47

Directed Reading: "Flowers After the Flames" pp. 94–101

TAKE FLIGHT
pp. 94–101

Pages 94–95

Ask a volunteer to read aloud the title of the selection. Read pages 94–95 while students listen. Ask: **What words does the author use to help you picture what the fires were like in Yellowstone?** (*fierce, red-hot.*) **LITERARY ANALYSIS**

Ask: **How does the illustration help you better understand the text?** (*The illustration helps to show how big the fire was.*) **GRAPHIC AIDS**

Pages 96–97

Read aloud page 97. Then say,

> **MODEL** I wonder how the wildlife in the park could survive after the fire. As I read the selection, I notice words and phrases such as "In the beginning," and "then." This tells me that the author has used sequence as a text structure. Reading the events in order helps me understand how the animals in Yellowstone were able to survive after the fire. **USE TEXT STRUCTURE AND FORMAT**

Ask: **How did elk adapt to the blackened forest?** (*They licked the ash for minerals and then ate the grasses that sprang up.*) **IMPORTANT DETAILS**

Pages 98–99

Ask: **What had to happen before seeds hidden under the scorched earth could sprout?** (*The sun had to melt the snow. Then the water from the snow had to trickle underground, soaking the seeds.*) **SEQUENCE**

Page 100

Ask: **Do you think the policy to let the fires burn was a good one? Explain.** (*Responses will vary.*) **MAKE JUDGMENTS/EXPRESS PERSONAL OPINIONS**

INTERVENTION PRACTICE BOOK

page 49

Summarize the selection. Ask students to summarize the selection by telling what happened before, during, and after the fires. Then have them complete the *Intervention Practice Book* page 49.

Answers to *Think About It* Questions

1. The forest fires made way for renewed life at Yellowstone. The heat of the fires popped open pinecones, spilling seeds for animals to eat. The fires made way for more sunshine so more flowers and trees could grow. **SUMMARY**

2. Possible response: People probably felt afraid of the fires. The next summer, people probably felt glad that the fires had made way for renewed life. **INTERPRETATION**

3. Postcards should describe the scenery and the plant and animal life and should express personal reactions to the park. **WRITE A POSTCARD**

AFTER

Skill Review
pages 294–295

USE SKILL CARD 12B

(Focus Skill) Graphic Aids

Have students look at **side B of Skill Card 12: Graphic Aids.** Read aloud the skill reminder. Direct students to look at the bar. Tell them that this is called a bar graph. It is a good way to show comparisons in amounts or to show how things change over time. Tell students to examine the graph. Ask:

1. **How many students were there for each computer during the 1990–1991 school year?** (*20*)

2. **How many students were there for each computer during the 1995–1996 school year?** (*10*)

3. **What happens to the number of students per computer every two years?** (*The number decreases as the years get closer to the present.*)

Ask students to develop a summary of the information in the bar graph. Then ask for volunteers to read aloud their answers. (*Possible response: The chart shows how much things have changed since 1990, when there was only one computer for every 20 students in U.S. public schools. There is now a computer for every six students.*) Remind students that when they read, it is important to notice graphic sources and to be able to interpret the information they contain.

FLUENCY BUILDER Use *Intervention Practice Book* page 47. Explain that students will practice the sentences at the bottom of the page by recording them on tape. Have students choose partners. Tell them to take turns reading the sentences aloud to each other and then reading them on tape. After listening to the tape, have each person tell how his or her recording has improved. Then have them record the sentences again.

INTERVENTION PRACTICE BOOK

page 47

Writing: Persuasive Paragraph

Build on prior knowledge. Tell students that you will be working together to write a short paragraph persuading people to be careful not to start forest fires. Remind students that when writing to persuade, they should include a reason that explains why the reader should agree with the writer's opinion, and details that support the reason. Start a list on the board like the one below:

Why It Is Important to Follow Fire Safety Rules

　1. Unattended campfires could cause forest fires.

　2. Forest fires kill plants and animals.

Ask students to name other reasons why they should follow fire safety rules. As they name other reasons, add them to the list.

Construct the text. "Share the pen" with students. Use the following steps to guide students through the process.

- ■ Help students write an introductory sentence for the paragraph. The sentence should capture the reader's attention and tell their opinion on the topic.

- ■ Have students use the items on the list to write sentences for the paragraph. Then help students draft the paragraph, making sure that the order of the sentences makes sense. For example, students should state their opinion, then tell why the reader should share that opinion.

- ■ Students should include a concluding sentence that restates their opinion.

Revisit the text. As students revise their paragraph, remind them to focus on whether they have included details to support their opinion. Ask them to evaluate their sentences to make sure that they clearly convey their opinion. Have students read aloud the completed paragraph.

> **On Your Own**
>
> Have each student write a persuasive paragraph on a topic of his or her choice. Have students work individually. When they have completed their paragraphs, ask volunteers to read them aloud.

Connect Spelling and Phonics

RETEACH **vowel diphthongs /ou/ *ou, ow*.** Remind students that the /ou/ sound can be spelled with the letters *ou* or *ow*. Have students number a piece of paper from 1–8. Dictate the following words and have students write them on their papers. After the students write each word, display the correct spelling of the word so students can proofread their work. They should draw a line through a misspelled word and write the correct spelling beside it.

1. out*	2. ground	3. sprout*	4. sounds*
5. brown*	6. now*	7. flowers*	8. however

*Word appears in "Flowers After the Flames."

Dictate the following sentences for students to write: *I dug the weeds out of the ground with my trowel. Now I can plant these flowers.*

Build and Read Longer Words

Write the following words on the board: *power, outdoors.* Have volunteers identify the letters that stand for the /ou/ sound in *power.* (*ow*) Tell students that when they read a longer word with the letters *ow* and *ou*, these letter combinations usually stay together when the word is broken into syllables. Ask: **Which part of the first word sounds like /pou/? Which part sounds like /ər/?** Draw your hand under the entire word as students read it. Then have students identify the two consonants that are next to each other in *outdoors.* (*t* and *d*) Draw a line between *t* and *d*, and remind students that words that have this pattern are usually divided into syllables between the two consonants. Frame *out* and have students read it. Frame *doors* and have students read it. Ask students to read the whole word. Repeat the procedure with *cloudburst, cowhand, outside,* and *plowshare.*

INTERVENTION
ASSESSMENT
BOOK

FLUENCY BUILDER Have students choose a passage from "Flowers After the Flames" to read aloud to a partner. You may have students choose passages they found particularly interesting or you can assign them a particular passage, such as:

- Read the second paragraph on page 96 to the end of the third paragraph on page 97. (From *"The fire had not . . .* through *. . . birds and small animals.* (Total words: 110)

- Read all of pages 98 and 99 (Total words: 124)

Ask students to read the passage aloud to their partners three times. Have students rate each reading on a scale of 1 to 4. Encourage students to note their improvement from one reading to the next.

Review Vocabulary

Read the questions to students and ask them to write the correct answers. Go over the answers and discuss why each is correct.

1. When they were hiking, they came upon a geyser, which is
   a. a small rodent.
   b. a natural spring that shoots a fountain of hot water.

2. If she veered to the right, she
   a. turned to the right.
   b. looked to the right.

3. They found shelter under a canopy of leaves, which is
   a. an overhead covering.
   b. a hideout.

4. They used old newspapers for tinder because newspapers
   a. had to be thrown away.
   b. would easily catch fire.

5. In the evening, the amount of light dwindled. That means
   a. it got less and less.
   b. it was more noticeable.

6. She looked at the embers of the dying fire. Embers are
   a. bits of glowing wood.
   b. the ashes.

7. She started a new policy for her club. A policy is
   a. a plan of action.
   b. an idea they would vote on.

   Correct responses: 1b, **2**a, **3**a, **4**b, **5**a, **6**a, **7**a

 Review Graphic Aids

INTERVENTION
PRACTICE
BOOK

page 50

To review graphic aids before the weekly assessment, use *Intervention Practice Book*, page 50. Call attention to the title *Graphic Aids*. Ask a volunteer to read the first line and fill in the first two blanks. Then have another student complete the next blank. Make sure each student writes out the answers on their papers. Direct students' attention to the bar graph. Have volunteers read and answer each question.

Review Test Prep

INTERVENTION
ASSESSMENT
BOOK

Ask students to turn to page 295 of the *Pupil Edition*. Point out the Tips for answering the test questions. Tell students to pay attention to these tips because they can help them answer not only the test questions on this page but also other test questions like these. Remind them that, when they are asked on a test to interpret information from a graphic source, they should look carefully at both the graphic and the question before giving an answer.

DISTANT VOYAGES
page 295

Self-Selected Reading

Encourage students to select books to read on their own. If students have difficulty selecting a book, suggest titles such as these:

- *Heroes in the Flames* by Kate Fisher. (Lesson plan available on page 295M of the *Teacher's Edition*.)

- *Everglades: Buffalo Tiger and the River of Glass* by Peter Lourie. Boyds Mills Press, 1994.

- *Fire!: My Parents' Story* by Jessie Haas. Greenwillow, 1998.

You may wish to suggest books that are the same genre, by the same author, or have the same kind of text structure as the selection.

Have each student fill in the information at the top of their personal copy of My Reading Log, found on page R38 in the back of the *Teacher's Edition*. Tell students to use the log to keep track of their reading and to record their responses to the literature.

Conduct student-teacher conferences. Arrange for an individual conference time with each student when you can discuss his or her self-selected reading. Have students bring their Reading Logs to share during the conference. You may also want to have the student choose a favorite passage to read aloud to you. Have students tell why they selected the book and whether they enjoyed it.

FLUENCY PERFORMANCE Have students read aloud the passage from "Flowers from the Flame" that they have practiced. Keep track of the number of words the student reads correctly. Ask each student to rate his or her performance on the 1–4 scale. If students aren't happy with their oral reading, give them an opportunity for additional practice.

See *Oral Reading Fluency Assessment* for monitoring progress.

**Building
Background
and Vocabulary**

Use with

"Oceans"

Review Phonics: Long Vowel /ī/*igh, ie*

Identify the sound. Have students repeat the following sentence twice: *They lie under the bright light of summer skies.* Ask students to identify the words that have the /ī/ sound. (*lie, bright, light, skies*)

Associate letters to sounds. Write the sentence above on the board. Underline the letters *igh* in the words *bright* and *light*. Tell students that the letter combination *igh* stands for the /ī/ sound. Point out that the letters *gh* are silent. Then underline the letters *ie* in *lie* and *skies*, and point out that this is also a long *i* letter pattern.

Word blending. Model how to blend and read the word *skies*. Point to the initial *s* and say /s/. Point to the *k* and say /k/. Slide your hand under *ie* and say /ī/. Point to the final *s* and say /z/. Slide your hand under the whole word as you elongate the sounds: /sskkīīzz/. Then say the word naturally—*skies*. Repeat the procedure with *light*.

**INTERVENTION
PRACTICE
BOOK**
page 52

Apply the skill. *Letter Substitution* Write each of the following words on the board and have students read it aloud. Make the changes necessary to form the words in parentheses. Have a volunteer say each new word.

fit (fight)   **mitt** (might)   **frill** (fright)   **trip** (tried)
pit (pie)   **sit** (sight)   **spin** (spies)   **slit** (slight)

Introduce Vocabulary

PRETEACH **lesson vocabulary.** Tell students they are going to learn six new words that they will see again when they read a story called "Oceans." Teach each Vocabulary Word using the following process.

Use the following suggestions or similar ideas to give the meaning or context.

gravitational Explain that this word is related to *gravity* and is the describing form of the word.

> Write the word.
> Say the word.
> Track the word and have students repeat it.
> Give the meaning or context.

bulge Tell students that a bulge is a swelling or an area of something that bends out.

inlet Relate this word to its two word parts, *in* and *let*, and tell students that an inlet is a place on the coast where the water is *let in*. An inlet is like a bay.

generated If an earthquake causes a huge tidal wave, we say that the earthquake generated the tidal wave, or caused it. *Generated* is the past form of *generate*.

energy	We refer to the power of the sun as its energy. The wind has the energy to push sailboats, and water has the energy to cut canyons through rock.
shallow	Along a sandy beach the ocean water is shallow, or not deep. Shallow ocean water might be a few feet deep, but deep ocean water might be a few miles deep.

For vocabulary activities, see Vocabulary Games on pages 2–7.

Vocabulary Words

gravitational having to do with gravity, or the pull of the sun and moon on the earth

bulge swelled area; place that bends out

inlet bay; opening in a coastline

generated caused; produced

energy power; ability to do work

shallow not deep

AFTER

Building Background and Vocabulary

Apply Vocabulary Strategies

Use reference sources. Write the word *gravitational* on the board. Tell students that when they see words that are very long or unusual, they can use reference sources to help them understand it.

> **MODEL** This word is very long, and I need to find out how to say it and what it means. I can use a dictionary to find out how to say it and what it means. I can use a print or online encyclopedia to find out how the word is used in science.

RETEACH lesson vocabulary. Make sure each student has a set of word cards for the vocabulary. Say the following sentences, and have students hold up the word cards that complete them. Reread the sentences aloud with the correct word choices, and discuss how the meaning of the Vocabulary Word fits the sentence.

1. The force that keeps the earth in orbit around the sun is the (gravitational) force.
2. The marbles in the sock made a (bulge) at the toe.
3. The ships sailed out of the ocean and docked in the (inlet).
4. The windmills (generated) electricity for the town.
5. Plants make their own food using the (energy) of the sun.
6. She waded in the creek because the water was (shallow).

FLUENCY BUILDER Use *Intervention Practice Book* page 51. Read aloud each of the words in the first column, and then have students repeat it as a group. Ask partners to read the words in the first column aloud to each other. Then proceed to the other two columns. After the pairs have practiced reading aloud the words in each separate column, have them practice the entire list.

INTERVENTION PRACTICE BOOK
page 51

Text Structure: Main Idea and Details

PRETEACH **the skill.** Tell students that to understand their reading, they must be able to sort the main idea from the supporting details.

Have students look at **side A of Skill Card 13: Text Structure: Main Idea and Details.** Read the explanation of main idea and details, and then have students read it aloud with you. Point students' attention to the diagram. Explain that a paragraph or an entire selection is built like a house is built: The details are like the foundation and the walls, and the roof is the main idea.

Ask a volunteer to read the first sentence of the passage. Say that this is the main idea of the paragraph—the grandmother's house is scary. As each following sentence is read (without the explanations in parentheses), ask whether it supports the idea that the house is scary.

Prepare to Read: "Oceans"

Preview. Tell students that they will read a selection called "Oceans." Explain that it is nonfiction and is written to give information to the reader. Then preview the selection.

DISTANT VOYAGES

pages 298–310

- **Pages 298–299:** I look at the illustration and see a wave with a crest. I see the title "Oceans," and I am sure this is going to be a story about the ocean.

- **Pages 300–301:** I think this piece is going to have a lot of graphics to explain tides and how the moon affects tides.

- **Pages 302–303:** The photographs seem to show the differences between high and low tides. I would like to find out how much difference there is in the depth of the water from high to low tide.

- **Pages 304–305:** I think these pages will tell about ocean storms.

- **Pages 306–307:** The diagram seems to explain big waves, so I am sure the text will tell about what really happens to the ocean in a storm and why.

- **Pages 308–309:** These photographs show the surf. In the smaller photograph there is a surfer. I think this page will tell about why the surf is the way it is and why it changes at times.

Set purpose. Model setting a purpose for reading "Oceans."

MODEL I think this selection will give me a lot of information about the ocean. I want to read to find out facts I didn't know before.

Reread and Summarize

Have students reread and summarize "Oceans" in sections, as described in the chart below.

> **Pages 298–301**
>
> **Let's reread pages 298–301 to remember how the author starts his article about the ocean.**
>
> Summary: Ocean covers more than 70 percent of the earth. High tides come twice a day and are a result of gravitational pull. The tides are biggest when the sun and moon are lined up just right with the earth.
>
> ⋯⋯⋯⋯⋯⋯⋯⋯⋯⋯⋯⋯⋯⋯⋯⋯⋯⋯⋯⋯⋯⋯⋯⋯⋯⋯⋯⋯⋯⋯⋯⋯⋯⋯⋯⋯⋯⋯
>
> **Pages 302–303**
>
> **Let's read pages 302–303 again to remember what else the author tells us about tides.**
>
> Summary: Tides are different in different areas of the ocean. A tsunami, or tidal wave, is caused by an earthquake or by the eruption of a volcano and can be very destructive.
>
> ⋯⋯⋯⋯⋯⋯⋯⋯⋯⋯⋯⋯⋯⋯⋯⋯⋯⋯⋯⋯⋯⋯⋯⋯⋯⋯⋯⋯⋯⋯⋯⋯⋯⋯⋯⋯⋯⋯
>
> **Pages 304–307**
>
> **Now let's reread pages 304–307 to recall information about waves and storms on the ocean.**
>
> Summary: Wind creates waves of different sizes. The energy of the waves moves across the ocean, but the water itself doesn't move very far. Waves can get higher than 100 feet tall.
>
> ⋯⋯⋯⋯⋯⋯⋯⋯⋯⋯⋯⋯⋯⋯⋯⋯⋯⋯⋯⋯⋯⋯⋯⋯⋯⋯⋯⋯⋯⋯⋯⋯⋯⋯⋯⋯⋯⋯
>
> **Pages 308–310**
>
> **As we reread pages 308–310, let's remember what happens when waves come to land.**
>
> Summary: Waves slow down when they come close to shore. A wave may fall over on itself, breaking on the shore. This surf can form hundreds of yards out to sea. It can also pound into rocky coastlines and slowly eat away at them.

Fluency Builder Reuse *Intervention Practice Book* page 51. Bring to students' attention the sentences on the bottom of the page, and tell them that the goal is to read each phrase smoothly. Model the appropriate pace, expression, and phrasing as you read aloud each of the sentences. Then have students practice reading aloud each sentence two or three times to a partner.

SEE
INTERVENTION
PRACTICE
BOOK
page 51

Directed Reading: "The Krakatoa Wave" pp. 102–108

Read aloud the title of the story. Then point out the volcano in the illustration on pages 102–103 and explain that this volcano is called Krakatoa. Have students read pages 102–103 to check their predictions. Ask: **Why weren't the people of Java and Sumatra worried when they saw smoke and heard explosions coming from the volcano?** (*Possible response: They were used to this. For years, the volcano did this without a major eruption.*) **DRAW CONCLUSIONS**

Pages 102–103

TAKE FLIGHT
pp. 102–108

Ask: **What happened on August 26, 1883?** (*Possible response: Krakatoa erupted violently.*) **MAKE PREDICTIONS-UNDERSTAND FIGURATIVE LANGUAGE**

Pages 104–105

Have students read pages 104–105 to see if they predicted correctly. Ask: **What happened on the day Krakatoa "woke up"?** (*Possible response: There was a huge explosion of steam, smoke, and hot ash, followed by several earthquakes.*) (Focus Skill) **MAIN IDEA AND DETAILS**

Ask a volunteer to read aloud the first paragraph of page 105 while students listen to find out how a tsunami is different from an ordinary high wave. Model using the Adjust Reading Rate strategy:

> **MODEL** The first few pages are very exciting, and I have been reading them quickly. However, now I read that a tsunami is different from an ordinary wave. I think this is important information, so I will read more slowly and carefully to find out how it is different. The second sentence says that an ordinary wave is caused by the gravitational pull of the moon. The next sentence tells that a tsunami is caused by the earthquakes that the volcanic explosion caused. (Focus Strategy) **ADJUST READING RATE**

Ask: **Why did people rush to higher ground?** (*They were afraid that the lowlands near the shore would be flooded by the wave.*) **CAUSE/EFFECT**

Page 106

Have students read page 106 to find out what happened next. (*Huge explosions blew Krakatoa apart. A new tsunami formed and grew to be over 120 feet high.*) To help students visualize how far 2,500 miles is, point out that this is almost the distance from one coast of the United States to the other. Ask: **Which do you think was the greater threat to humans—the explosion or the tsunami? Why?** (*Possible response: the tsunami; because its size and force devastated buildings and caused great loss of human life*) **STORY EVENTS**

Page 107

Have students read page 107 to find out what happened when the tsunami hit land. (*It wiped out towns and killed thousands of people.*) Ask: **What do you think Krakatoa's wave teaches us about nature?** (*Possible response: Nature is an awesome force that should be respected and, at times, feared.*) **THEME**

Summarize the selection. Have students think about the sequence of events leading up to the tsunami. Then ask them to summarize the story in a few sentences by telling about this sequence of events.

Answers to *Think About It* Questions

1. A tsunami is a very high wave made by the energy of an under-ground earthquake. When the tsunami hit, towns were wiped out and people died. **SUMMARY**

2. Possible response: The wave was so large, it traveled so far and so fast, and it killed so many people that people will always talk and write about it. **INTERPRETATION**

3. Accept reasonable responses. Lists and paragraphs should show an understanding that the island was lush and green before the volcano's eruption and barren after the eruption. **MAKE A LIST/ WRITE A PARAGRAPH**

(Focus Skill) Text Structure: Main Idea and Details

RETEACH the skill. Have students look at **side B of Skill Card 13: Text Structure: Main Idea and Details.** Ask students to read the skill reminder silently. Read the skill reminder aloud. Then ask a student to read aloud the paragraph.

Help students start the activity. Have them number their papers as instructed on the skill card. Read the first sentence aloud: *People go to the ocean for many reasons.* Ask: **Do you think this is the main idea, or is it a supporting detail?** (*the main idea*) Ask them to write the answer on their papers. Repeat with the second sentence. (*supporting detail*)

Ask students to create a diagram like the one on the skill card and fill in the spaces. Tell them not to write whole sentences, but just a couple of words for the details.

FLUENCY BUILDER Use *Intervention Practice Book* page 51. Explain that today each student will practice the sentences on the bottom half of the page by reading them aloud on tape. Assign partners, and have them take turns reading the sentences aloud to each other and then on tape. After students listen to the tape, have them tell how their reading has improved. Then have them read the sentences aloud on tape again, focusing on improved pacing and tone.

**INTERVENTION
PRACTICE
BOOK**

page 51

Persuasive Writing: Persuasive Paragraph

Build on prior knowledge. Tell students that they are going to write a persuasive paragraph that is based on true information. Tell them that in the paragraph, they will persuade someone to do something.

Explain that it is important to understand who they are writing to and what they are asking for. Tell students that the paragraph could be part of a letter to someone. Suggest a topic and an audience, such as asking the school principal to help them organize a school clean-up day. Students may also propose a topic of their own.

Construct the text. "Share the pen" with students in a collaborative writing effort. As students dictate sentences, write them on the board or on chart paper. Guide the process by asking questions and making suggestions. Use the following points:

- **Remember to be polite and respectful.**

- **Tell exactly what you would like the person to do.**

- **Give reasons why the person would want to do this.**

- **Tell how your project is helpful.**

- **End by asking the person to do what you have asked.**

Revisit the text. Reread the paragraph together. Ask: **Do I say exactly what I want and why it is helpful?**

- Guide students to decide whether they have included enough reasons or details to persuade the reader. Ask: **How can I make my reasons stronger?** (*Possible response: put the most important reason last*) Make the appropriate changes.

- Help students assess the order of the sentences. Ask: **Which ideas should come first, next, and last?** (*Possible response: main idea first, reasons or details next, and request for action last*)

- Have students read the completed paragraph aloud.

On Your Own

Ask students to write their own persuasive paragraphs that could be parts of a letter to members of Congress. Students should choose topics of personal interest and tell lawmakers why they should work toward these issues.

Connect Spelling and Phonics

RETEACH **long vowel /ī/ *igh, ie*.** Write the word *light* on the board, and tell students that in the first four words you will say, the /ī/ sound is spelled *igh*. Dictate words 1–4, and have students write them. Display the correct spellings so students can proofread their work. Then write the word *pie* on the board, and tell students that in the next four words you will say, the /ī/ sound is spelled *ie*. Dictate words 5–8, and have students proofread as before.

1. high*	2. night*	3. flight	4. brighter*
5. tie	6. cried	7. tries	8. denies

*Word appears in "The Krakatoa Wave."

Dictate the following sentence for students to write: *She tied a bright light on her bike for a night ride.*

Build and Read Longer Words

INTERVENTION
ASSESSMENT
BOOK

Write the word *oversight* on the board. Remind students that when they come to a longer word, they can check to see if it is made up of two shorter words. Ask students to tell which part of the word sounds like /ō'vər/ (*first*) and which part sounds like /sīt/ (*second*). Ask what the words *over* and *sight* together sound like. Have students blend the longer word parts to read the longer word *oversight*. Follow a similar procedure with *nightcap, limelight,* and *sightseeing.* Give students other /ī/ words to read, such as *searchlight, upright*, and *frightened*.

FLUENCY BUILDER Have students choose a passage from "The Krakatoa Wave" to read aloud to a partner. You may have students choose passages they found very interesting. Or you can assign them a particular passage, such as:

- Pages 102–103. (From *Krakatoa was . . .* through . . . *asleep again.* Total: 119 words)

- Pages 105–106. (From *The tsunami wasn't . . .* through . . . *on Earth.* Total: 113 words)

Ask students to read the selection aloud to their partners three times. Have students rate their own readings on a scale of 1 to 4.

Encourage students to note their improvement from one reading to the next by completing the sentence *I know my reading has improved because* _____ . Encourage the listening partner to offer positive feedback about improvements.

Review Vocabulary

To revisit Vocabulary Words prior to the weekly assessment, read the following sentences and ask students to identify the correct choice and then explain why that choice makes sense in that sentence. Ask them to write down the letter of that choice.

1. The **gravitational** force of the earth
   a. makes you sink.   b. keeps you on the ground.

2. My shirt sleeve had a **bulge**
   a. where it was dirty.   b. where my elbow had been.

3. My dad took us fishing at the
   a. **inlet**.   b. skating rink.

4. The wind **generated** enough power to
   a. blow the building over.   b. cause a flood.

5. People get their **energy** from
   a. eating food.   b. feeding their pets.

6. A **shallow** stream is
   a. deep enough for ships.   b. good for wading.

Correct responses: lb, 2b, 3a, 4a, 5a, 6b

This is a good time to show the Vocabulary Words and definitions on page 129. Have students copy them to use for studying for the vocabulary test.

Review Text Structure: Main Idea and Details

**INTERVENTION
PRACTICE
BOOK**
page 54

To review finding the main idea and supporting details before the weekly assessment, distribute *Intervention Practice Book*, page 54. Call attention to the title Main Idea and Details. Ask students to read the selection and follow the directions. Ask them to look at the illustration, too, and decide what the main idea is.

Help students decide whether each sentence is a detail or the main idea and label it. Have them write the main idea sentence in their own words. Ask for volunteers to read aloud their answers.

Review Test Prep

**INTERVENTION
ASSESSMENT
BOOK**

Ask students to turn to page 319 of the *Pupil Edition*. Point out the tips for answering the test questions. Tell students to pay attention to these tips because they can help them answer not only the test questions on this page but also on other tests.

**DISTANT
VOYAGES**
page 319

Remind students to look at fill-in-the-blank questions carefully to decide whether to fill in one word, several words, or a whole sentence. Have students follow along as you read aloud each test question and the tip that goes with it.

Self-Selected Reading

Encourage students to select their own books to read on their own. They may choose books from your classroom library shelf, or you may select a group of appropriate books from which your students can choose.

- *Energy from Water* (See page 319M of the *Teacher's Edition* for a lesson plan.)

- *Seal Surfer* by Michael Foreman. Harcourt, 1997.

- *Tornado* by Betsy Byars. HarperCollins, 1996.

After students have chosen their books, give them copies of My Reading Log, found on page R38 in the back of the *Teacher's Edition*. Have students fill in the information at the top of the form. Then have students use the log to keep track of their reading and to record their responses to the literature.

Conduct student-teacher conferences. Arrange for an individual conference time with each student to discuss his or her self-selected reading. Have students bring their Reading Logs to share during the conference. You may also want to have the student choose a favorite passage to read aloud to you. Then ask questions designed to stimulate discussion. For example, you might question what information the student learned from a nonfiction text, how the author structured the text, or how the artwork helped the student understand the topic.

FLUENCY PERFORMANCE Have students read aloud to you the passage from "The Krakatoa Wave" they have selected and practiced previously with their partners. Keep track of the number of words the student reads correctly. Ask each student to rate his or her performance on the 1–4 scale. If students aren't happy with their oral reading, give them an opportunity to practice some more and to reread the passage to you.

See *Oral Reading Fluency Assessment* for monitoring progress.

LESSON 14

BEFORE

Building
Background
and Vocabulary

Use with

"Seeing Earth from Space"

Review Phonics: Consonant /j/g, dge

Identify the sound. Have students repeat the following sentence aloud three times: *The giant engine uses steam energy to pull the huge train over the bridge.* Have students identify the words that have the /j/ sound. (*giant, engine, energy, huge, bridge*)

Associate letters to sound. Write the sentence from above on the board. Underline *g* in *giant, engine, energy,* and *huge,* and *dge* in *bridge.* Explain that in these words, the letters *g* and *dge* stand for the /j/ sound. Point out that in general, the letter *g* followed by the letter *e, i,* or *y* stands for the /j/ sound.

Word Blending. Write the words *giant, general, ledge,* and *stingy* on the board. Model how to blend and read the word *giant.* Slide your hand under the whole word as you elongate the sounds: /jjīīənnt/. Then say the word naturally—*giant.* Follow a similar procedure for the other words.

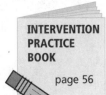

INTERVENTION
PRACTICE
BOOK

page 56

Apply the skill. *Letter Substitution* Write the following words on the board, and have students read each aloud. Then make the changes necessary to form the words in parentheses. Have a volunteer read each new word aloud.

going (ginger)	**wag** (wage)	**bag** (badge)	**lag** (large)
gum (gem)	**rag** (rage)	**rig** (ridges)	**guppy** (gypsy)

Introduce Vocabulary

PRETEACH **lesson vocabulary.** Tell students that they are going to learn six new words they will see again when they read a story called "Seeing Earth from Space." Teach each Vocabulary Word using the following process.

Use the following sentences to give the meaning or context.

sensors	As we walked toward the store entrance, sensors opened the door.
atoll	The atoll was formed when the middle of the island sank into the ocean.
reef	When we walked in the ocean, we reached a sandy reef, and the water was only as high as our ankles.
lagoon	In the middle of the island there was a calm lagoon surrounded by coral, which protected it from the waves of the ocean.

> Write the word.
> Say the word.
> Track the word and have students repeat it.
> Give the meaning or context.

meander   Lost in the woods, the man continued to meander, going in one direction and then another.

barren   When we say the moon is a barren place, we mean that there is nothing living there.

For vocabulary activities see Vocabulary Games on pages 2–7.

For vocabulary activities see Vocabulary Games on pages 2–7.

Vocabulary Words

sensors devices that detect information

atoll a doughnut-shaped coral island

reef a ridge of sand, rocks, or coral at or near the surface of the water

lagoon a body of water enclosed by a ring-shaped coral island

meander to wind and turn

barren having no life

AFTER

Building Background and Vocabulary

Apply Vocabulary Strategies

Use context to define words. Explain to students that a good way to define words is to look at other words in the sentence or paragraph. Model using the information in the sentence from Introduce Vocabulary to help define the word *atoll*.

> **MODEL**   The sentence says that the atoll was formed when the middle of the island sank. I imagine an island that is high in the middle. Then I think about the high part sinking down. I think this would leave a ring-shaped island that has water in the middle. That must be what an atoll is.

Tell students to use context to define other words in the selection.

RETEACH lesson vocabulary. Give each student a set of vocabulary cards, and then read the following sentences aloud. Ask students to hold up the appropriate word card. Reread the sentences with the correct word choices.

1. Divers saw millions of sea animals near the coral __(reef)__ .
2. The __(barren)__ desert had not one plant or animal.
3. Our house lights have __(sensors)__ that turn them on at night.
4. The stream began to __(meander)__ when it reached flat land.
5. The water in the peaceful __(lagoon)__ was a good place to fish.
6. No one lived on the __(atoll)__ because it had very little land.

FLUENCY BUILDER Distribute copies of *Intervention Practice Book* page 55. Read each word in the first column and have students repeat it. Then have students work in pairs and take turns reading the words to each other. Follow the same procedure with each of the remaining columns. After partners have practiced reading aloud the words in each column separately, have them practice the entire list.

INTERVENTION PRACTICE BOOK

page 55

★ (Focus Skill) **Graphic Aids**

PRETEACH **the skill.** Tell students that graphic aids such as photographs, charts, diagrams, illustrations, and maps can help readers understand a reading selection.

Have students look at **side A of Skill Card 14: Graphic Aids.** Read aloud the explanation, and ask students to look at the illustration and to read the story to themselves. Ask:

- **What do you see in the illustration?** (*Possible response: mountains, snow, streams, a river, a delta, farms, homes*)

- **How does the illustration support the paragraph and make it clear?** (*Possible response: All the things discussed in the paragraph are shown in the picture. Reading information and seeing it in pictures helps me understand it.*)

Have volunteers read aloud the chart entries, and discuss how each idea is supported by the illustration. Students may want to suggest other ideas that could be listed. (*Possible response: Idea—mountains and melting snow; how the graphic helped—The water in the streams and rivers comes from snow melting on the mountains.*)

Prepare to Read: "Seeing Earth from Space"

Preview. Tell students that they are going to read a selection called "Seeing Earth from Space." Explain that in this nonfiction selection, the photographs help us understand the information. Then preview the selection.

DISTANT VOYAGES
pages 322–338

- **Pages 322–325:** On these four pages I see photographs of the Earth. Some seem to be taken farther from the Earth than others. I also see a picture of the space shuttle. I wonder if the photographs were taken from the space shuttle.

- **Pages 326–327:** These pictures of Earth seem to be of a storm and of the ocean. I wonder what the golden color is in the picture on the right.

- **Pages 328–331:** The pictures on these four pages look like islands. Some of the islands seem to have sandy beaches. I wonder which islands these are.

Set purpose. Model setting a purpose for reading "Seeing Earth from Space."

MODEL I want to read this selection to find out about the things in the photographs. I also want to know what the different colors in the photographs are.

Reread and Summarize

Have students reread and summarize "Seeing Earth from Space" in sections, as described in the chart below.

Pages 322–325

Let's reread pages 322–325 to learn about the photographs of the Earth.

Summary: The Apollo astronauts took the first photos of the Earth as a planet. Satellites and other astronauts have taken pictures of parts of the Earth. People use the photos to learn about the Earth.

Pages 326–327

Let's reread to see some things we learn from the pictures.

Summary: We can see what typhoons and pollution look like from the pictures.

Pages 328–332

Let's reread pages 328–332 to learn about the islands.

Summary: Many islands were made from volcanoes. When these volcanoes are no longer active, the islands they have formed gradually sink and become atolls surrounded by coral reefs.

Page 333

Let's reread page 333 to find out about the mountains.

Summary: The plates of the Earth are always moving. The Himalaya Mountains are still being formed by the crashing of two plates.

Pages 334–338

Let's reread these pages to see what we can learn from the pictures.

Summary: Scientists can learn how the things people do are changing the Earth. The photos help us see that things like pollution, oil spills, erosion, and cutting down forests affect the whole Earth. They help us know that we must take care of our planet.

FLUENCY BUILDER Be sure students have copies of *Intervention Practice Book* page 55. Call attention to the sentences at the bottom of the page. Model appropriate pace, expression, and phrasing as you read each sentence, and have students read it after you. Then have students practice by reading the sentences aloud to a partner.

INTERVENTION PRACTICE BOOK

page 55

Directed Reading: "Gardens of the Sea: Coral Reefs," pp. 110–117

TAKE FLIGHT
pp. 110–117

Tell students that they will read a nonfiction selection with graphic aids that give information. Explain that as they read the story, they will practice interpreting graphic aids.

Pages 110–111

Have students read aloud the story title and preview the story by looking at the illustrations and photos and reading the captions. Have them predict what the selection is about. Then read page 110 aloud, and ask: **In what kind of water are coral reefs found?** (*warm, shallow, clean, clear water*) **IMPORTANT DETAILS**

How do corals get food? (*Possible response: Tentacles around their mouths catch tiny sea animals that float by in the water.*) **MAIN IDEA**

Page 112

Read page 112 aloud to students, asking them to listen to find out how a coral reef is formed. Say: **In one sentence, summarize how coral reefs are formed.** (*Possible response: Corals grow on top of the skeletons of dead corals; over time a reef builds up.*) **SUMMARIZE**

Page 113

Have students study the diagram on page 113 to learn how a coral atoll forms. Model using the Reread to Clarify strategy:

> **MODEL** This page has a series of three steps. I think I should read each step closely and study its diagram before I move on to the next one. Since this important information seems to be in time order, I will reread the steps to make sure I understand the steps and the order. After I reread, I understand that first, a fringing reef grows around a volcanic island. Then, the island sinks and forms a barrier reef and a lagoon. Finally, the island disappears and leaves a ring-shaped reef, which is the coral atoll. (Focus Strategy) **REREAD TO CLARIFY**

Ask: **Does the diagram make the text on this page easier to understand? In what way?** (*Possible response: Yes, the steps in the text are easy to see in the diagram.*) (Focus Skill) **GRAPHIC AIDS**

Pages 114–115

Ask students to study the map on page 114, and help them locate the Great Barrier Reef. Then have them read the first paragraph on page 114 to find out about the Great Barrier Reef. Ask: **Why is the Great Barrier Reef so important?** (*Possible response: It's the largest coral reef on Earth and the richest in sea life.*) **MAIN IDEA**

Ask volunteers to read the caption for each animal picture on pages 114–115. Ask: **What animals live along the Great Barrier Reef?** (*Possible response: sea horses, green sea turtles, crown-of-thorns sea stars, giant clams, longnose butterfly fish*) **IMPORTANT DETAILS**

Page 116

Read page 116 aloud to students, and have them listen to find out what is harming and killing the world's coral reefs. Ask: **Why are the living coral reefs in danger of dying?** (*Possible response: Corals need clean water, and*

ocean pollution kills the corals.) **CAUSE-EFFECT**

Ask: **How can the world's coral reefs be saved?** (*Possible response: Stop pollution of the oceans.*) **DRAW CONCLUSIONS**

Summarize the selection. Ask students to think about where coral reefs grow, how they are formed, why they are important, and why they are in danger. Then have students write four sentences to summarize the selection.

Answers to *Think About It* Questions

1. Coral reefs grow in oceans around the world, but only where the water is warm, shallow, clean, and clear. **SUMMARY**

2. Possible responses: A coral reef is like a garden in that it grows in one place. It's different from a garden of plants because the living things are animals. **INTERPRETATION**

3. Remind students to present specific reasons for choosing that animal. **WRITE A PARAGRAPH**

AFTER

Skill Review
pages 347A–347B

USE SKILL CARD 14B

⭐ Focus Skill Graphic Aids

RETEACH the skill. Have students look at **side B of Skill Card 14: Graphic Aids.** Read the skill reminder to them. Ask a student to read the skill reminder aloud.

Have students look at the illustration, and ask: **What does this illustration show?** (*Possible responses: the lake, the river, the delta, and the formation of a bayou.*) Read the story to students as they read it silently. Then ask a volunteer to read the story aloud to the group. Ask students to answer the two questions at the bottom of the card and write the letter of the answer on their own paper. Remind them to look for the answers in both the story and the illustration. Call on students to share their answers.

FLUENCY BUILDER Distribute *Intervention Practice Book* page 55. Explain that students will practice the sentences at the bottom of the page by reading them aloud on tape. Assign new partners. Have students take turns reading the sentences aloud to each other. Listeners should report on what their partners did well and make suggestions for improvement. Students should then read the sentences again and report whether they feel they improved.

INTERVENTION
PRACTICE
BOOK

page 55

Persuasive Writing: Persuasive Paragraph

Build on prior knowledge. Tell students that they will write a paragraph to persuade the principal to allow the fifth graders to "adopt" a street to keep clean. Display the following sentence:

> It would be good for the community and good for the fifth graders to "adopt" a street to keep clean.

Construct the text. "Share the pen" with students in a collaborative writing effort. As students dictate phrases and sentences, write them on the board or on chart paper. Guide the process by asking questions and making suggestions as needed. Have students build detail sentences from the main idea sentence given. Ask: **What are some ways this project would help the community? What are some ways it would help the fifth graders? What action do we want the principal to take?** For example, begin by writing:

> **It would be good for our community and for fifth graders to "adopt" a street to keep clean. This project would get students involved in keeping the environment clean. It would also make the community look better. When other people see students trying to help the environment, it might inspire them to clean up their own streets.**

Revisit the text. Go back and read the paragraph with students. Ask: **How can we make our sentences flow together smoothly?** (*Possible response: We could add words and phrases such as* first, the most important reason, *and* also.)

- Guide students to decide whether they have included enough strong reasons to have such a project. Ask: **How can we make our reasons stronger?** (*Possible response: We could tell good things about how other students have cleaned up streets.*)

- Remind students that the paragraph should end with a request for something. If needed, ask: **What action should we ask the principal to take?** (*Possible response: ask him or her to help us start or join a project*)

- Read aloud the completed paragraph with students.

On Your Own

Ask students to write paragraphs of their own that persuade someone to do something. They should begin with a sentence that tells the main idea and follow with sentences that tell reasons why the person should help them. They should conclude with a sentence asking the person to do something specific.

Connect Spelling and Phonics

RETEACH **consonant /j/g, dge.** Write *barge* on the board, and point out the *g*. Tell students that in the first six words you will read, the /j/ sound is spelled with a *g*. Dictate words 1–6, and have students write them. After each one, display the correct spelling for students to proofread against. Then write *badge* on the board, and point out the letters *dge*. Tell students that the next two words have the /j/ sound spelled *dge*. Dictate words 7–8, and have students write and proofread as before.

1. change   2. gently*   3. giant   4. largest*

5. fringe*   6. gems   7. ridges*   8. edge*

*Word appears in "Gardens of the Sea: Coral Reefs."

Build and Read Longer Words

Write the words *villager* and *dangerous* on the board, and say them aloud. Guide students to identify the VCCV pattern in each. (*illa; ange*) Remind students that words that have two consonants between two vowels are usually broken into syllables between the consonants. Demonstrate breaking the words into syllables: *vil-lag-er; dan-ger-ous*. Say each syllable and word with students. Repeat the procedure with *gesture, litterbug,* and *kindergarten*.

FLUENCY BUILDER Have students choose a passage from "Gardens of the Sea: Coral Reefs" to read aloud to a partner. You may have students choose passages that they found particularly interesting, or have them choose one of the following options.

■ Read page 110. (From *If you could . . .* through *. . . clean, and clear.* Total: 108 words)

■ Read page 113. (From *There are three . . .* through *. . . is a coral atoll.* Total: 105 words)

■ Read page 115. (From *Green Sea Turtle . . .* through *. . . to the reefs.* Total: 119 words)

Have students read a selected passage aloud to their partners three times. Then have students rate each reading on a scale from 1 to 4.

Encourage students to note their improvement from one reading to the next by completing the sentence *I know my reading has improved because* _____. Encourage the listeners to offer positive feedback.

Review Vocabulary

To revisit Vocabulary Words prior to the weekly assessment, use these sentence frames. Read the statements to students, and ask them to respond by writing the letters of the correct answers. Go over each answer, and discuss why it is correct.

1. The deep-ocean submarine had **sensors** to tell the people above
   a. when to come back up.   b. how deep it was.

2. The **atoll** was the island that was left after the volcano had
   a. sunk into the water.   b. exploded.

3. The huge **reef** off the coast of Australia is a rich place to see
   a. corals and other sea animals.   b. skyscrapers.

4. The children swam safely in the **lagoon** because it was
   a. in the pounding waves.   b. protected from big waves.

5. The speed of water flowing in rivers that **meander** is usually
   a. very fast.   b. very slow.

6. The surface of Mars seems to be **barren**. That is, Mars
   a. seems to have forests.   b. seems to have no life.

Correct responses: lb, 2a, 3a, 4b, 5b, 6b

You may want to display the Vocabulary Words and definitions on page 139, and have students copy them to study for the vocabulary test.

Review Graphic Aids

**INTERVENTION
PRACTICE
BOOK**

page 58

Before the weekly assessment on graphic aids, distribute *Intervention Practice Book* page 58. Ask students to read the story silently and look at the diagram to help them understand the information in the selection. Then have a student read the story aloud. Guide students in answering the first question. Then ask them to finish on their own.

Review Test Prep

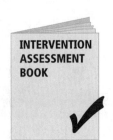

**INTERVENTION
ASSESSMENT
BOOK**

Ask students to turn to page 347 of the *Pupil Edition*. Call attention to the tips for answering the test questions. Tell students that paying attention to these tips can help them answer not only the test questions on this page but also questions on other tests. Have students look at the first tip and read it silently as you read it aloud. Direct students to look at the next tip. Have students read the story and answer each question. Remind them to use the tips when answering the questions.

**DISTANT
VOYAGES**

page 347

Self-Selected Reading

Have students select their own books to read independently. They may choose books from the classroom library shelf or you may wish to offer a group of appropriate books such as these from which students can choose.

- *The Great Barrier Reef.* (See page 347M of the *Teacher's Edition* for a lesson plan.)

- *Destination: Jupiter* by Seymour Simon. William Morrow, 1998.

- *Adventure in Space: The Flight to Fix the Hubble* by Elaine Scott. Hyperion, 1995.

After students have chosen their books, give each student a copy of My Reading Log, which can be found on page R38 in the back of the *Teacher's Edition*. Have students fill in the information at the top of the form. Then have them use the log to keep track of their reading and to record their responses to the literature.

Conduct student-teacher conferences. Arrange time for each student to confer with you individually about his or her selected reading. Have students bring their Reading Logs to share with you at the conference. Students might also like to choose a favorite passage to read aloud to you. To give students more practice with summarizing and paraphrasing, ask them to read a short section and to summarize and then paraphrase it.

FLUENCY PERFORMANCE Have students read aloud to you the passage from "Gardens of the Sea: Coral Reefs" that they selected and practiced with their partners. Keep track of the number of words students read correctly. Ask each student to rate his or her own performance on the 1–4 scale. If students are not happy with their oral reading, give them an opportunity to continue practicing and to reread the passage to you again.

See *Oral Reading Fluency Assessment* for monitoring progress.

Use with

"The Case of the Flying-Saucer People"

Review Phonics: Consonant /s/c

Identify the sound. Have students repeat the following sentence aloud three times: *The circus clown rode on a unicycle in the center ring.* Ask students to identify the words that have the /s/ sound. (*circus, unicycle, center*)

Associate letters to sound. Write on the board the sentence above. Underline the *c* with the /s/ sound in *circus, unicycle,* and *center* as you say each word aloud. Explain that in these cases the *c* stands for the /s/ sound. Guide students to understand that *c* followed by *e, i,* or *y* usually stands for the /s/ sound. Remind students that *y* can act as a vowel, as it does in the word *unicycle.*

Word blending. Model how to blend the letters and sounds to read the word *cinder.* Point to each letter and say its sound. Slide your hand under the whole word as you elongate the sounds: /ssiinndərr/. Then say the word naturally—*cinder.*

INTERVENTION PRACTICE BOOK

page 60

Apply the skill. *Letter Substitution* Write the following words on the board, and have students say them. Make the changes necessary to form the words in parentheses. Ask volunteers to read the new words.

call (cell)   **crater** (center)   **cave** (civil)   **collar** (cellar)

Introduce Vocabulary

PRETEACH **lesson vocabulary.** Tell students that they are going to learn five new words they will see again when they read a story called "The Case of the Flying-Saucer People." Teach each Vocabulary Word using the following process.

Use the following suggestions or similar ideas to give the meaning or context.

> Write the word.
> Say the word.
> Track the word and have students repeat it.
> Give the meaning or context.

translation	The translation of the book from English to Spanish was hard work.
advanced	Eight baseball teams advanced to the playoffs.
features	Identical twins look alike and have the same facial features.
piercing	The mother heard her baby's piercing cry from upstairs.
publicity	The announcement in the newspaper gave our art fair a lot of publicity.

For vocabulary activities, see Vocabulary Games on pages 2–7.

Vocabulary Words

advanced highly developed or complex

features facial characteristics

translation words changed from one language to another

piercing penetrating

publicity information intended to attract public interest

AFTER

Building Background and Vocabulary

Apply Vocabulary Strategies

Use suffixes. Tell students that when the suffix *-ion*, *-tion*, or *-ation* is added to a root word, the new word has a different meaning and is a different part of speech. Write these words on the board: *translate, determine.* Model how to add the suffix *-ion*, *-tion*, or *-ation* to *translate* and *examine.*

> **MODEL** I know that *translate* is a root word. If I drop the final *e* and add *-ion*, I make a new word: *translation*. When I add *-ation* to *determine*, I need to drop the *e* to make *determination*. I have changed the meaning of both root words and changed the part of speech from action words to naming words.

Tell students to use this strategy as they read.

RETEACH **lesson vocabulary.** Make sure each student has a set of vocabulary cards. As you read the following sentences, have students listen and hold up the appropriate word card. Reread each sentence with the correct word choice.

I. We read a <u>(*translation*)</u> of the story that had been written in French.
2. The calendar of the Mayas was as <u>(*advanced*)</u> as today's calendars.
3. Often, the facial <u>(*features*)</u> of sisters and brothers are similar.
4. My mother gives me a <u>(*piercing*)</u> look when I am in trouble.
5. Our <u>(*publicity*)</u> posters drew many people to our concert.

FLUENCY BUILDER Distribute *Intervention Practice Book* page 59. Read each word in the first column, and have students repeat it. Then have partners take turns reading the words to each other. Follow the same procedure with each of the remaining columns. After partners have practiced reading aloud each column separately, have them practice the entire list.

INTERVENTION PRACTICE BOOK

page 59

(Focus Skill) Text Structure: Main Idea and Details

PRETEACH **the skill.** Tell students that writers often organize their ideas by giving main ideas and supporting details. Explain that if a passage doesn't state the main idea clearly, readers must use the details to form a main idea statement.

Have students look at **side A of Skill Card 15: Text Structure: Main Idea and Details**. Read the explanation aloud. Direct students' attention to the illustration, and have students tell what they see. Have volunteers take turns reading sentences of the paragraph aloud. Then guide a discussion of the chart. Ask:

- **Is the main idea stated clearly in this paragraph? How do you know?** (*Possible response: Yes; it tells in a general way what the rest of the sentences are about.*)

- **How does each detail add to the main idea?** (*Possible response: It supports the information in the main idea sentence, or gives an example of it.*)

Remind students that not all passages have main idea sentences and that sometimes the main ideas must be figured out.

Prepare to Read: "The Case of the Flying-Saucer People"

Preview. Tell students that they are going to read a selection called "The Case of the Flying-Saucer People." Explain that in this fiction story one of the characters reports an encounter with space people. This adds an element of science fiction to the selection. Then preview the story.

DISTANT VOYAGES

pages 350–361

- **Pages 350–351:** I see a space alien in the picture and a man with a very surprised look on his face. I think I would have this kind of look, too, if I saw a space alien.

- **Pages 352–353:** A boy and a woman are having a telephone conversation. I wonder if they are talking about the man who saw the space alien.

- **Pages 354–355:** I see a man telling the boy something. The boy seems surprised. Maybe the man is telling the boy about the aliens.

Set purpose. Model setting a purpose for reading "The Case of the Flying-Saucer People."

MODEL I can tell from the title that this is a detective mystery. I want to read to see if I can solve the mystery myself.

Reread and Summarize

Have students reread and summarize "The Case of the Flying-Saucer
People" in sections, as described in the chart below.

Pages 350–353

Let's reread pages 350-353 to find out how the story starts.

Summary: Einstein Anderson's mother calls Einstein to ask him to be
with her as she interviews Mr. Janus for a newspaper article. This man
says he has spoken with space aliens while on the moon, and she
wants to know what Einstein thinks. Mr. Janus shows up for dinner.

Pages 354–355

Let's reread these pages to see what Mr. Janus says about the aliens.

Summary: Mr. Janus tells how he met and spoke with the aliens on the
moon. He says he heard some hammering and went to see what
it was.

Pages 356–358

Let's reread to see if we can solve the mystery.

Summary: Mr. Janus says the aliens were knocking down their base and
were leaving. Einstein asks to go outside to play. Einstein's mother
speaks to Einstein alone and asks his opinion. Then the reader is asked
what the error in Mr. Janus's story is.

Pages 360–361

Reread to find out how Einstein figured the mystery out.

Summary: Einstein tells his mother that Mr. Janus's error is in saying
that he heard hammering on the moon. This is not possible, since the
moon has no atmosphere.

FLUENCY BUILDER Be sure students have copies
of *Intervention Practice Book* page 59, which you used
for the Fluency Builder activity. Call attention to the
sentences at the bottom of the page. Model appropriate pace, expression, and phrasing as you read each
sentence, and have students read it after you. Then
have students practice by reading the sentences aloud
to a partner.

INTERVENTION
PRACTICE
BOOK

page 59

Directed Reading: "An Encounter with Space People," pp. 118–125

TAKE FLIGHT
pp. 118–125

Tell students that they will read a science fiction story. People read science-fiction for enjoyment since it often has make-believe characters from outer space doing things that can't really happen. Point out that the writer includes details that help readers understand the main idea. Remind students to look for details that help them identify the main idea.

Page 118

Have students read aloud the story title and preview the story by looking at the illustrations and code writing in the story. Then ask students to read page 118. Ask: **How do Miss Clancy and the students react to the space giants?** (*Miss Clancy and the students are calm. She talks to them and then asks Vince for help.*) **CHARACTERS' TRAITS**

Page 119

Have students read page 119 to find out why Miss Clancy calls on Vince to help and how he helps. Ask: **Why does Vince know so much about space people?** (*Vince studies space people.*) **CAUSE/EFFECT**

Ask: **What are the space giants going to do after they receive help?** (*continue their trip*) **SEQUENCE**

Page 120

Have students look at the code in the picture on page 120 and then read the page. Ask: **What does Miss Clancy give the space giant?** (*a pen and a notepad*) **IMPORTANT DETAILS**

Ask: **Do you think Vince will understand the space giant's message? Why?** (*Possible response: Yes; he seems to know about the space giants.*) Ask: **What do you think the letters V•R•MT mean?** (*Responses will vary.*) **EXPRESS PERSONAL OPINIONS**

Page 121

Ask students to read page 121 to learn the main reason for the giants' visit. Ask: **What is the main idea of the giants' message? What details support this main idea?** (*Possible response: They are hungry; they nod when Vince explains that they need food and have used up their supplies. They are also impatient.*) (Focus Skill) **MAIN IDEA AND DETAILS**

Page 122

Ask students to read the page. Ask: **How are the codes on pages 120 and 122 alike?** (*They both have V•R.*) **COMPARE AND CONTRAST**

Page 123

Ask students to read aloud the final sentence on page 123, and draw students' attention to the word *encounter*. Model using the strategy Use Decoding/Phonics.

> **MODEL** This is a long word, so I will look at and say each part. I know that *en-* is pronounced /en/ and that *-ter* is pronounced /tər/. The syllable *coun* looks like /koun/. So, I can put these parts together to get /en-koun-tər/. This sounds like a word I know—*encounter*. (Focus Strategy) **USE DECODING/PHONICS**

Have students look at the picture and read the letters on the notepad. Ask: **How do they spell** *easy*? (*EZ*) **GRAPHIC AIDS**

Ask students to read the page to find out how Vince breaks the code. Ask: **Is it possible for Vince to know that the space giants are from Mars and that they like to have fun?** (*Possible response: No; this story is make-believe and could never happen.*) **FANTASY/REALITY**

Summarize the selection. Ask students to think about the details that describe the space giants and the detail that describes Vince as an expert on space people. Then have students write four sentences to summarize the selection.

INTERVENTION PRACTICE BOOK

page 61

Answers to *Think About It* Questions

1. Vince figures out that they need food. **IMPORTANT DETAILS**
2. Possible response: She feels nervous but wants to keep calm so the students aren't frightened. **MAKE JUDGMENTS**
3. Responses will vary. **CREATE A MENU**

AFTER

Skill Review
pages 364–365

USE SKILL CARD 15B

(Focus Skill) Text Structure: Main Idea and Details

RETEACH the skill. Have students look at **side B of Skill Card 15: Text Structure: Main Idea and Details.** Read the skill reminder to them and ask a student to read the story aloud.

Direct students' attention to the questions at the bottom of the page. Have a volunteer read question 1 aloud, and ask students to choose the answer. (*choice c*) If necessary, point out that choices *a, b,* and *d* give true information about parts of the story but are not the main ideas. Then read question 2 aloud, and draw attention to the word *not*. Ask students to choose the answer. (*choice a*) If students are confused by the word *not* in the question, tell them that they can look at each choice and ask themselves, "Does this detail support the idea of playing the alphabet game?" The choice they respond to by saying "no" is the answer.

FLUENCY BUILDER Reuse *Intervention Practice Book* page 59. Explain that students will practice the sentences at the bottom of the page by reading them aloud on tape. Assign new partners. Have students read the sentences aloud to each other. Tell students to comment on each other's performance. Listeners should report on what their partners did well and make suggestions for improvement. Students should then read the sentences again and report whether they feel they improved.

INTERVENTION PRACTICE BOOK

page 59

Timed or Tested Writing: Persuasive Paragraph

Build on prior knowledge. Tell students that they will write a paragraph that could be part of a letter to people in their city government. The letter would ask the city to start a tree-planting program. Display the following graphic organizer:

> **Why We Should Plant Trees**
>
> to make the city more beautiful
>
> to provide homes for small animals
>
> to add oxygen to the air

Construct the text. Discuss the ideas, and invite students to add their own. "Share the pen" with students in a collaborative writing effort. As students dictate sentences, write them on the board. Guide the process by asking questions and making suggestions. Help students construct a main idea sentence and follow it with the details. They should end with a request for action. For example:

> We think it **would be a good idea if the city started a tree-planting program. Trees help people and the environment in many ways. First, trees make places look more beautiful. Second, trees provide homes for birds, squirrels, and other small animals. Third, trees make oxygen and help keep the air clean. We would like to meet with you to talk about how students can help.**

Revisit the text. Reread the paragraph with students. Ask: **Why do we use a main idea sentence at the beginning?** (*Possible response: It lets the reader know right away what the paragraph is about.*)

- Guide students to make the sentences flow together. Ask: **What other connecting words could we use besides *Second* and *Third*?** (*Possible responses: Next; Last; Also*) Make any revisions students request.

- Ask: **How did using a graphic organizer help you?** (*Possible response: It helped me organize my thoughts so I could finish on time.*)

- Read aloud the completed paragraph with students.

> ### On Your Own
>
> Ask students to write paragraphs of their own in which they try to persuade a friend that there are or are not creatures on other planets. Remind students to use a graphic organizer to list their reasons and to begin their paragraphs with main idea sentences.

Connect Spelling and Phonics

RETEACH **consonant /s/c.** Write *nice* and *cent* on the board. Tell students that the words you will say have the /s/ sound spelled with *c*. Then dictate the following words, and have students write them. After students write each word, display the correct spelling so students can proofread their work. Have them draw a line through a misspelled word and write the correct spelling beside it.

I. trace	2. bicycle	3. space*	4. slices
5. lace	6. cells	7. center	8. faces*

*Word appears in "An Encounter with Space People."

Dictate the following sentence, and have students write it: *Place your bicycle in the center of the space.*

Build and Read Longer Words

Write *celebrate* on the board and read it aloud. Review open syllables by reminding students that words such as *bicep* and *protest* that have a long vowel sound in the first syllable are divided right after the vowel in the first syllable. Demonstrate by writing *bi-cep* and *pro-test* on the board. Then discuss open syllables by using the word *celebrate*. Point out that the first syllable of *celebrate* is divided after the *l* because it has a short vowel sound. Repeat the procedure by having students read *precise*, *civil*, *pencil*, *Pacific*, and *icy*.

INTERVENTION
ASSESSMENT
BOOK

FLUENCY BUILDER Have students choose a passage from "An Encounter with Space People" to read aloud to a partner. You may have students choose passages that they found particularly interesting or have them choose one of the following options.

- Read page 119. (From *I'm Vince* . . . through . . . *with their trip.* Total: 115 words)

- Read pages 120–121. (From *"Can't they speak* . . . through . . . *wanted to eat.* Total: 117 words)

- Read pages 122–123. (From *Miss Clancy* . . . through . . . *for their trip.* Total: 114 words)

Have students read a selected passage aloud to their partners three times. Have students rate each of their own readings on a scale from 1 to 4. Encourage students to note their improvement from one reading to the next by completing the sentence *I know my reading has improved because* _____. Encourage listeners to offer positive feedback about improvements.

Review Vocabulary

To revisit the Vocabulary Words prior to the weekly assessment, use these sentence frames. Read the statements to students, and ask them to write the letter of the answer. Go over each answer and discuss why it is correct.

1. The **piercing** roar of the jet's engines made us
   a. cover our ears.   b. sing and dance.

2. The **features** of a man's face might include
   a. blue eyes and a beard.   b. glasses.

3. As I **advanced** toward the plate of cupcakes, I could
   a. smell them better.   b. smell them less.

4. Someone was there to give a **translation** for the woman who
   a. spoke our language.   b. spoke another language.

5. Movie companies use **publicity** posters to get people to
   a. see the movies.   b. eat popcorn.

   Correct responses: la, 2a, 3a, 4b, 5a

You may want to display the Vocabulary Words and definitions on page 149 and have students copy them to use when they study for the vocabulary test.

 Review Main Idea and Details

INTERVENTION
PRACTICE
BOOK

page 62

Before the weekly assessment on main idea and details, distribute *Intervention Practice Book* page 62. Ask students to read the passage silently as one student reads the passage aloud. Read the first question aloud. Have students read the four choices silently and circle the letter of the answer. Follow the same procedure for question 2. When students are finished, call on volunteers to share their answers.

Review Test Prep

INTERVENTION
ASSESSMENT
BOOK

Ask students to turn to page 365 of the *Pupil Edition*. Call attention to the tips for answering the test questions. Tell students that paying attention to these tips can help them answer not only the test questions on this page but also questions on other tests. Have students look at the first tip and read it silently as you read it aloud. Direct students to look at the next tip. Have students read the story and answer each question. Remind them to use the tips when answering the questions.

**DISTANT
VOYAGES**

page 365

Self-Selected Reading

Have students select their own books to read independently. They may choose books from the classroom library shelf or you may wish to offer a group of appropriate books from which students can choose.

- *Apollo: To the Moon.* (See page 365M of the *Teacher's Edition* for a lesson plan.)

- *June 29, 1999* by David Wiesner. Clarion, 1992.

- *Time Machine and Other Cases* by Seymour Simon. William Morrow, 1997.

After students have chosen their books, give each student a copy of My Reading Log, which can be found on page R38 in the back of the *Teacher's Edition*. Have students fill in the information at the top of the form. Then have them use the log to keep track of their reading and to record their responses to literature.

Conduct student-teacher conferences. Arrange time for each student to confer with you individually about his or her selected reading. Have students bring their Reading Logs to share with you at the conference. Students might also like to choose a favorite passage to read aloud to you. To give students more practice with summarizing and paraphrasing, ask them to read a short section and to summarize and then paraphrase it.

FLUENCY PERFORMANCE Have students read aloud to you the passage from "An Encounter with Space People" that they selected and practiced with their partners. Keep track of the number of words each student reads correctly. Ask each student to rate his or her own performance on the 1–4 scale. If students are not happy with their oral reading, give them an opportunity to continue practicing and to reread the passage to you.

See *Oral Reading Fluency Assessment* for monitoring progress.

LESSON 16

"Hattie's Birthday Box"

BEFORE

Building Background and Vocabulary

Review Phonics: Vowel Diphthong /oi/*oi, oy*

Identify the sound. Have students say the following sentence three times: *Roy annoys Joy with his loud noises.* Have students identify the words that have the /oi/ sound. (*Roy, annoys, Joy, noises*)

Associate letters to sound. Write the sentence *Roy annoys Joy with his loud noises* on the board. Underline the letters *oy* or *oi* in each word. Tell students that the vowel combinations *oi* and *oy* do not follow the rule that two vowels between consonants usually stand for a long vowel sound, as in *coat* and *grain*. The combinations *oi* and *oy* usually stand for the /oi/ sound in *Roy* and *noises*.

Word blending. Write *coil, oyster,* and *moist* on the board. Model how to blend and read the word *coil*. Draw your hand under the whole word as you elongate sounds: /koill/. Then say the word naturally—*coil*. Repeat the process for the remaining words.

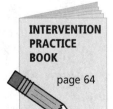

INTERVENTION PRACTICE BOOK

page 64

Apply the skill. *Letter Substitution* Write the following words on the board and have students read each aloud. Make the changes necessary to form the words in parentheses. Have a volunteer read aloud each new word. Try to give every student an opportunity to respond.

jay (joy)	**fowl** (foil)	**nose** (noise)	**layer** (loyal)
mist (moist)	**pint** (point)	**Jon** (join)	**decay** (decoy)

Introduce Vocabulary

PRETEACH **lesson vocabulary.** Tell students they are going to learn seven words that they will see again when they read the story "Hattie's Birthday Box." Teach each vocabulary word using the following process.

Use the following suggestions or similar ideas to give the meaning or context.

> Write the word.
> Say the word.
> Track the word and have students repeat it.
> Give the meaning or context.

undeniable	It was *undeniable* that she had eaten the cookies because she still had crumbs on her mouth.
rations	Our family's weekly *rations* of sugar and meat had to last for seven days.
brooded	If a person thought deeply for a long time before deciding, we say he or she *brooded* over the decision.
concocted	When he caught his first fish, the boy *concocted* a tale about catching a shark.

despair	The farmer felt *despair* after a prairie fire burned his crops and his barn.
homestead	The settlers went west to *homestead* on the prairie and start a farm on the land.
perch	From my *perch* high in the tree house I could see the roofs of all the houses in the neighborhood.

For vocabulary activities, see Vocabulary Games on pages 2–7.

AFTER

Building Background and Vocabulary

Apply Vocabulary Strategies

Interpret figurative language. Point out to students that this selection has several figurative expressions. Write the following sentence on the board: *"Oh, I love her to pieces."* Tell students that writers sometimes use figurative language to mean things other than what the words actually say.

MODEL I know that writers sometimes use language in colorful ways to get their meaning across. In the sentence *"Oh, I love her to pieces,"* I know that Grandaddy means that he loves Hattie very much.

Tell students to watch for figurative language as they read the selection.

RETEACH lesson vocabulary. Give each student a set of vocabulary cards. Read aloud the following sentences, substituting "blank" for the Vocabulary Word. Ask students to hold up the appropriate card. Then reread each sentence aloud, using the correct word.

1. It was (undeniable) that the championship team was the best.
2. The army sent the soldiers (rations) to last three days.
3. Dad (brooded) over his decision to change jobs.
4. After Grandpa died, Grandma had feelings of (despair).
5. The government gave each farmer forty acres to (homestead).
6. She (concocted) an excuse for not finishing her homework.
7. We watched the fireworks from our (perch) on the top floor.

FLUENCY BUILDER Use *Intervention Practice Book* page 63.
Read aloud each of the words in the first column, and have students repeat it. Then have partners take turns reading the words aloud. Follow the same procedure with each of the remaining columns. After each partner has had a turn reading aloud the words in each column, have them practice reading the entire list and time themselves.

INTERVENTION
PRACTICE
BOOK

page 63

USE SKILL CARD 16A

(Focus Skill) Word Relationships: Antonyms

PRETEACH the skill. Have students look at **side A of Skill Card 16: Word Relationships: Antonyms.** Ask a volunteer to read the explanation aloud. Then direct students' attention to the illustration. Ask:

- **What can you say that compares the two trees in the picture?** Draw students' attention to the first sentence, and tell them that the words in dark print are antonyms.

- Ask: **What are some other antonym pairs that could describe the trees?** (Possible responses: *big—small; giant—tiny*)

- Repeat the procedure with the other two sentences that tell about the picture. Then ask students to name any other antonym pairs they know.

Point out that knowing how words relate to each other is an important part of understanding language.

Prepare to read: "Hattie's Birthday Box"

Preview. Tell students that they are going to read a selection called "Hattie's Birthday Box." Explain that this is a realistic fiction selection, which means that the characters and events are like those in real life, but were made up by the author.

DISTANT
VOYAGES

pages
370–380

- **Pages 370–371:** In the picture I see an old man sitting in a rocking chair. He has a large wrapped present in his lap and there are balloons, so I think it must be his birthday.

- **Pages 372–373:** Now I see a girl with the old man. I wonder if these people are Hattie and her grandfather. On page 373 I see an old-fashioned wedding picture.

- **Pages 374–375:** The colors in these pictures are different, and they have frames drawn around them. Maybe the grandfather is telling about things he did in the past. I also see a box.

- **Pages 376–377:** The pictures are colorful again, and the grandfather is there, too. I see a gift, so I'm pretty sure this is the man's birthday party. He seems to be looking very hard at something.

- **Pages 378–380:** An old woman is hugging the man, and the girl is looking at them. I wonder if Hattie is the girl or the woman. On page 380 I see an open box. I want to know what was inside the box and how the story ends.

Set purpose. Model setting a purpose for reading "Hattie's Birthday Box."

MODEL From my preview, I think something special happens at the man's birthday party. I want to read to find out what happens.

Reread and Summarize

Have students reread and summarize "Hattie's Birthday Box" in sections, as described in the chart below.

Pages 370–372

Let's look again at pages 370–371 to remember who this man is and why he is nervous before his birthday party.

Summary: The narrator and her mother go to the nursing home to celebrate the hundredth birthday of the narrator's great-great-grandfather. He is worried about the arrival of his younger sister, Hattie, whom he has not seen in 76 years.

Pages 373–375

Let's reread the story the narrator's grandaddy tells.

Summary: Grandaddy's younger sister was leaving to homestead in Nebraska. As a gift, Grandaddy made a box by hand and carved her initials in it. He couldn't afford a gift to put inside, but he told Hattie that she should open it when times were hard.

Pages 376–377

Let's reread these pages to recall Hattie's arrival at the party.

Summary: People begin arriving at the party, but Grandaddy can't pay much attention because he is so worried about Hattie's arrival. Finally she arrives, and she and Grandaddy see each other.

Pages 378–380

Reread the ending of the story to see what Hattie thinks of the empty box.

Grandaddy asks Hattie to forgive him for giving her an empty box. Hattie explains that the empty box has represented hope to her, which was the best present anyone could give.

FLUENCY BUILDER Reuse *Intervention Practice Book* page 63. Call attention to the sentences at the bottom of the page. State that the goal is to have each student read each phrase smoothly. Model the appropriate pace, expression, and phrasing as you read aloud each of the sentences. Then have students practice reading aloud each sentence two or three times to a partner.

INTERVENTION PRACTICE BOOK

page 63

Directed Reading: "Peppermint-Peanut-Butter Fudge" pp. 126–132

Read aloud the title of the story. Ask students what is unusual about the title. (*Peppermint and peanut butter do not normally go together.*) Have them read page 126. Ask: **Why aren't Roy and Pearl enjoying the occasion?** (*They have no gift for Granny.*) **CAUSE/EFFECT**

TAKE FLIGHT
pages
126–132

Page 126

Page 127

Have students read page 127 to find out what Roy and his sister do about a birthday gift for Granny. **What does Roy mean when he says, "You're looking at a boy who can't boil water"?** (*He knows nothing about cooking.*) **UNDERSTAND FIGURATIVE LANGUAGE**

Ask a volunteer to read aloud the last paragraph on page 127 and ask themselves the same question. Model using the self-question strategy:

> **MODEL** I read that Roy asks Pearl whether butter isn't "the same as peanut butter." I ask myself the same question. I don't think they would make the fudge turn out the same at all. I think it will ruin the fudge.
> ★ (Focus Strategy) **SELF-QUESTION**

Page 128

Ask students to read page 128 to find out what happens next to the fudge. (*Peppermints are accidentally spilled into the fudge.*) Ask: **How does Roy feel when the peppermints spill into the fudge? How can you tell?** (*He feels guilty and embarrassed; he nearly cries; he says, "I've spoiled it!"*) **CHARACTERS' EMOTIONS**

Page 129

Ask: **What do Roy and Pearl each think they should do with the fudge?** (*Roy thinks they should throw it away. Pearl thinks they should feed it to the pigs later.*) **IMPORTANT DETAILS**

Page 130

Ask students to view the illustration on page 130 and describe it. Have them read page 130 to find out what happens when Granny tastes the fudge.

Ask: **How can you use the words in the first two sentences of the second paragraph to tell what Granny thinks of the fudge?** (*The story says that Roy waited for Granny to make a terrible face. The word but in that sentence helps me know that something with an opposite meaning will be said next. Then I read that Granny made a face of pure bliss. So, a face of pure bliss is like an antonym for a terrible face. Granny liked the fudge.*)
★ (Focus Skill) **WORD RELATIONSHIPS: ANTONYMS**

Page 131

Have students read page 131 to see who wins the kitchen contest. (*Pearl and Roy*) **What do Pearl and Roy do with the prize-winning fudge?** (*They give it to Granny as a birthday gift.*) **SUMMARIZE**

Summarize the selection. Ask students to discuss what Pearl and Roy think will happen with their fudge and what actually happens. Then help them summarize the story in three or four sentences.

INTERVENTION PRACTICE BOOK

page 65

Answers to *Think About It* Questions

1. Roy and Pearl don't like the fudge because it is too sweet. Granny likes it because she missed sweets as a child and enjoys very sweet things now. **SUMMARY**

2. Possible response: They think everyone will make fun of them. **INTERPRETATION**

3. Responses will vary but should use the correct format for a friendly letter. **WRITE A LETTER**

AFTER

Skill Review
pages 388–389

USE SKILL CARD 16B

⭐ (Focus Skill) Word Relationships: Antonyms

Have students look at **side B of Skill Card 16: Word Relationships: Antonyms.** Ask a volunteer to read the skill reminder aloud, and have students look at the illustration.

Point out the underlined words in the paragraph. Tell students to think about the context of the sentences and write their own antonyms that make sense. Read aloud the first sentence, and guide students to understand that the words *evening* and *sets* are antonyms for *morning* and *rises* and that these words make sense in the sentence. If necessary, guide students through the second and third sentences. Have them complete the sentences on their own. (Possible responses for the remaining sentences: *clear; smooth; few; high; fresh water; end, noisy; happiness; free*)

FLUENCY BUILDER Reuse *Intervention Practice Book* page 63. Explain that each student will practice the sentences at the bottom of the page by reading them aloud on tape. Assign new partners, and have them take turns reading the sentences aloud to each other and then reading them on tape. After students listen to the tape, have them tell how they have improved their reading. Then have them tape themselves again, focusing on improved pacing and tone.

INTERVENTION
PRACTICE
BOOK

page 63

Expository Writing: Sentences That Compare

Build on prior knowledge. Tell students that being able to compare things is an important skill not only in school but also in life. Explain that they will write sentences that compare the two parties in "Hattie's Birthday Box" and "Peppermint-Peanut-Butter Fudge." Begin by having students list some of the features of each party. For example:

"Hattie's Birthday Box"	"Peppermint-Peanut-Butter Fudge"
given for Grandaddy	given for Granny
took place inside	took place outside
happy event	happy event
many party-goers	many party-goers

Construct the text. "Share the pen" with students in a collaborative writing effort. As students dictate phrases and sentences, write them on the board or on chart paper. Guide the process by asking questions and making suggestions as needed. Be sure to include sentences that reflect both similarities and differences, and encourage students to come up with their own comparisons. For example:

- One party was for a man. The other party was for a woman.

- One party was held inside. The other party was held outside.

- Both of the parties were happy events.

- Each party had many people.

Revisit the text. Reread the sentences orally with students. Point out any antonym pairs, such as *man—woman* and *inside—outside.*

Guide students to decide whether they need to combine any sentences. Ask: **How would we combine two sentences into one?** (Possible response: by using connecting words, such as *and, but,* and *while,* and comparison words, such as *also, too,* and *both*)

Have partners proofread the sentences to check for any errors in capitalization and punctuation.

Read the sentences aloud with students.

> ### On Your Own
>
> Have students choose another pair of stories to write comparison sentences about. They may choose stories from the *Pupil Edition* or from their independent reading. Tell students to include the titles of the stories with their sentences.

Connect Spelling and Phonics

RETEACH **vowel diphthong /oi/***oi, oy.* Write *oil* on the board, and tell students that in the first four words you will say, the /oi/ sound is spelled *oi.* Dictate words 1–4, and have students write them. After they write each word, display the correct spelling so students can proofread their work. Then write the word *boy* on the board and say that in the next four words, the /oi/ sound is spelled *oy.* Proceed as before.

1. foil
2. spoiled*
3. moist*
4. broil
5. annoyed*
6. enjoying*
7. royal
8. employ

*Word appears in "Peppermint-Peanut-Butter Fudge."

Dictate the following sentences, and have students write them: *We had our choice of oysters or broiled fish. The boys pointed to the oysters.*

Build and Read Longer Words

Write these words on the board: *employment, asteroid.* Have a volunteer identify the letters that stand for the /oi/ sound in *employment* (*oy*) and in *asteroid.* (*oi*) Underline the letters *oy* and *oi,* and tell students that these letter combinations stay together when a word is broken into syllables. Help students identify the syllables in *employment* by asking: **Which letters stand for /em/? Which letters stand for /ploi/? Which letters stand for /ment/?** Then draw your hand under the whole word as students read it aloud. Repeat the procedure for *asteroid, overjoyed* and *disappoint.*

INTERVENTION
ASSESSMENT
BOOK

FLUENCY BUILDER Have students choose a passage from "Peppermint-Peanut-Butter Fudge" to read aloud to a partner. You may have students choose passages they found particularly interesting, or assign one of these passages:

- Read pages 127–128. (From *From our perch . . .* through . . . *I said.* Total: 113 words)
- Read pages 130–131. (From *I waited for . . .* through . . . *wondrous sweets!* Total: 114 words)

Ask students to read the selection aloud to their partners three times. Have students rate their own readings on a scale of 1–4. Encourage students to note their improvement from one reading to the next by completing the sentence *I know my reading has improved because* _____. Encourage listeners to offer positive feedback about improvements.

Review Vocabulary

To revisit the Vocabulary Words prior to the weekly assessment, use these sentence frames. Read the sentences to students, and ask them to write the answers on their papers. Go over the answers, and discuss why they are correct.

1. It was **undeniable** that the man was the thief because his fingerprints

   a. were on the door.   b. weren't found.

2. When **rations** of oil and gasoline were low, people had to

   a. drive less.   b. drive long distances.

3. My cat **brooded** over the new cat food I gave her. She

   a. loved the food.   b. didn't like it.

4. The storyteller **concocted** a tall tale in which a princess

   a. rode a bike.   b. became a queen on Mars.

5. With **despair** in her voice, my mom said to my dad,

   a. "Our car can't be fixed." b. "Let's have pizza."

6. When the government let settlers **homestead** the new land, the people

   a. built homes and farms.   b. built ships.

7. From its **perch** high in the branch of a tree, the eagle could see

   a. just a few things.   b. for miles around.

Correct responses: la, 2a, 3b, 4b, 5a, 6a, 7b

This is a good time to show the Vocabulary Words and definitions on page 159. Have students copy them to use for studying for the vocabulary test.

 Word Relationships: Antonyms

To review antonyms before the weekly assessment, use *Intervention Practice Book* page 66. Have a volunteer read the first item aloud, and guide students to fill in the blank. Remind students to use context clues as they complete the remaining items on their own. When students finish, ask volunteers to share their answers.

Students may refer to the story "Peppermint-Peanut-Butter Fudge" to answer the last question. Ask a volunteer to give an answer when the class has finished.

Review Test Prep

Ask students to turn to page 389 of the *Pupil Edition.* Point out the tips for answering the test questions. Tell students that paying attention to these tips can help them on this and other tests. Remind students to read the entire story and use context clues to find the answers.

INTERVENTION
PRACTICE
BOOK

page 66

INTERVENTION
ASSESSMENT
BOOK

DISTANT
VOYAGES

page 389

Self-Selected Reading

Encourage students to select books to read on their own. They may choose books from your classroom library shelf or you may select a group of appropriate books from which your students can choose.

- *Taming the Land.* (See page 389K of the *Teacher's Edition* for a lesson plan.)

- *Staying Nine* by Pam Conrad. HarperCollins, 1988.

- *Happy Birthday, Everywhere* by Arlene Erlbach. Millbrook, 1998.

After students have chosen their books, give each student a copy of My Reading Log, found on page R38 in the back of the *Teacher's Edition*. Have each student fill in the information at the top of the form. Then have students use the log to keep track of their reading and to record their responses to the literature.

Conduct student-teacher conferences. Arrange for an individual conference time with each student to discuss his or her self-selected reading. Have students bring their Reading Logs to share during the conference. You may also want to have the student choose a favorite passage to read aloud to you. Then ask questions designed to stimulate discussion. For example, you might question what information the student learned from a nonfiction text, how the author structured the text, or how the artwork helped the student understand the topic.

FLUENCY PERFORMANCE Have students read aloud to you the passage from "Peppermint-Peanut-Butter Fudge" they selected and practiced previously with their partners. Keep track of the number of words each student reads correctly. Ask each student to rate his or her performance on the 1–4 scale. If students aren't happy with their oral reading, give them an opportunity to practice some more and then to reread the passage to you.

See *Oral Reading Fluency Assessment* for monitoring progress.

LESSON 17

Use with

"William Shakespeare & the Globe"

Review Phonics: Vowel Variant /ô/aw, au(gh)

Identify the sound. Ask students to repeat the following sentence aloud several times: *Paul taught the hawk to hide its claws.* Have them identify words with the /ô/ sound. (*Paul, taught, hawk, claw*)

Associate letters to sound. Write on the board the sentence *Paul taught the hawk to hide its claws*, and underline the letters *au*, *augh*, and *aw*. Tell students that in these words the letters *au*, *aw*, and *augh* stand for the /ô/ sound. Point out that the letters *gh* in *taught* are silent.

Word blending. Model how to blend and read the word *hawk*. Point to *h* and say /h/. Point to *aw* and say /ô/. Point to *k* and say /k/. Slide your hand under the whole word as you elongate the sounds: /hhôôk/. Then say the word naturally—*hawk*. Follow a similar procedure for the words *Paul* and *taught*.

Apply the skill. *Letter Substitution* Write the following words on the board, and have students read each aloud. Make the changes necessary to form the words in parentheses. Have a volunteer read aloud each new word.

INTERVENTION PRACTICE BOOK

page 68

sack (saw)   **claim** (claw)   **lunch** (launch)   **cat** (caught)

Introduce Vocabulary

PRETEACH **lesson vocabulary.** Tell students that they are going to learn seven new words that they will see again when they read a story called "William Shakespeare & the Globe." Teach each Vocabulary Word using the following process.

Use the following suggestions or similar ideas to give the meaning or context.

> Write the word.
> Say the word.
> Track the word and have students repeat it.
> Give the meaning or context.

patron	The artist thanked his patron for providing him with money.
shareholder	Each shareholder was an owner of part of the company.
critical	An audience for an opera expects a better show and is much more critical than an audience for a school play.
lavish	The people who went to the king's party wore lavish costumes and the finest jewels.
congested	The streets of the huge city were congested with traffic during rush hour.

adornment	The adornment for the queen's head was a crown of gold, rubies, and diamonds.
dismantle	Workers at the fair began to dismantle the merry-go-round to take it to another place.

For vocabulary activities, see Vocabulary Games on pages 2–7.

For vocabulary activities, see Vocabulary Games on pages 2–7.

AFTER
Building Background and Vocabulary

Apply Vocabulary Strategies

Use prefixes, suffixes, and roots. Write the words *critical* and *dismantle* on the board. Point out to students that knowing prefixes and suffixes will help them understand these words. Underline the suffix *-al* in *critical* and the prefix *dis-* in *dismantle*.

> **MODEL** I know that the prefix *-al* means "like," so I can use the prefix plus the root word *critic* to know that *critical* means "like a critic." I also know that the prefix *dis-* means "opposite." This gives me a clue about what *dismantle* means. When I look up *dismantle*, I see that it means "take apart," which means something like "opposite of *build*."

RETEACH **lesson vocabulary.** Be sure each student has a set of vocabulary cards. Read aloud the following sentences, saying "blank" for each blank. Ask students to hold up the correct word card. Reread each sentence with the appropriate word.

1. Their ___(patron)___ paid all the costs for making the movie.
2. Each ___(shareholder)___ owns stock in the company.
3. The company was ___(critical)___ of workers who wore T-shirts.
4. When I saw the ___(lavish)___ buffet, I was glad I was hungry.
5. The road was ___(congested)___ because of the accident.
6. The only ___(adornment)___ for her outfit was a necklace.
7. It was a sad day when we had to ___(dismantle)___ our fort.

Vocabulary Words

patron wealthy person who supports an artist or writer

shareholder person who owns part of a business

critical likely to judge severely

lavish extremely showy, expensive, or abundant

congested crowded; too full

adornment decoration

dismantle take apart

FLUENCY BUILDER Use *Intervention Practice Book* page 67. Read aloud each of the words in the first column, and have students repeat it. Then have partners read the words to each other. Repeat for the remaining columns. Then have partners practice reading the entire list while timing themselves.

INTERVENTION PRACTICE BOOK

page 67

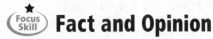

Fact and Opinion

PRETEACH **the skill.** Explain that knowing the difference between fact and opinion will help students understand what they read. It will also help them to determine how reliable the information is.

Have students look at **side A of Skill Card 17: Fact and Opinion.** Ask a volunteer to read the explanation aloud. Then have other students read aloud the text under Words That Signal Opinions and under Words That May Signal Opinions. Students may want to name other signal words. Then call attention to the two sentences at the bottom of the page. Ask:

- **Why is the first sentence a fact?** (Records would prove it.)

- **Why is the second sentence an opinion?** (Possible responses: It cannot be proved; other people might disagree.)

Point out that writers sometimes include both facts and opinions and that facts can be used to support opinions.

Prepare to Read: "William Shakespeare & the Globe"

Preview. Tell students that they are going to read "William Shakespeare & the Globe." Explain that this is a biography, which is the story of someone's life.

DISTANT VOYAGES
pages
392–411

- **Pages 392–395:** The man on these pages must be William Shakespeare. I think he was a writer, because he has a pen.

- **Pages 396–399:** Maybe the places shown on pages 396-397 are where William Shakespeare lived. I also see Queen Elizabeth I and performers of some kind. Maybe he wrote stories about them.

- **Pages 400–403:** The caption says the places on the left are play-houses. I wonder if *playhouse* means "theatre." I also see more performers. Next I see Shakespeare writing and a building going up. Maybe it's a theatre.

- **Pages 404–407:** I see that the Globe in the story title is a theatre. In one scene it is burning. Page 406 must show Shakespeare's stories.

Set purpose. Model setting a purpose for reading "William Shakespeare & the Globe."

MODEL I will read this selection to find out who William Shakespeare was and why he was important. I also want to know what "the Globe" is.

Reread and Summarize

Have students reread and summarize "William Shakespeare and the Globe" in sections, as described in the chart below.

Pages 392–395

Let's reread to recall who William Shakespeare was.

Summary: William Shakespeare, who lived in the 1500s and 1600s, was one of the greatest storytellers of all times.

Pages 396–399

Let's reread pages 396-399 to recall Shakespeare's early life and his move to London.

Summary: Shakespeare grew up in a large family and then moved to London. The arts were important to the people there.

Pages 400–403

Let's reread pages 400-403 to learn about Shakespeare's early experiences with the theatre in London.

Summary: Shakespeare's plays became well known, and a patron supported him. When the owner wanted to take down the theatre, Shakespeare helped take the theatre apart and move it.

Pages 404–407

Let's reread pages 404-407 to find out about the Globe.

Summary: Shakespeare's new theatre, the Globe, was successful, but after several years it burned down. He moved out of the city.

Pages 408–411

Reread pages 408-411 to recall how Shakespeare enjoyed the results of his work.

Summary: Shakespeare wrote plays until he died at the age of 52. He also invented many words and expressions still used today.

FLUENCY BUILDER Reuse *Intervention Practice Book* page 67. Call attention to the sentences at the bottom of the page. State that the goal is to have each student read each phrase smoothly. Model the appropriate pace, expression, and phrasing as you read aloud each of the sentences. Then have students practice reading aloud each sentence two or three times to a partner.

INTERVENTION PRACTICE BOOK

page 67

Directed Reading: "A Man of the Theater" pp. 134–141

TAKE FLIGHT
pages
134–141

Page 134

Ask a student to read aloud the title of the story. Then read page 134 aloud. Ask: **What did people do for entertainment in the 1600s in France?** (*Possible response: They went to plays.*) **IMPORTANT DETAILS**

Page 135

Ask students to read page 135 to find out how Molière got started in the theater. Ask: **What was Molière studying to become?** (*lawyer*) Ask: **What do you think his family thought about his going into the theater? Why?** (*Possible response: Disappointed and upset; he was sent to college to study law.*) **SPECULATE**

Page 136

Have students read page 136 to understand the difficulties Molière had in Paris. Model using the strategy Adjust Reading Rate:

> MODEL **I will read these paragraphs slowly to make sure I understand the problems Molière had in Paris. Since actors were not well thought of, they soon ran out of money. So, Molière was put in jail because he could not pay his bills. After his family paid the debt, he got out of jail. Now that I understand the problems, I can speed up my reading.** ⭐(Focus Strategy) **ADJUST READING RATE**

Ask: **What was the result of failing in Paris?** (*Possible response: Molière and his group performed all over France, and eventually the king saw a play and liked it. He gave Molière a theater to do his plays in.*) **CAUSE/EFFECT**

Page 138

Ask a volunteer to read aloud page 138. Ask: **How did Molière succeed with his plays?** (*Possible response: He created comedies in which he made fun of people, especially important people. Audiences loved the comedies.*) **DRAW CONCLUSIONS**

Page 139

Read page 139 aloud. Ask students to listen to find out why some people were angry with Molière's plays. Ask: **Who didn't like his work?** (*the people whom he made fun of in his plays*) **IMPORTANT DETAILS**

Ask: **Did the people whom Molière poked fun at deserve it?** (*Possible response: He thought so, but not everyone agreed.*) ⭐(Focus Skill) **FACT AND OPINION**

Page 140

Read page 140 aloud to students so they can notice the result of Molière's work. Ask: **In what ways was Molière honored for his work?** (*Possible response: A theater was named for him, and his work is performed all over the world.*) **SUMMARIZE**

Summarize the selection. Ask students to think about what happened in the beginning, in the middle, and at the end of Molière's life. Then have students write three or four sentences to summarize his life.

INTERVENTION
PRACTICE
BOOK

page 69

Answers to *Think About It* Questions

1. He wrote about people and situations in France, particularly rich people. **SUMMARY**

2. Possible response: They were embarrassed and then angry about the way he made fun of them. **INTERPRETATION**

3. Responses will vary, but questions and answers should focus on all stages of his career. **WRITE QUESTIONS AND ANSWERS**

Skill Review
pages 420–421

USE SKILL CARD 17B

(Focus Skill) Fact and Opinion

RETEACH the skill. Have students look at **side B of Skill Card 17: Fact and Opinion.** Ask students to read the explanation aloud together. Mention that both facts and opinions may be included in a paragraph and that the author may not tell which is which. Ask a volunteer to read aloud the paragraph. Ask students to use their own paper to make a fact-and-opinion chart as stated on the card.

When students have finished, have them share their responses. Charts should look like the following:

Facts	Opinions
New York City is the largest city in the United States.	I am very excited to be going to New York City this summer.
New York is the center of the fashion industry in this country.	It is absolutely the most exciting city in the whole world!
The clothes designed in New York are the clothes that will be sold to people all over the country.	The fashions there are the coolest and the latest.
The designers in New York decide what colors the latest fashions should be.	I think everyone should buy the latest colors and fashions to look their best.

FLUENCY BUILDER Reuse *Intervention Practice Book* page 67. Each student should practice reading the sentences at the bottom of the page by recording them onto a cassette. Have partners take turns reading the sentences aloud to each other and then record them onto a cassette. After students listen to the cassette, have them tell how they have improved their reading. Then have them record themselves again, focusing on improved pacing and tone.

INTERVENTION PRACTICE BOOK

page 67

Expository Writing: News Paragraph

Build on prior knowledge. Tell students that they will talk about a special event that happened recently at school. Then they will write a paragraph about the event for the school newspaper. Display the five *W* questions:

> What happened?
> When did it happen?
> Where did it happen?
> Who was there?
> Why did it happen?

Construct the text. Discuss a recent school event, such as a performance of a play, that students are familiar with. Then "share the pen" with students in a collaborative writing effort. As students dictate phrases and sentences about the event, write them on the board or on chart paper. Guide the process by asking questions and giving suggestions as needed. For example:

> **MODEL** Our fifth grade class put on a musical play last Friday
> night. We performed the play in the cafeteria. Most of the students and
> their parents were there. Many teachers from other grades were also
> there. The play gave us a chance to learn how to speak and sing in
> front of people. We also got to learn some new songs.

Revisit the text. Go back and reread the paragraph with students. Ask: **How can we make sure we have included all the information a news article needs?** (We can check to make sure we have answered all the five *W* questions.) Do we have to tell about the facts in any special order? Explain. (Possible response: No; we only need to answer all the questions.)

- Guide students to assess whether they need to combine any sentences. Ask: **How would we combine the first two sentences?** (Possible response: Combine the ideas in the sentences: *Our fifth grade class put on a musical play last Friday night in the cafeteria.*) Make any revisions that students request.

- Tell students that news articles should contain only facts. Guide them to make sure they have not included opinions.

- Reread the paragraph aloud with students.

On Your Own

Have students write a news paragraph about an event in your school, town, or city. Remind them to answer the five *W* questions, and to include only facts, not opinions. Ask for volunteers to read their stories aloud to the class.

Connecting Spelling and Phonics

RETEACH **vowel variants /ô/ aw, au(gh).** Write the word *raw* on the board. Tell students that in the first four words you will say, the /ô/ sound is spelled *aw*, as in *raw*. Dictate words 1–4, and have students write them. After they write each word, display the correct spelling so students can proofread their work. Continue the procedure with the word *haul* for words 5–6 and the word *caught* for words 7–8.

1. claws   2. thaw   3. dawn   4. straw
5. fraud*   6. launched*   7. taught*   8. haughty*

*Word appears in "A Man of the Theater."

Build and Read Longer Words

Write these words on the board: *author, naughty, clawing, astronaut, strawberry.* Tell students that the letter combinations *au* and *aw* usually stay together when a word is broken into syllables. Point to *author* and ask: **Which part of the word stands for /ô/?** (*au*) **Which part stands for /thər/?** (*thor*) Then point to *naughty*, and tell students that the letters *augh* stay together when this word is divided. Have students read this word aloud. Continue by having them read the remaining words aloud and explain how they figured out how to break each one.

FLUENCY BUILDER Have students choose a passage from "A Man of the Theater" to read aloud to a partner. You may have students choose passages they found particularly interesting, or have them choose one of the following options:

- Read page 136. (From *After about a year* . . . through . . . *on his plays.* Total: 103 words)

- Read pages 138–139. (From *Over the next* . . . through . . . *parts of it.* Total: 107 words)

Ask students to read the selection aloud to their partners three times. Have students rate their own readings on a scale of 1–4. Encourage students to note their improvement from one reading to the next by completing the sentence *I know my reading has improved because* _____. Encourage listeners to offer positive feedback about improvements.

Review Vocabulary

To revisit the Vocabulary Words prior to the weekly assessment, use these sentence frames. Read the statements to students, and ask them to write the answers on their papers. Go over the answers, and discuss why they are correct.

I. The wealthy art **patron** gave money to

   a. poor people.   b. artists and writers.

2. The people who were the **shareholders** in the company

   a. didn't own anything.   b. owned the business.

3. She was used to judging the best art, so she was **critical** of

   a. the beginner's work.   b. the great artist.

4. If someone promised you a **lavish** allowance, you'd expect

   a. very little money.   b. plenty of money.

5. The airport was **congested** because of holiday travelers, so the

   a. flights were early.   b. flights were late.

6. An example of an **adornment** on a queen's hand might be

   a. a gold ring.   b. a spot of dirt.

7. If a crane comes to **dismantle** a building, it comes to

   a. make it stronger.   b. take it apart.

Correct responses: lb, 2b, 3a, 4b, 5b, 6a, 7b

This is a good time to show the vocabulary words and definitions on page 169. Have students copy them to use for studying for the vocabulary test.

Fact and Opinion

To review fact and opinion before the weekly assessment, use *Intervention Practice Book* page 70. Have a different student read aloud each sentence and fill in the blank.

INTERVENTION
PRACTICE
BOOK

page 70

Direct students' attention to the next section. Tell students to use "A Man of the Theater" to answer the questions. Read aloud each item, and ask students to circle "Fact" or "Opinion." Remind them to think about whether something can be proved. Review the answers, and discuss any differences of opinion.

DISTANT
VOYAGES

page 421

Review Test Prep

Ask students to turn to page 421 of the *Pupil Edition*. Point out the tips for answering the test questions. Tell students that paying attention to these tips can help them answer these and other test questions.

INTERVENTION
ASSESSMENT
BOOK

Have students follow along as you read aloud each test question and the tip that goes with it. Mention that to answer these questions they need to look back at the passage. Remind students to watch for words that signal opinions. Also remind them that facts are statements that can be proved by using information outside the passage.

Self-Selected Reading

Encourage students to select their own books
to read on their own. They may choose books
from your classroom library shelf or you may select
a group of appropriate books from which your
students can choose.

- *Is All the World Really a Stage?*
  (See page 421M of the *Teacher's Edition*
  for a lesson plan.)

- *Laura Ingalls Wilder by* Alexandra Wallner.
  Holiday House, 1997.

- *Davy Crockett: Young Pioneer* by Laurence
  Santrey. Troll, 1989.

After students have chosen their books, give each
student a copy of My Reading Log, found on page
R38 in the back of the *Teacher's Edition*. Have each
student fill in the information at the top of the
form. Then have students use the log to keep track
of their reading and to record their responses to the
literature.

Conduct student-teacher conferences. Arrange for an individual
conference time with each student when you can discuss his or her self-
selected reading. Have students bring their Reading Logs to share during
the conference. You may also want to have the
student choose a favorite passage to read aloud
to you. Then ask questions designed to stimulate
discussion. For example, you might ask the student
what he or she learned from a nonfiction text,
how the author structured the text, or how the
artwork helped the student understand the topic.

FLUENCY PERFORMANCE Have students read aloud to you
the passage from "A Man of the Theater" they have selected and practiced previously with their partners. Keep track of the number of words
students read correctly. Ask each student to rate his or her performance on the 1–4 scale. If students aren't happy with their oral reading,
give them an opportunity to practice and reread the passage to you.

See *Oral Reading Fluency Assessment* for monitoring progress.

Use with

"The World of William Joyce Scrapbook"

Review Phonics: Vowel Variant /o͝o/*oo, ou*

Identify the sound. Read the following sentence aloud three times: *Tom should take in some wood to make a cooking fire.* Ask students to identify the words that have the vowel sound heard in *hood.* (*should, wood, cooking*)

Associate letters to sound. Write on the board the sentence *Tom should take in some wood to make a cooking fire.* Underline the vowels *oo* in *wood* and *cooking.* Tell students that although most words with two vowels together have a long vowel sound, the letters *oo* do not follow the same rule. In these words, they stand for the /o͝o/ sound heard in *look.* Next, underline the vowels *ou* in *should.* Explain that in this word, the letters *ou* also stand for the /o͝o/ sound. Also explain that the *l* in *should* is silent. Point to each word with the /o͝o/ sound, and have students read it aloud.

Word blending. Model how to blend and read the word *should.* Slide your hand under the whole word as you elongate the sounds: /sshho͝odd/. Then read the word naturally—*should.* Follow a similar procedure with the word *wood.*

Apply the skill. *Letter Substitution* Write the following words on the board, and have students read each aloud. Make the changes necessary to form the words in parentheses. Have a volunteer read aloud each new word. Try to give every student an opportunity to respond.

feet (foot)	**show** (should)	**coal** (cook)	**goal** (good)
woke (would)	**cold** (could)	**croak** (crook)	**shock** (shook)

Introduce Vocabulary

PRETEACH **lesson vocabulary.** Tell students they are going to learn five new words that they will see again when they read a story called "The World of William Joyce Scrapbook." Teach each vocabulary word using the following process.

Use the following suggestions or similar ideas to give the meaning or context.

> Write the word.
> Say the word.
> Track the word and have students repeat it.
> Give the meaning or context.

encouraged   She was learning to play the piano so easily that her mom encouraged her to keep taking lessons.

illustrating   A person who is illustrating a book is drawing pictures for it.

series	A comic strip usually has a series of three or more scenes.
charcoal	After our campfire had turned cold, I noticed that the burned wood had become black charcoal.
pastels	The set of pastels that my brother bought for his high school art class looked like big crayons to me.

For vocabulary activities, see Vocabulary Games on pages 2–7.

AFTER

Building Background and Vocabulary

Apply Vocabulary Strategies

Use compound words. Tell students that a number of words in the selection are compound words, or words made up of two smaller words. Write the words *spaceships*, *watercolors*, *baseball*, and *airplane* on the board. Point out that compound words can be figured out by looking at each part by itself.

> **MODEL** The word *spaceships* looks like a very long word to me, but when I look more closely I see the words *space* and *ships*. I know how to say both of these words, so I just put them together to say the whole word: /spās-ships/. I know I can figure out other compound words in this way, too.

RETEACH **lesson vocabulary.** Give students vocabulary cards. Say each sentence, substituting "blank" for each blank, and have students hold up the correct card. Then read the sentence aloud with the correct choice.

1. Dad __(encouraged)__ me to add labels to my rock collection.
2. The pictures __(illustrating)__ the car showed how the motor works.
3. The author wrote a __(series)__ of books about the same group of friends.
4. Keep the paper on the __(charcoal)__ crayon or your fingers will get dirty.
5. Artists use __(pastels)__ to create colorful pictures of flowers.

FLUENCY BUILDER Use *Intervention Practice Book* page 71. Read aloud each of the words in the first column, and have students repeat it. Then have partners take turns reading the words to each other. Repeat for the remaining columns. After students have practiced the words in each column, have them practice reading the entire list and time themselves.

INTERVENTION PRACTICE BOOK

page 71

See *Oral Reading Fluency Assessment* for monitoring progress.

(Focus Skill) **Word Relationships: Synonyms**

PRETEACH the skill. Have students look at **side A of Skill Card 18: Word Relationships: Synonyms.** Read the definition aloud to students. Then have volunteers read aloud the next two sentences.

Tell students that to be good readers and good writers, they need to recognize synonyms for words. Point out that some synonyms have stronger or weaker meanings than others. Draw students' attention to the word web, and have volunteers read the words aloud. Use the words *small* and *microscopic* to demonstrate how synonyms can show different degrees of meaning. Ask:

- **Would you expect something *small* to be bigger than or larger than something *microscopic*?** (Possible response: bigger than)

- **How would you compare a *miniature* chair to a *wee* chair?** (Possible response: A *miniature* chair might be littler than a *wee* chair.)

Explain that some synonyms, such as *tiny* and *petite*, might be about the same in meaning. Discuss the other synonyms in the web, and invite students to name other synonyms for *diminutive* that they can think of.

Prepare to Read: "The World of William Joyce Scrapbook"

Preview. Tell students that they are going to read "The World of William Joyce Scrapbook," which is an autobiography, or a true story of a person's life written by that person. Then preview the selection.

DISTANT VOYAGES
pages 424–434

- **Pages 424–425:** I read the title and see the author's name. I see that he has written this selection and drawn the illustrations. I think the man in the photograph must be the author. The illustrations look fun, and I wonder what the story of his life is.

- **Pages 426–429:** On these pages, I can see that he tells about when he was a child. I think he will tell how he got started drawing.

- **Pages 430–431:** The heading "How I Do a Book" makes me think he is going to explain his process. I think this will be very interesting. It probably isn't as easy as it seems.

Set purpose. Model setting a purpose for reading "The World of William Joyce Scrapbook."

(MODEL) This story seems to be about how an illustrator got started. I want to read to find out how he learned to draw pictures and write books.

Reread and Summarize

Have students reread and summarize "The World of William Joyce Scrapbook" in sections, as described in the chart below.

Pages 424–427

Let's look again at pages 424–427 to remember how William Joyce started to write and illustrate books.

Summary: William Joyce started writing stories and drawing pictures when he was a child. He loved books and TV and got ideas from them.

Pages 428–429

As we read over pages 428–429 again, let's recall how William Joyce learned to draw well.

Summary: Joyce took art lessons and copied his favorite artists to figure out how they drew. He tried different media, and he realized he wanted to write books and draw pictures about things that weren't real.

Pages 430–431

On pages 430–431, let's see how Joyce makes a book.

Summary: He starts with a story and then sketches it. Then he makes paintings of the drawings.

Pages 432–433

Let's reread pages 432–433 and see how he used something he loved as a child.

Summary: He'd always loved dinosaurs, so he created a character, Dinosaur Bob, who could play baseball, play the trumpet, and dance.

Page 434

Reread page 434 to see why Joyce wrote this.

Summary: Joyce wrote the selection to answer questions people ask.

FLUENCY BUILDER Reuse *Intervention Practice Book* page 71. Call attention to the sentences at the bottom of the page. State that the goal is to have each student read each phrase smoothly. Model the appropriate pace, expression, and phrasing as you read aloud each of the sentences. Then have students practice reading aloud each sentence two or three times to a partner.

INTERVENTION PRACTICE BOOK

page 71

Directed Reading: "My Imaginary World," pp. 142–148

Read aloud the title of the story. Explain that this selection tells about a real person, Istvan Banyai. Ask students what sort of job Istvan Banyai might have and why they think this. (*Possible response: He must be a writer or painter who makes up things in his imagination, because the story is called "My Imaginary World."*) **DRAW CONCLUSIONS**

TAKE FLIGHT
pages
142–148

Page 142

Then read aloud page 142. Tell students to listen to confirm their predictions. (*Istvan Banyai is an illustrator*.) **What things helped Istvan develop his imagination during his childhood?** (*Possible response: Since he didn't have TV or brothers and sisters, he had to make up lots of things to do by himself. This made him good at imagining things.*) **IMPORTANT DETAILS/SPECULATE**

Page 143

Have students read page 143. Ask: **How can you use the synonyms in the first paragraph to know the age of the items in the grandmother's boxes?** (*Possible response: The words* old, ancient, *and* past *all let me know that the things were old.*) (Focus Skill) **WORD RELATIONSHIPS: SYNONYMS**

What was Istvan's favorite thing at his grandmother's house? Why was it his favorite? (*her slide lantern, because it made images on the wall*) **IMPORTANT DETAILS**

Page 145

Read aloud page 145. Ask: **What kinds of things did Istvan draw as a child?** (*both scary and funny scenes from his imagination*) **IMPORTANT DETAILS**

What steps does he take to create his illustrations today? (*He makes a series of drawings first. Next, he transfers these to clear plastic sheets. Then he paints in the colors on the plastic sheets.*) **SEQUENCE**

Page 146

Ask a volunteer to read aloud page 146. Ask: **What do you think Istvan Banyai means when he says, "I . . .take a shower in ideas"?** (*Possible response: His imagination is active even when he's doing ordinary activities.*) **AUTHOR'S CRAFT/FIGURATIVE LANGUAGE**

Page 147

Have volunteers take turns reading aloud sentences from page 147. Ask: **Why does Istvan describe his books as "windows into (his) imaginary world?"** (*Possible response: His stories and illustrations show what he thinks, feels, and sees inside his mind.*) **AUTHOR'S CRAFT/IMAGERY**

Page 148

Before students read page 148, ask them to use text structure and format to tell what kind of information is found at the top right of page 148. Model using the strategy Use Text Structure and Format:

> **MODEL** I look at the top of page 148 and see a label with a colon following it. I know that a colon sometimes carries the meaning "here it is." So, the label "Books by Istvan Banyai:" tells me that here is a list of books that have been written and illustrated by him.
>
> (Focus Strategy) **USE TEXT STRUCTURE AND FORMAT**

Summarize the selection. Have students name the things in Istvan Banyai's childhood that helped him develop his imagination and become an illustrator. Then ask them to summarize the selection in two or three sentences.

Answers to *Think About It* Questions

1. Possible response: Istvan Banyai had no brothers or sisters, so he often played alone. He played with old things in his grandmother's house. He spent hours drawing. **SUMMARY**

2. Possible response: He is happy; he seems to enjoy describing the process of illustrating and writing. **INTERPRETATION**

3. Responses will vary. **WRITE QUESTIONS**

AFTER

Skill Review
pages 438–439

USE SKILL CARD 18B

(Focus Skill) Word Relationships: Synonyms

RETEACH **the skill.** Have students look at **side B of Skill Card 18: Word Relationships: Synonyms.** Read aloud the skill reminder, and have a volunteer read the text that follows it. Then draw students' attention to the directions and the sentences, and guide them through the first item. Discuss the various synonyms students name, and have them write their choices on their own paper. (Possible responses: 1. *tough; challenging; complicated* 2. *hurry; dash; rush* 3. *grab; grasp; clench* 4. *furry; hairy; shaggy* 5. *consider; brood*)

FLUENCY BUILDER Reuse *Intervention Practice Book*, page 71. Explain that students will practice the sentences at the bottom of the page by reading them aloud on tape. Assign new partners, and have them take turns reading the sentences aloud to each other and then reading them on tape. After listening to the tape, have students tell how they have improved their reading. Then have them tape themselves again, focusing on improved pacing and tone.

INTERVENTION
PRACTICE
BOOK
page 71

Expository Writing: Sentences That Compare and Contrast

Build on prior knowledge. Tell students that they will talk and write about ways things are alike and ways things are different. Ask students to help you brainstorm a list of things that can be compared and contrasted. Choose things from the list that have both likenesses and similarities. For example:

> **Things to Compare and Contrast**
>
> apple pie—spinach pie
> car—truck
> paper plates—glass plates

Construct the text. "Share the pen" with students in a collaborative writing effort. As students dictate phrases and sentences, write them on the board or on chart paper. Guide the process by asking questions and making suggestions. Help students construct two sentences for each topic. For example:

- **Apple pie and spinach pie are both baked in a pie crust. Apple pie is eaten for dessert, but spinach pie is eaten for dinner.**

- **A car and a truck are both forms of transportation. All of a car is covered by a roof, but the back of a truck is not covered by a roof.**

- **You eat things on both paper plates and glass plates. You throw paper plates away, but you wash glass plates and use them again.**

Revisit the text. Go back and reread the sentences with students.

- Guide students to recognize words that signal comparisons and contrasts. Ask: **What words signal that we are comparing something?** (Possible responses: *and; both*) **What word signals that we are contrasting something?** (Possible response: *but*)

- Review punctuation of compound sentences by asking: **Why do we use a comma in each second sentence but not in each first sentence?** (Compound sentences need commas between the main parts.)

- Read the sentences aloud with students.

On Your Own

Ask students to come up with two or three other sets of things that can be compared and contrasted. Have them write pairs of sentences that tell about the likeness and differences.

Connect Spelling and Phonics

RETEACH **vowel variant /o͝o/ *oo, ou*.** Write *could* on the board. Tell students that in the first two words you will say, the /o͝o/ sound is spelled *ou* as in *could*. Dictate words 1–2, and have students write them. After they write each word, display the correct spelling so students can proofread their work. Then write the word *took* on the board. Tell students that in the next six words you will say, the /o͝o/ sound is spelled *oo* as in *took*. Dictate words 3–8, and have students proofread as before.

1. would*	2. should	3. book*	4. looking
5. stood	6. cook	7. hooked	8. wooden*

*Word appears in "My Imaginary World."

Dictate the following sentence for students to write: *Would you take a good look at the crooked fence?*

Build and Read Longer Words

Write these words on the board: *goodwill, overlook, dogwood*. Point to *goodwill* and read it aloud. Ask: **Which part of the word sounds like /go͝od/? Which part sounds like /wil/?** Draw a vertical line between the two syllables. Remind students that when two consonants come together between two vowels, the word is usually divided into syllables between the two consonants. Follow a similar process with *overlook* and *dogwood*.

FLUENCY BUILDER Have students choose a passage from "My Imaginary World" to read aloud to a partner. You may have students choose passages they found particularly interesting or assign them one of the following options:

- Read page 145. (From *When I was . . .* through *. . . in pencil.* Total: 118 words)

- Read pages 146–147. (From *Illustrating is . . .* through *. . . that never ends.* Total: 102 words)

Ask students to read the selection aloud to their partners three times. Have students rate their own readings on a scale of 1–4. Encourage students to note their improvement from one reading to the next by completing the sentence *I know my reading has improved because* _____. Encourage listeners to offer positive feedback about improvements.

Review Vocabulary

To revisit the Vocabulary Words prior to the weekly assessments, use these sentence frames. Read the statements to students, and ask them to write the correct answers on their papers. Go over the answers, and discuss why they are correct.

1. Once he had sold several of his paintings, he felt **encouraged**

    a. to quit painting.   b. to keep painting.

2. A person **illustrating** a book about volcanoes learns

    a. the best words to use.   b. how a real volcano looks.

3. If a person takes a **series** of karate lessons, he or she might take

    a. one or two lessons.   b. thirty or forty lessons.

4. In my picture of the white polar bear I used **charcoal** for

    a. the snow.   b. its eyes.

5. My little brother took my set of **pastels** because he thought

    a. they were crayons.   b. he could build with them.

Correct responses: 1b, 2b, 3b, 4b, 5a

Show the Vocabulary Words and definitions on page 179. Have students copy them to use for studying for the vocabulary test.

Word Relationships: Synonyms

To review synonyms before the weekly assessment, use *Intervention Practice Book* page 74. Have volunteers read the first two items aloud and give their responses. Tell students that they should refer to the story "My Imaginary World" to answer the next section. Have partners locate the words on page 145 and decide on a synonym for each. (Responses will vary.) For any responses that don't fit, point out why the meanings are not the same.

INTERVENTION PRACTICE BOOK

page 74

Review Test Prep

Ask students to turn to page 439 of the *Pupil Edition*. Point out the tips for answering the test questions. Tell students that paying attention to these tips can help them answer these and other test questions.

DISTANT VOYAGES

page 439

INTERVENTION ASSESSMENT BOOK

Before students answer the questions, remind them to think carefully about the difference between a synonym and an antonym. Tell students, for example, that a multiple-choice item that asks for a synonym may have an antonym as an incorrect choice.

Self-Selected Reading

Encourage students to select their own books to read on their own. They may choose books from your classroom library shelf, or you may select a group of appropriate books from which your students can choose.

- *A Story by Dorie.* (See page 439M of the *Teacher's Edition* for a lesson plan.)

- *Buddy* by William Joyce. HarperCollins, 1999.

- *How Artists See People* by Colleen Carroll. Abbeville Press, 1996.

After students have chosen their books, give each student a copy of My Reading Log, found on page R38 in the back of the *Teacher's Edition*. Have each student fill in the information at the top of the form. Then have students use the log to keep track of their reading and to record their responses to the literature.

Conduct student-teacher conferences. Arrange for an individual conference time with each student when you can discuss his or her self-selected reading. Have students bring their Reading Logs to share during the conference. You may also want to have the student choose a favorite passage to read aloud to you. Then ask questions designed to stimulate discussion. For example, you might question what information the student learned from a nonfiction text, how the author structured the text, or how the artwork helped the student understand the topic.

FLUENCY PERFORMANCE Have students read aloud to you the passage from "My Imaginary World" they have selected and practiced previously with their partners. Keep track of the number of words each student reads correctly. Ask each student to rate his or her performance on the 1–4 scale. If students aren't happy with their oral reading, give them an opportunity to practice some more and to reread the passage to you.

Use with

"Satchmo's Blues"

Review Phonics: Vowel Variant /o͞o/ *oo, ue, ew, ui, u*

Identify the sound. Have students repeat the following sentence aloud three times: *Ruth wore a new blue swimsuit to the pool party.* Ask students to name the words that have the same /o͞o/ sound they hear in *soon.* (*Ruth, new, blue, swimsuit, pool*)

Associate letters to sound. Write the above sentence on the board. Explain that many combinations of letters stand for the /o͞o/ sound. Underline the letter *u* in *Ruth*, the letters *ew* in *new*, the letters *ue* in *blue*, the letters *ui* in *swimsuit*, and the letters *oo* in *pool*. Point out that these letters and combinations can all stand for the /o͞o/ sound.

Word blending. Write *ruby, drew, clue, bruise,* and *bamboo* on the board. Model how to blend and read the word *ruby.* Slide your hand under the letters as you elongate the sounds: /rro͞obē͞e/. Then say the word naturally—*ruby.* Follow a similar procedure for the remaining words.

Apply the skill. *Letter Substitution* Write the following words on the board, and have students read each aloud. Make the changes necessary to form the words in parentheses. Have volunteers say each new word.

club (clue)   **step** (stew)   **hop** (hoop)   **trust** (truth)

INTERVENTION
PRACTICE
BOOK

page 76

Introduce Vocabulary

PRETEACH **lesson vocabulary.** Tell students they are going to learn six new words that they will see again when they read a story called "Satchmo's Blues." Teach each Vocabulary Word using the following process.

Use the following sentences or similar ideas to give the meaning or context.

> Write the word.
> Say the word.
> Track the word and have students repeat it.
> Give the meaning or context.

pawnshop	The man took some tools that he didn't need to the pawnshop and got money for them.
produce	There were all kinds of beautiful fruits and vegetables at the produce stand.
errands	Her errands for Saturday morning were to go to the post office and to return her brother's library book.
numerous	The park was crowded with numerous people having picnics and playing ball.
international	An international airplane flight is one that goes between different countries.

gravelly   When I had a cold, my throat
was so sore that my voice
sounded gravelly.

For vocabulary activities, see Vocabulary Games on pp. 2–7.

For vocabulary activities, see Vocabulary Games on pp. 2–7.

AFTER
Building Background and Vocabulary

Apply Vocabulary Strategies

Use affixes and root words. Write the word *international* on the board, and read it aloud. Remind students that they can sometimes figure out the meaning of an unfamiliar word by breaking it into its root word and its prefix or suffix.

> **MODEL** This is a very long word that I'm not familiar with. I can see the word *nation* in the middle. Then I notice that the first two syllables are the prefix *inter-*. I think *inter-* means "between." Then I see the *-al* on the end, a suffix, which I think means "related to." So, *international* must mean "relating to something between two or more nations." I will check the dictionary to see if I am right.

Have students use this strategy when they come across other unfamiliar words as they read. Remind them to use a dictionary or glossary to confirm word meanings.

RETEACH lesson vocabulary. Give each student a set of vocabulary cards. Read aloud the following sentences, saying "blank" for each blank. Then ask students to hold up the correct word card. Reread the sentence with the appropriate word.

 1. He went to the <u>(pawnshop)</u> to look for a radio.
 2. We found the best <u>(produce)</u> at the farmer's market.
 3. I loved it when Mom let me go on <u>(errands)</u> with her.
 4. The complaints about the noise in that apartment were <u>(numerous)</u>.
 5. The <u>(international)</u> flights from the United States are always long.
 6. The cheerleader's voice sounded <u>(gravelly)</u> after the football game.

Vocabulary Words

pawnshop place where personal goods are exchanged for money

produce vegetables and fruit grown for market

errands short trips to carry out tasks

numerous very many

international between two or more nations

gravelly harsh, as a voice

FLUENCY BUILDER Use *Intervention Practice Book* page 75. Read aloud each of the words in the first column, and have students repeat it. Then have partners read the words to each other. Repeat for the remaining columns. After each partner has had a turn reading aloud the words in each column, have them practice reading the entire list and time themselves.

INTERVENTION PRACTICE BOOK

page 75

USE SKILL CARD 19A

★
(Focus Skill) **Fact and Opinion**

PRETEACH **the skill.** Explain to students that it is important to understand what is fact and what is opinion.

Have students look at **side A of Skill Card 19: Fact and Opinion**. Read the explanation of fact and opinion, and have students read it aloud with you. Point out the two illustrations. Ask students if it can be proved how many Senators there are. (*Yes, there are statistics.*) Ask if it can be proved that a certain kind of sneaker hurts your feet. (*maybe after a lot of testing, which may not have been done*) Have a volunteer read the items listed under Facts. Then ask a volunteer to read the items under Opinions.

Prepare to Read: "Satchmo's Blues"

Preview. Tell students that they are going to read a selection called "Satchmo's Blues." Explain that this is historical fiction. Point out that this kind of story has real-life characters but some of the events are made up. Then preview the selection.

DISTANT VOYAGES

pages
442–455

- **Pages 442–443:** Right away my eye is drawn to the illustration of an African American boy holding a horn. The horn seems important to him, and I wonder how he was able to get it.

- **Pages 444–445:** I see musicians, with a banjo, a violin, and a drum. I think these men are important to the boy. There is the dim outline of a city in the background. I think I will find out about where the boy is from.

- **Pages 446–447:** The boy is playing a horn again. He seems to be putting a lot of energy into playing. I wonder what kind of event is taking place in this city.

- **Pages 448–449:** I see a city neighborhood and a little boy. It is probably the same boy who was playing the horn. I am curious about what he is saying to the man with the cart.

- **Pages 450–451:** I think this picture shows the same boy sitting with his mother or grandmother. Because the house is small and the steps rickety, I think he may be from a poor family. I wonder where his horn is now.

- **Pages 452–453:** These pages show a happy boy. In the background is a shiny brass horn. Falling from his hands are coins. I wonder if he is buying a new horn or if he earned the money playing the horn.

Set purpose. Model setting a purpose for reading "Satchmo's Blues."

MODEL **I know this story is about a real person. I want to read about how he got his horn and how he learned to play it.**

Reread and Summarize

Have students reread and summarize "Satchmo's Blues" in sections, as described in the chart below.

Pages 442–445

Let's reread pages 442–445 to recall the setting of the story and why Louis is sad.

Summary: Louis Armstrong, a boy in New Orleans, loves jazz music and hopes to play the horn someday. However, his family is poor, and the $5 cornet in the pawnshop window seems out of reach for him.

Pages 446–447

Let's reread these pages to see how Louis gets ready to play a horn.

Summary: Louis tries to play someone's horn, but it sounds bad. So, he practices blowing his lips and dreams of playing in bands.

Pages 448–449

Let's reread pages 448–449 to see how Louis tries to earn the cornet.

Summary: Louis does all kinds of odd jobs for people to earn the $5 for the pawnshop cornet.

Pages 450–451

Reread pages 450–451 to find out how Louis's plans get pushed back.

Summary: Louis's mother asks him for a quarter to help her buy food for his sister's birthday party. He sadly gives it to her but enjoys the food. Later, his mother gives him a silver dollar.

Pages 452–455

Let's reread the end of the story to see if Louis's dream comes true.

Summary: Louis takes the money and buys the horn at the pawnshop. He begins to practice and plans to learn to play very well.

FLUENCY BUILDER Reuse *Intervention Practice Book* page 75. Call attention to the sentences at the bottom of the page. State that the goal is to have each student read each phrase smoothly. Model the appropriate pace, expression, and phrasing as you read aloud each of the sentences. Then have students practice reading aloud each sentence two or three times to a partner.

INTERVENTION PRACTICE BOOK

page 75

Directed Reading: "With Love from Ella," pp. 150–157

TAKE FLIGHT
pages
150–157

Page 150

Read aloud the title of the selection. Explain that it tells about a real person, Ella Fitzgerald. The author imagines a letter Ella might have written to a fan and includes real facts about Ella's life in the letter. Read aloud page 150 as students follow along. Ask: **What clues tell you that Ella is a musician?** (*Possible clues:* composer, want to know about my career, love music) **CONTEXT CLUES**

Page 151

Have students read page 151 to find out what Ella's childhood is like. Remind them to picture story details in their minds. Ask: **Is it fact or opinion that she had a happy childhood? Explain.** (*Possible response: Opinion; although she gives reasons, they cannot be proved.*) (Focus Skill) **FACT AND OPINION**

Ask: **How does Ella become a good singer?** (*She sings at church, sings with friends after school, and copies styles of singers on the radio.*) **SUMMARIZE**

Ask students to think about whether Ella's interest in dancing or her ability at singing will end up making her famous. Model using the Read Ahead Strategy:

> **MODEL** I know that Ella is interested in dancing but that she has a gift of singing. It's hard to say if just having an interest in something will make a person famous. However, I know that a person has to have a natural gift for something to be successful. I will read ahead to see if her career will be singing or dancing. (Focus Strategy) **READ AHEAD**

Page 152

Read page 152 aloud. Ask students to listen to find out what happens when Ella goes on stage. Ask: **What happens when Ella tries to dance on stage?** (*She can't dance, so she sings instead and wins first place.*) **SUMMARIZE**

Page 153

Call on volunteers to read page 153. Ask: **How does Chick Webb help Ella?** (*She joins his band; he helps her develop her rhythm and style; he introduces her to important people.*) **SUMMARIZE**

How can you tell that Ella is world famous? (*The clue "international star"*) **IMPORTANT DETAILS**

Page 154

How does Ella's life change after Chick Webb dies? (*She becomes the leader of the band. After three years, she goes solo.*) **CAUSE/EFFECT**

Page 155

Ask students to read page 155 to find out Ella's message to her fans. Ask: **What is special about "scat" singing?** (*The voice sounds like musical instruments.*) **IMPORTANT DETAILS**

Page 156

Read aloud page 156 as students follow along. Point out that this is the author's note about Ella. Ask: **How can you tell that the author admires Ella Fitzgerald?** (*The author mentions her career highlights, some of her honors, and her famous style of "scat" singing.*) **AUTHOR'S VIEWPOINT**

INTERVENTION PRACTICE BOOK

page 77

Does this story make you want to hear Ella's "scat" singing? Why or why not? (Possible response: *Yes, I think it would be fun to hear a voice that sounds like an instrument.*) **EXPRESS PERSONAL OPINIONS**

Summarize the selection. Ask students to discuss the important events in Ella Fitzgerald's life. Then have them summarize the story in three sentences. Next, help them complete *Intervention Practice Book* page 77.

Page 157

Answers to *Think About It* Questions

1. She was surrounded by music from an early age. Even as a child, she enjoyed singing and knew she sang well. **SUMMARY**

2. She wanted to be a dancer until she tried to dance in a contest. She was too scared to dance, so she sang—and won first prize in the contest. **INTERPRETATION**

3. Responses will vary. **WRITE A PARAGRAPH**

AFTER

Skills Review *pages 462–463*

USE SKILL CARD 19B

(Focus Skill) Fact and Opinion

RETEACH the skill. Have students look at **side B of Skill Card 19: Fact and Opinion.** Read the skill reminder aloud, and have a volunteer read the two sentences that follow.

Direct students' attention to the first instruction and the illustration. Have students tell which statement is fact and which is opinion. (The first is a fact; the second is an opinion.) Then have students read the next instruction and the statements. Ask partners to decide whether each statement can be proved and, if so, where they could look to check each one. (Statements 1, 3, and 6 are facts that could be checked in an encyclopedia or textbook; statements 2, 4, and 5 are opinions.)

Remind students that it's important to think carefully about the difference between fact and opinion in what they read and hear.

FLUENCY BUILDER Use *Intervention Practice Book* page 75. Explain that each student will practice the sentences at the bottom of the page by reading them aloud on tape. Assign new partners, and have them take turns reading the sentences aloud to each other and then reading them on tape. After students listen to the tape, have them tell how they have improved their reading. Then have them tape themselves again, focusing on improved pacing and tone.

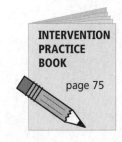

INTERVENTION PRACTICE BOOK

page 75

Expository Writing: Response to Literature

Build on prior knowledge. Tell students that they are going to write their opinions about "With Love from Ella." Brainstorm with students ideas to write in a paragraph about the selection. For example:

What the story makes me think about:

I want to hear Ella's music.
I want to listen to some jazz.
I want to hear Chick's music.

Construct the text. "Share the pen" with students in a collaborative writing effort. As students dictate phrases and sentences, write them on the board or on chart paper. Guide the process by asking questions and making suggestions. Begin by helping students construct a main idea sentence for their paragraphs. For example:

> MODEL The story "With Love from Ella" makes me want to hear jazz music. The way Ella's letter describes jazz makes it seem like a fun and exciting kind of music. I especially want to hear Ella's famous song "A-Tisket, A-Tasket." I also want to hear some of Chick Webb's music. I think he must have been a great musician if he was able to teach Ella how to use her talent to become famous.

Revisit the text. Go back and reread the paragraph with students. Ask: **How can we add variety to our sentences?** (Possible response: Change the beginning of some of the sentences since two begin with *The* and three begin with *I*.)

Guide students to make sure they have written titles correctly. Ask: **How should we show the story title and any song titles?** (Possible response: Use quotation marks; check capitalization and punctuation against the story.) Make the appropriate changes.

Ask students to make sure the opinions expressed refer to specific points in the story.

Read the completed paragraph aloud with students.

On Your Own

Ask students to write a paragraph of their own about another story they have read. Tell them to make sure their opinions refer to specific points in the story.

Connect Spelling and Phonics

RETEACH **vowel variant /ōō/oo, ue, ew, ui, u.** Dictate the following words, and have students write them on their papers. After students write each word, display the correct spelling so students can proofread their work. Have them draw a line through a misspelled word and write the correct spelling beside it.

| 1. stoop* | 2. smooth* | 3. Drew* | 4. brew |
| 5. ruby | 6. duty | 7. juice | 8. blue* |

*Word appears in "With Love from Ella."

Dictate the following sentence, and have students write it: *Sue hears a rumor that the new fruit-flavored gum will be in stores soon.*

Build and Read Longer Words

Write these words on the board: *soonest, jewelry, suitcases.* Remind students that when breaking most words that have two vowels together standing for one sound, the vowels stay together. Point out the *oo* in *soonest,* and read the word aloud. Then cover the suffix *–est* and have a volunteer read *soon;* cover *soon* and have a volunteer read *est.* Draw your hand under each word as students read aloud the remaining words.

Write *fruitful* on the board. Remind students that when two consonants appear between vowels, the word usually is broken into syllables between the consonants. Cover the word part *–ful* and have a volunteer read *fruit.* Then cover *fruit* and have a student read *ful.* Draw your hand under the entire word as students read it aloud.

FLUENCY BUILDER Have students choose a passage from "With Love from Ella" to read aloud to a partner. You may have students choose passages they found particularly interesting or you can assign one of the following options:

- Read pages 150–151. (From *Thank you . . .* through *. . .sing at church.* Total: 112 words)

- Read pages 152–153. (From *The truth is . . .* through *. . . hear me sing.* Total: 122 words)

Ask students to read the selection aloud to their partners three times. Have students rate their own readings on a scale of 1–4. Encourage students to note their improvement from one reading to the next by completing the sentence *I know my reading has improved because* _____ . Encourage listeners to offer positive feedback about improvements.

Review Vocabulary

Read the questions to your students and ask them to write the correct answers on their papers. Go over the answers and discuss why the answer is correct.

I. At a **pawnshop** people get money for

    a. their fruit and vegetables.   b. their belongings.

2. My mother went to the **produce** market to buy

    a. bananas and apples.   b. a new dress.

3. I have a few **errands** to run, so I will be back in

    a. about an hour.   b. about a week.

4. His awards for playing football were so **numerous** that they

    a. all fit in his hand.   b. needed a display case.

5. Someone who makes an **international** telephone call might call

    a. across town.   b. Mexico or France.

6. Having a **gravelly** voice might be a sign that you have

    a. had the flu.   b. been eating lemons.

Correct responses: Ib, 2a, 3a, 4b, 5b, 6a

This is a good time to show the vocabulary words and definitions on page 189. Have students copy them to use for studying for the vocabulary test.

Fact and Opinion

INTERVENTION PRACTICE BOOK

page 78

To review fact and opinion before the weekly assessment, use *Intervention Practice Book* page 78. Ask volunteers to read the first two items aloud and give the answers. Then proceed through the text by asking whether each statement is a fact or opinion. Discuss each answer as it is given. Remind students to ask themselves, "Can this statement be proved?" If it cannot, it is an opinion.

Review Test Prep

INTERVENTION ASSESSMENT BOOK

Ask students to turn to page 463 of the *Pupil Edition.* Point out the tips for answering the test questions. Tell students that paying attention to these tips can help them answer not only the test questions on this page but also questions on other tests. Tell students that when taking tests in which they must read passages, they should think about whether statements are facts or opinions, because the test questions may ask about them.

DISTANT VOYAGES

page 463

Self-Selected Reading

Encourage students to select their own books to read on their own. They may choose books from your classroom library shelf or you may select a group of appropriate books from which your students can choose.

- *Always in Style.* (See page 463K of the *Teacher's Edition* for a lesson plan.)

- *Tchaikovsky Discovers America* by Esther Kalman. Orchard, 1994.

- *Alvin Ailey* by Andrea Davis Pinkney. Hyperion, 1993.

After students have chosen their books, give each student a copy of My Reading Log, found on page R38 in the back of the *Teacher's Edition*. Have each student fill in the information at the top of the form. Then have students use the log to keep track of their reading and to record their responses to the literature.

Conduct student-teacher conferences. Arrange for an individual conference time with each student when you can discuss his or her self-selected reading. Have students bring their Reading Logs to share during the conference. You may also want to have each student choose a favorite passage to read aloud to you. Then ask questions designed to stimulate discussion. For example, you might question what information the student learned from a nonfiction text, how the author structured the text, or how the artwork helped the student understand the topic.

FLUENCY PERFORMANCE Have students read aloud to you the passage from "With Love from Ella" they have selected and practiced previously with their partners. Keep track of the number of words each student reads correctly. Ask each student to rate his or her performance on the 1–4 scale. If students aren't happy with their oral reading, give them an opportunity to practice some more and to reread the passage to you.

See *Oral Reading Fluency Assessment* for monitoring progress.

Use with

"Evelyn Cisneros"

Review Phonics: Digraphs /n/kn, gn; /r/wr

Identify the sound. Have students repeat the following sentence aloud three times: *The gnat flew from Carl's knee to his wrist.* Have students identify the words that begin with the /n/ sound. (*gnat, knee*) Then read the sentence again, and ask students which word begins with the /r/ sound. (*wrist*)

Associate letters to sounds. Write on the board the sentence above. Underline the letters *gn* in *gnat* and *kn* in *knee.* Tell students that the letters *gn* and *kn* can stand for the /n/ sound; the *k* and *g* are silent. Next, underline the letters *wr* in *wrist,* and tell students that the letters *wr* stand for the /r/ sound; the *w* in *wr* is silent.

Word blending. Write the words *knot, gnome,* and *wrap* on the board, and model how to blend and read them. Slide your hand under the word as you elongate the sounds /nnoott/. Then read the word naturally—*knot.* Follow a similar process for *gnome* and *wrap.*

Apply the skill. *Consonant Substitution* Write the following words on the board and have students read each aloud. Make the changes necessary to form the words in parentheses. Have a volunteer read aloud each new word.

fit (knit) **stack** (wrack) **block** (knock) **flash** (gnash)

INTERVENTION
PRACTICE
BOOK

page 80

Introduce Vocabulary

PRETEACH **lesson vocabulary.** Tell students they are going to learn seven new words that they will see again when they read a story called "Evelyn Cisneros." Teach each Vocabulary Word using the following process.

Use the following suggestions or similar ideas to give the meaning or context.

> Write the word.
> Say the word.
> Track the word and have students repeat it.
> Give the meaning or context.

flexibility Mention the root word *flex,* which means "to bend," and *flexible,* which means "able to bend."

migrant Point out the word *migrate* and mention how birds *migrate* south in the winter.

timid Mention that this word has its origin in the Latin word *timere,* meaning "to fear."

thrived Relate to the way a plant would grow in a brightly lit place. Plants *thrive* in sunlight.

scholarship	Mention the related word *scholar*, which refers to someone who is studying something.
devote	This comes from the Latin word *devovere*, which means "to vow."
apprentice	The origin of this word is in the Latin word *apprendere*, "to learn."

For vocabulary activities, see Vocabulary Games on pp. 2–7.

For vocabulary activities, see Vocabulary Games on pp. 2–7.

AFTER
Building Background and Vocabulary

Apply Vocabulary Strategies

Use word origins and derivation. Write the word *migrant* on the board. Remind students that an effective way to increase their vocabulary is to learn the origins of words and from what other words they may have been derived.

MODEL The word *migrant* sounds familiar. In the dictionary I see that *migrant* comes from the Latin word *migrare*, which means "to move from place to place." Now I can figure out that *migrant* has something to do with moving around, and it makes sense to me when I read that this word means "moving around to find work."

RETEACH lesson vocabulary. Read aloud the following sentences. Then ask students to hold up the word card with the word that correctly completes the sentence. Reread the sentence with the correct word choice.

1. She knew that _____ (*flexibility*) was important to a dancer.
2. His parents had been _____ (*migrant*) workers in the bean fields.
3. The kitten was so _____ (*timid*) it wouldn't come out from under the bed.
4. The students _____ (*thrived*) when they were allowed to pick their own schedules.
5. She received a _____ (*scholarship*) to go to summer music camp.
6. He decided to _____ (*devote*) himself to working for an end to violence.
7. His father had been an _____ (*apprentice*) stonemason for seven years.

Vocabulary Words

flexibility the ability to bend or twist without breaking

migrant moving around to find work, especially in harvesting crops

timid fearful or shy

thrived progressed toward a goal

scholarship money awarded to a student to help pay for his or her education

devote to give up one's time to an activity

apprentice a person who works for another to learn a skill

FLUENCY BUILDER Use *Intervention Practice Book* page 79. Read aloud each of the words in the first column and have students repeat it. Then have students read the words aloud. Follow the same procedure with each of the remaining columns. After students have practiced reading aloud the words in each column, have them practice reading the entire list.

INTERVENTION PRACTICE BOOK

page 79

Evelyn Cisneros/Lourdes López: Ballet Star **199**

(Focus Skill) **Main Idea and Details**

PRETEACH the skill. Have students look at **side A of Skill Card 20: Main Idea and Details**. Read the first two sentences aloud to students. Then have volunteers read aloud the next two sentences. Stress that the main idea may not be written directly. If it is in the paragraph, it could be the first sentence, the last sentence, or somewhere in the middle. Now call attention to the diagram. Have students read aloud the supporting details. Then read aloud the main idea.

■ Ask: **Do all of these details support the main idea: that Jamie wants to be a tennis champion?** (*Possible response: Yes, except for the sentence about her family.*)

■ Ask: **How do you think the sentence about her family fits into the main idea?** (*Possible response: Jamie knows that family support is necessary to be a champion.*)

Have students look at the details again. Ask them to write down a main idea using their own words. Have volunteers read aloud their sentences.

Prepare to Read: "Evelyn Cisneros"

Preview. Tell students that they are going to read a selection called "Evelyn Cisneros." Explain that this is a biography. This selection gives true information about a person and uses photographs to help tell the story. Then preview the selection.

DISTANT VOYAGES

pages 466–480

■ **Pages 466–467:** I see the title and the author's name. I know this is a biography so I think the photograph of the ballerina is of Evelyn Cisneros.

■ **Pages 468–469:** On this page, there is another photograph of this ballerina with a male partner. She is on her toes. There is a large quotation about the audience clapping a lot. I think that this dancer was a big success.

■ **Pages 470–47 I:** The story evidently goes back to when she was young. There is a photograph of Evelyn when she was nine, wearing dancing clothes. I wonder how she started dancing and how long she took lessons.

Set purpose. Model setting a purpose for reading "Evelyn Cisneros."

(MODEL) From previewing these pages, I can see that I will learn about a little girl who worked hard to become a prima ballerina. I know that one purpose for reading biographies is to learn more about a certain person. I will read to learn about how being Hispanic affected Evelyn Cisneros's goal of being a dancer.

Reread and Summarize

Have students reread and summarize "Evelyn Cisneros" in sections, as described in the chart below.

Pages 466–469

Let's look again at pages 466–469 to remember the information on where this dancer came from.

Summary: The photographs and story start out showing a triumphant Evelyn Cisneros, ballerina. But she came from a Mexican American family that was not rich or especially artistic.

Pages 470–473

As we read pages 470–473 again, let's recall what Evelyn was like as a young child and how ballet became the most important thing in her life.

Summary: Because she was Hispanic, she seemed different and she became quite shy. Her mother sent her to dance classes to help that. At fourteen, she decided to give up other after-school activities to devote herself to dance. This paid off and she studied at ballet companies' summer dance programs.

Pages 474–477

Let's reread pages 474–477 and remember the highlights of Evelyn's career after she decided dance was most important.

Summary: As a member of the San Francisco Ballet company, she got good reviews when she took over for a principal dancer during a show.

Pages 478–480

Read again pages 478–480 to remember the conclusion of this dancer's story.

Summary: Evelyn became a fine representative of Hispanic culture and received honors. She is married and has achieved much. She has come a long way from being the shy little Mexican American girl who was afraid to speak in class.

FLUENCY BUILDER Reuse *Intervention Practice Book* page 79. Call attention to the sentences on the bottom half of the page. Model the appropriate pace, expression, and phrasing as you read aloud each of the sentences. Then have students practice reading each sentence aloud two or three times to a partner.

INTERVENTION PRACTICE BOOK

page 79

Directed Reading: "Lourdes López: Ballet Star," pp. 158–165

TAKE FLIGHT
pp. 158–165

Page 158

Read aloud the title of the story. Tell students that this selection is about a real person, Lourdes López. Then have them read page 158 to find out where Lourdes López's family came from and where Lourdes grew up. (*Cuba, Florida*) Ask: **What problem did young Lourdes have that might have made it hard to become a dancer?** (*She had a problem with her feet.*) **SYNTHESIZE**

Pages 159–160

Have students read page 159 to find out why Lourdes first started taking ballet classes. (*Her doctor said dance lessons would make her legs stronger.*) Ask: **Why do you think Lourdes felt triumphant about her recital?** (*Her friends could finally understand how good she was and why dancing mattered to her so much.*) **CAUSE-EFFECT**

Where did Lourdes study next? (*the School of American Ballet in New York City*) Ask: **Who noticed Lourdes's talent at the school?** (*the founder, George Balanchine*) **IMPORTANT DETAILS**

What do you think this shows about Lourdes? (*Possible response: It shows that she was an especially good dancer.*) **DRAW CONCLUSIONS**

Page 163

Ask a volunteer to read aloud page 163 while other students read along silently. Then have students summarize the information on the page. If students have difficulty, model the Summarize strategy.

> **MODEL** As I read page 163 I see that there is a lot of information here. To make sure I understand it all, I'll try to summarize it in a few lines. When Lourdes began her career in New York at age 15, she never thought she'd be a star. But with hard work, her own confidence and her popularity grew with each new ballet. By the time she was 23, she was a ballerina, and dance critics were calling her a star. (Focus Strategy) **SUMMARIZE**

What abilities and qualities did critics praise in Lourdes? (*her artistic talent, technique, and flexibility*) **IMPORTANT DETAILS**

What is the main idea on this page? (*Possible response: Lourdes worked her way to the top of the company and won critics' praise.*)
(Focus Skill) **MAIN IDEA AND DETAILS**

Page 164

After students read page 164, ask: **What happened to threaten Lourdes's career?** (*She hurt her foot.*) **IMPORTANT DETAILS**

What does Lourdes do now, after having stopped dancing professionally? (*She teaches ballet to children in New York City.*) **IMPORTANT DETAILS**

Summarize the selection. Have students each share a goal they would like to accomplish. Then have them summarize the selection.

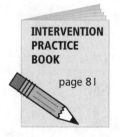

INTERVENTION PRACTICE BOOK

page 81

Answers to *Think About It* Questions

1. She moved to New York City to study at the School of American Ballet. Before long, she joined the New York City Ballet. There she became a soloist, a ballerina, and finally a ballet star. **SUMMARY**

2. Possible responses: Yes; she was very drawn to ballet and seemed to have a natural ability. No; her parents probably would not have sent her to ballet classes. **INTERPRETATION**

3. Accept reasonable responses. Diary entries should be written in the first person, from Lourdes López's point of view. They should express the dancer's excitement and pleasure. **WRITE A DIARY ENTRY**

AFTER

Skill Review
pages 486–487

USE SKILL CARD 20B

(Focus Skill) Main Idea and Details

RETEACH **the skill.** Have students look at **side B of Skill Card 20: Main Idea and Details**. Read the skill reminder aloud to them. Ask students why it helps to be able to pick out the main idea. (*It helps you understand the selection better.*) Ask for a volunteer to read aloud the paragraph on the skill card. Then ask students to draw the diagram from the skill card on their papers and to fill in the supporting detail circles.

Point out that this paragraph doesn't have a sentence that tells the main idea. In fact, it needs one, either at the beginning or the end of the passage. Ask: **What would be a good sentence for the main idea of this paragraph?** (*Possible response: Alex and Maddie were determined to raise money for cancer research.*) You may want to have students give suggestions for possible main idea sentences before they arrive at the one they find most satisfying. Ask them to write the sentence on their papers.

FLUENCY BUILDER Reuse *Intervention Practice Book*, page 79. Explain that today each student will practice the sentences on the bottom half of the page by reading them aloud on tape. Assign new partners. Have students take turns reading the sentences aloud to each other and then reading them on tape.

INTERVENTION PRACTICE BOOK

page 79

Expository Writing: Compare and Contrast

Build on prior knowledge. Point out that for some essays, students may be asked to compare and contrast two different things or people or ideas. In this type of essay, it is important for students to organize the material in a way that uses what they know about main ideas and details.

Construct the text. Tell students that as a group they are going to work on a short essay comparing and contrasting the two women whose biographies they have read. Draw on the board two columns, the first one labeled "Similarities," the second one labeled "Differences." Ask students to help you fill in the first column with the similarities between the two ballerinas. Here are some of the possible responses for the Similarities column:

- *Hispanic background*
- *started dance classes when young*
- *worked hard at dance and had little time for other things*
- *studied at School of American Ballet*

Then work on a Differences column. You may want to make two sub-columns, one for Lourdes and one for Evelyn.

Go back to the Similarities column and with students write a paragraph describing how these two women are alike. Write the text on the board and have students write it on their papers. Make sure that students include a main idea sentence in the paragraph.

Revisit the text. Go back and reread the paragraph with students.

- Ask students to pick out words that signal comparison in the paragraph. (Possible responses: and, both, also) Ask: **Does the paragraph include information from the "Similarities" column?**

- Guide students in picking out the main idea and supporting details. Ask: **Do the details in the paragraph support the main idea?**

On Your Own

Now have students individually write a paragraph contrasting Lourdes and Evelyn. Ask them to use the list they have constructed. Mention that they need to have a main idea sentence and supporting details. When students have completed their writing, ask for a volunteer to read a sample paragraph.

Connect Spelling and Phonics

RETEACH **digraphs /n/kn, gn; /r/wr.** Have students number a piece of paper 1 through 8. Tell them that in the first three words you will say, the /n/ sound is spelled *kn*. Dictate words 1–3, and have students write them. Then tell students that in the next three words you will say, the /n/ sound is spelled *gn*. Dictate words 4–6. Then tell students that in the last two words you will say, the /r/ sound is spelled *wr*. Dictate words 7–8. When they are finished, help students proofread their work.

1. knob	2. knew*	3. kneecap	4. gnaw
5. gnat	6. resign	7. wriggled*	8. wrong

*Word appears in "Lourdes López: Ballet Star."

Dictate the following sentences for students to write: *Meg laid the blanket in the shade of a gnarled tree. Then she kneeled on it and unwrapped the sandwiches.*

Build and Read Longer Words

Write these words on the board:

knapsack   wrapper   knothole

Remind students that when two or more consonants appear between vowels, usually the word is broken into syllables between the consonants. Point to the word *knapsack*. Cover the word part *sack*, and have a volunteer read *knap*. Then cover *knap* and ask a volunteer to read *sack*. Draw your hand under the whole word as students read it aloud. Call on volunteers to read the remaining two words and tell how they figured them out.

**INTERVENTION
ASSESSMENT
BOOK**

FLUENCY BUILDER Have students choose a passage from "Lourdes López: Ballet Star" to read aloud to a partner. You may have students choose passages they found particularly interesting or you can assign them a particular passage, such as:

- Pages 158–159. Starting with *When Lourdes was . . .* through *. . . more than ever.* (Total: 116 words)

- Pages 160–163. Starting with *Lourdes took classes . . .* through *. . . thrived on it.* (Total: 113 words)

Ask students to read the selection aloud to their partners three times. Have students rate their own readings on a scale of 1 to 4.

Review Vocabulary

Read the sentences to students and ask them to write the correct answers on their papers. Go over the answers and discuss why each one is correct.

1. The new wire was noted for its **flexibility.** That means
   a. it conducted electricity well.
   b. it could bend or twist without breaking.

2. Things were very hard for **migrant** workers. These are workers
   a. who move around from job to job.
   b. who have full-time jobs in factories.

3. The violinist didn't like to go to parties because she was so **timid.** That means she was
   a. shy.
   b. bored.

4. The plants **thrived** in the greenhouse. That means
   a. they grew bigger and lusher.
   b. they didn't do very well.

5. A **scholarship** made it possible for her to go to college. The **scholarship** was
   a. a trophy for her sports excellence.
   b. money to help pay for her education.

6. The father wanted to **devote** himself to teaching his son to play baseball. He was going to
   a. give his time to do that.
   b. vote for the winners.

7. She would practice hard as an **apprentice.** This was a way
   a. to learn a skill by working for another.
   b. for her not to work.

Correct responses: 1b, 2a, 3a, 4a, 5b, 6a, 7a

This is a good time to show the vocabulary words and definitions on page 199. Have students copy them to use for studying for the vocabulary test.

Main Idea and Details

To review main idea and details before the weekly assessment, use *Intervention Practice Book*, page 82. Call attention to the title Main Idea and Details. Have a student read the first sentence and fill in the blank. Have a second student do the second sentence, and so on. Then direct students' attention to the Lourdes López story. In this review, they will find a main idea for each page of text and from that, determine a main idea for the selection. Have volunteers read their main idea for each page. Then give them time to complete the selection main idea.

INTERVENTION
PRACTICE
BOOK

page 82

Review Test Prep

INTERVENTION
ASSESSMENT
BOOK

Ask students to turn to page 487 of the *Pupil Edition*. Point out the tips for answering the test questions. Tell students to pay attention to these tips because they can help them answer not only the test questions on this page but also other test questions like these.

DISTANT
VOYAGES

page 487

Self-Selected Reading

Encourage students to select books to read on their own. They may choose books from your classroom library shelf, or you may select a group of appropriate books from which your students can choose.

- *Toe Shoes and Tutus* (See page 487K of the Teacher's Edition for an Independent Reading Plan.)

- *Alvin Ailey* by Andrea Davis Pinkney, Hyperion, 1993

- *Andrew Carnegie: Builder of Libraries* by Charnan Simon, Children's Press, 1997

After students have chosen their books, give each student a copy of My Reading Log, found on page R38 in the back of the Teacher's Edition. Have each student fill in the information at the top of the form. Then have students use the log to keep track of their reading and to record their responses to the literature.

Conduct student-teacher conferences. Arrange for an individual conference time with each student to discuss his or her self-selected reading. Have students bring their Reading Logs to share during the conference. You may also want to have students choose a favorite passage to read aloud to you. Ask questions about the reading to stimulate discussion. For example, you might ask what information the student learned from a nonfiction text, how the author structured the text, or how the artwork helped the student understand the topic.

FLUENCY PERFORMANCE Have students read aloud to you the passages they have selected and practiced previously with their partners. Keep track of the number of words each student reads correctly. Ask each student to rate his or her performance on the 1–4 scale. If students aren't happy with their oral reading, give them additional opportunities to practice and then reread the passage to you.

See *Oral Reading Fluency Assessment* for monitoring progress.

Use with
"Off and Running"

Review Phonics: Digraphs /f/ph, gh

Identify the sound. Have students repeat the following sentence aloud three times: *I always laugh at the phony elephants.* Ask them to identify the words with the /f/ sound. (*laugh, phony, elephants*)

Associate letters to sound. Write on the board this sentence: *I always laugh at the phony elephants.* Underline the letters *ph* in *phony* and *elephants.* Explain that the letters *ph* in these words stand for the /f/ sound. Next, underline the letters *gh* in *laugh,* and tell students that the letters *gh* stand for the /f/ sound in *laugh.*

Word blending. Model how to blend and read the word *laugh.* Point to the letter *l* and say /l/. Slide your hand under *au* and say /a/. Slide your hand under *gh* and say /f/. Next slide your hand under the whole word as you elongate the sounds: /llaaff/. Then say the word naturally—*laugh.* Follow a similar procedure with the words *phony* and *elephants.*

Apply the skill. *Letter Substitution* Write the following words on the board, and have students read each aloud. Make the changes necessary to form the words in parentheses. Have a volunteer read aloud each new word. Try to give each student an opportunity to respond.

INTERVENTION
PRACTICE
BOOK

page 84

elegant (elephant) **grab** (graph) **prone** (phone)

Introduce Vocabulary

PRETEACH **lesson vocabulary.** Tell students they are going to learn five new words that they will see again when they read a story called "Off and Running." Teach each vocabulary word using the following process.

Use the following suggestions or similar ideas to give the meaning or context.

	Write the word.
	Say the word.
	Track the word and have students repeat it.
	Give the meaning or context.

campaign The mayor's campaign promises included new traffic lights.

residence When a person goes home, we say he or she goes to his or her residence. Students can remember the word easily by memorizing the sentence *I reside at my residence.*

obnoxious Point out that this word is an adjective, or describing word. My little brother made obnoxious faces all during my performance in the school play.

endorse Advertisers sometimes pay sports stars to endorse their products. Companies hope that endorsements by sports stars will get people to buy their products.

graffiti Tell students that this word does not follow rules but that it must be memorized. The word is the plural form of *graffito*, which comes from an Italian word that means, loosely, "writing that is scratched onto something."

For vocabulary activities, see Vocabulary Games on pages 2–7.

For vocabulary activities, see Vocabulary Games on pages 2–7.

Vocabulary Words

campaign an organized series of activities or steps that has a set goal

residence home; house

obnoxious annoying; bothersome

endorse to support or approve of someone

graffiti writing or drawing done on some public surface

AFTER

Building Background and Vocabulary

Apply Vocabulary Strategies

Use context. Remind students that figuring out the meaning of some words can be like detective work. Just as a detective finds clues and uses them to solve a mystery, students can figure out what a word means. Clues they can use are the other words in the sentence and the other sentences nearby. Model the process.

> **MODEL** When I come to a word I don't know, I can try to get clues from the other words in the sentence. I also read the sentences around the word to look for clues. Sometimes other sentences tell meanings of words. Sometimes sentences give clues about opposite meanings.

Tell students to use this strategy as they encounter other unfamiliar words in their reading.

RETEACH **lesson vocabulary.** Provide students with word cards for all of the Vocabulary Words. Then read aloud this paragraph, saying "blank" in place of the underlined words. Then read it aloud again, and have students hold up the appropriate word cards for the blanks. Discuss why each answer fits where it does.

During my dad's _(campaign)_ to be elected to the town council, some interesting things happened. First, someone scribbled _(graffiti)_ on his office building. Then, we got some _(obnoxious)_ phone calls at our _(residence)_. Finally, the mayor said that she would _(endorse)_ my dad. With her support, Dad was elected.

FLUENCY BUILDER Use *Intervention Practice Book* page 83. Read aloud each of the words in the first column, and have students repeat it. Then have partners take turns reading the words to each other. Follow the same procedure with each of the remaining columns. Then have students practice reading the entire list and timing themselves.

INTERVENTION PRACTICE BOOK

page 83

Text Structure: Compare and Contrast

PRETEACH the skill. Explain to students that an important reading skill is comparing and contrasting. When you do this, you figure out how things are alike, and how they are different. For example, if you went to the grocery store and picked out an orange and an apple, you could notice how different they are even though they are about the same size and they are both sweet.

Have students look at **side A of Skill Card 21: Text Structure: Compare and Contrast.** Ask for a volunteer to read the explanation.

Direct students' attention to the two illustrations. Ask volunteers to tell what they think is happening in each illustration.

- Ask: **What are some things that are alike in the pictures?** (*Possible responses: both people could be going away to college or to work out of town; both could be feeling excited and scared.*)

- Ask: **What are some things that are different?** (*Possible response: different ways of communicating with parents back home*)

Have a student read the lists aloud and see how their own lists compare with the lists on the card.

Prepare to Read: "Off and Running"

Preview. Tell students that they are going to read a selection called "Off and Running." Explain that this is realistic fiction. Point out that this kind of story has characters that seem real and events that could really happen, but the author makes them up. Then preview the selection.

DISTANT VOYAGES
pages 492–506

- **Pages 492–493:** There are a girl and a boy with campaign flyers. So, this must be a story about an election at school.

- **Pages 494–495:** A girl is talking on the phone and feeding fish, and then she is talking to a man reading a newspaper. Maybe she is asking her dad's advice about the election.

- **Pages 496–497:** Now the girl and her family are having a meal, and the people seem happy.

- **Pages 498–499:** Someone is driving the girl to a store. I wonder how this trip is connected to the election.

- **Pages 500–501:** The girl is at someone's house. I wonder whose house it is and what is in the bag.

Set purpose. Model setting a purpose for reading "Off and Running."

MODEL I think this selection is about how the girl does in a school election. I will read to find out if she wins the election.

Reread and Summarize

Have students reread and summarize "Off and Running" in sections,
as described below.

Pages 492–495

**Let's reread pages 492–495 to remember the main character of the
story and what she is doing.**

Summary: Miata Ramirez is running for class president. She gets a crank
call at home from someone and then asks her father if he knows anyone important.

Pages 496–499

**Let's reread pages 496–499 to recall what Miata is doing to win the
election.**

Summary: Miata's mother knows a woman who had been a mayor in
the past. Her mother takes Miata to talk to the woman. On the way
they buy the woman a loaf of bread.

Pages 500–503

**As we reread pages 500–503, let's see what happens when Miata
meets the woman.**

Summary: Miata meets Doña Carmen and hears her story about how
she beat her husband for the position of mayor of the town.

Pages 504–506

**Let's reread the end of the story to find out what Miata learns from
Doña Carmen.**

Summary: As mayor, Doña Carmen worked to make the town better
and more beautiful. She offers to help Miata make her school more
beautiful. Miata leaves with a clear idea of how she can improve the
school.

FLUENCY BUILDER Reuse *Intervention Practice Book*
page 83. Call attention to the sentences at the bottom
of the page. State that the goal is to have each student
read each phrase smoothly. Model the appropriate
pace, expression, and phrasing as you read aloud each
of the sentences. Then have students practice reading
aloud each sentence two or three times to a partner.

INTERVENTION
PRACTICE
BOOK

page 83

Directed Reading: "Certain Steps" pp. 166–172

TAKE FLIGHT pp. 166–172

Page 166

Have a volunteer read the story title aloud. Help students identify Al and Murphy in the illustration. Then read page 166 aloud to students. Ask: **What does Al want Murphy to do?** (*help him on his campaign*) **IMPORTANT DETAILS**

Page 167

Ask students to read page 167 to find out more about Al's campaign platform. Model using the Use Context to Confirm Meaning strategy:

> **MODEL** I have read the word *platform* on these two pages, and I want to make sure I understand what it means. On page 166 I read that it is what a person plans to do if elected. On page 167 Murphy asks Al what he plans to do for his fellow students. So, a platform must be a set of ideas for what a person will do if elected. (Focus Strategy) **USE CONTEXT TO CONFIRM MEANING**

Page 168

Have a volunteer read page 168. Ask students to listen to find out what Murphy is thinking. Ask: **Why do you think Murphy is concerned about Al's campaign?** (*Possible response: He doesn't think Al is taking the election seriously.*) **STORY EVENTS**

How are Murphy's ideas different from Al's about what can be done for the school? (*Possible response: Al just wants to promise no homework, while Murphy is interested in making the school a better, more pleasant place.*) (Focus Skill) **TEXT STRUCTURE: COMPARE AND CONTRAST**

Page 169

Have them read page 169 to confirm their predictions. Ask: **How does Murphy feel about the school and its students? How do you know?** (*Possible response: He cares about the school and its students. He erases graffiti and picks up trash, and he tells Al he can't support the no-home-work campaign.*) **CHARACTERS' MOTIVATIONS**

Page 170

Have students read page 170 to find out what happens after lunch. Ask: **What does Murphy notice other students doing?** (*They are staring, giggling, and whispering about him.*) **IMPORTANT DETAILS**

Why do you think they are doing this? (*Possible response: Maybe they're making fun of Murphy for being so serious.*) **SPECULATE**

Page 171

Have students read page 171 to find out how the story ends. Ask: **What does Al do?** (*He withdraws from the election and tells students to vote for Murphy.*) **SUMMARIZE**

What do you think Al was doing earlier when he whispered to students about Murphy? (*He was campaigning for Murphy.*) **DRAW CONCLUSIONS**

INTERVENTION
PRACTICE
BOOK

page 85

Page 172

Who do you think won the election, Casey or Murphy? Why? (*Responses will vary.*) **SPECULATE**

Summarize the selection. Ask students to think about what happened on the first, second, and third days of the school election campaign. Then have them write three sentences to summarize the story.

Answers to *Think About It* Questions

1. Murphy sees that his friend Al is unwilling to work to improve the school. Al's only campaign promise is no homework. **SUMMARY**

2. He probably feels worried about what they're saying. He must think the other kids are making fun of him. **INTERPRETATION**

3. Webs and paragraphs should describe Murphy as an honest person who is willing to work hard to help others. **WRITE A PARAGRAPH**

AFTER

Skill Review
pages 510–511

USE SKILL CARD 21B

(Focus Skill) Text Structure: Compare and Contrast

RETEACH **the skill.** Have students look at **side B of Skill Card 21: Text Structure: Compare and Contrast.** Read the skill reminder aloud to them.

Have three volunteers read aloud the selection, each taking a paragraph. Then, with students, fill in the chart.

How they are alike:
- They are friends of Angela.
- They are artists.

How they are different:
- They have known Angela for different lengths of time.
- Ben likes to paint.
- Ben likes to hand-letter things.
- Tanya prefers to take photographs.
- Tanya wants to create type on the computer.

Ask students what they know about Tanya and Ben by comparing and contrasting them. (*Possible response: Tanya likes to use technology for quick results, while Ben likes to take the time to make things by hand.*)

FLUENCY BUILDER Use *Intervention Practice Book* page 83. Explain that students will practice the sentences at the bottom of the page by reading them aloud on tape. Assign partners, and have students take turns reading the sentences aloud to each other and then on tape. After students listen to the tape, have them tell how they have improved their reading. Then have students read the sentences aloud on tape again, focusing on improved pacing and tone.

INTERVENTION
PRACTICE
BOOK

page 83

Research Report: Prewrite

Build on prior knowledge. Announce that students will think of and write sentences for a speech Miata could use in her campaign for class president. Display on the board the sentences in the box.

> Hi. My name is Miata Ramirez, and I am running for fifth-grade class president.

Construct the text. As a class, brainstorm sentences. The sentences should be worded as Miata would say them, and they should tell what Miata is like and what she plans to do if she is elected. Students may use information from the selection and make up their own ideas. Write their suggestions on the board. For example:

- I have gone to this school since I was in kindergarten.
- I want to plant flowers and clean up the school.
- I want to get rid of the graffiti on the walls.
- I am not a clown like Rudy is.

Revisit the text. Review the list of ideas together. Discuss which items belong in a campaign speech, and identify any ideas that do not belong.

- Ask: **How can we make sure the speech focuses on why Miata should be elected?** (*Possible responses: delete the idea "I am not a clown like Rudy is"; change the last idea to tell only about Miata's good qualities*)

- Remind students that the ideas should be sentences. Ask: **What things does each complete sentence need?** (*Possible response: to begin with a capital letter; to end with a correct end mark; to have a subject and verb that go together*) Make any needed corrections.

- Reread the sentences aloud as a group.

On Your Own

Ask students to write several more sentences that tell about specific plans Miata wants to put in place if she is elected. Suggest that the final sentence ask students to vote for her.

After they have completed this exercise, ask for volunteers to read aloud their sentences.

Connect Spelling and Phonics

RETEACH **digraphs /f/ph, gh.** Have students number a sheet of paper 1 through 8. Tell them that the first word you will read has the /f/ sound spelled *gh*. Then dictate the first word, and have students write it. Display the correct spelling so students can proofread their work. Next, write the word *phone* on the board. Explain that in the next seven words you will read, the /f/ sound is spelled *ph*. Dictate the words, and have students write and proofread them as before. Have them draw lines through any misspelled words and write them correctly.

1. laughed*	2. photo*	3. telegraph	4. phrases*
5. asphalt	6. graphic	7. emphasis*	8. geography*

*Word appears in "Certain Steps."

Dictate the following sentence and have students write it:
The photograph made Philip laugh.

Build and Read Longer Words

Write *laughter* on the board. Remind students that when two or more consonants appear between vowels, the word usually is broken into syllables between the consonants that stand for different sounds. Point to the word *laughter*. Draw a line between the syllables: *laugh/ter*. Tell students that when dividing words that have the letters *gh* or *ph* to stand for the /f/ sound, these letters always stay together. As you slide your hand under each syllable, have students read the word aloud. Then ask students to read these words and explain how they figured them out: *alphabet*, *emphasis*. Give students other /f/ph, gh words to read, such as *pharmacy*, *physics*, and *enough*.

**INTERVENTION
ASSESSMENT
BOOK**

FLUENCY BUILDER Have students choose a passage from "Certain Steps" to read aloud to a partner. You may have students choose one of these passages or another they found particularly interesting.

- Pages 167–168. From "*What's your platform . . .* through . . . *he vowed silently.* (Total: 129 words)

- Pages 170–171. From *During geography . . .* through . . . *time to vote.* (Total: 152 words)

Ask students to read the selection aloud to their partners three times. Have students rate their own readings on a scale of 1 to 4.

Encourage students to note their improvement from one reading to the next by completing the sentence *I know my reading has improved because_____.* Encourage the listening partner to offer positive feedback about improvements.

Review Vocabulary

To revisit Vocabulary Words prior to the weekly assessment, use these sentences. Read the questions to students, and ask them to write the answers. Go over the answers, and discuss why each one is correct.

1. A **campaign** poster is one that
   a. is about a lost dog.
   b. is used for an election.

2. A person's **residence** is
   a. his or her home.
   b. in a classroom.

3. When Julio told his little brother that he was **obnoxious**, he meant that
   a. his brother was polite.
   b. his brother was annoying.

4. If someone **endorses** a person who is trying to be elected, he or she
   a. supports the person.
   b. works against the person.

5. The librarian said, "Anyone who writes **graffiti** on the table
   a. will have to sit in the corner."
   b. will get a prize."

Correct responses: 1b, 2a, 3b, 4a, 5a

This is a good time to show the Vocabulary Words and definitions on page 209. Have students copy them to use for studying for the vocabulary test.

 ## Review Compare and Contrast

INTERVENTION
PRACTICE
BOOK

page 86

To review comparing and contrasting before the weekly assessment, use *Intervention Practice Book* page 86. Ask a volunteer to read the first line, and help students fill in the first blank. Then have students work in pairs to answer the rest of the questions.

Review Test Prep

INTERVENTION
ASSESSMENT
BOOK

Ask students to turn to page 511 of the *Pupil Edition*. Point out the tips for answering the test questions. Tell students to pay attention to these tips because they can help them answer not only the test questions on this page but also the questions on other tests. Remind students to look at all the possible answers in multiple-choice questions and to cross out any that are clearly wrong. They should then read the remaining choices carefully before deciding on the correct one.

DISTANT
VOYAGES

page 511

Self-Selected Reading

Encourage students to select their own books
to read on their own. They may choose books
from your classroom library shelf, or you may select
a group of appropriate books such as the following
from which your students can choose.

- *The Best Candidate*. (See page 511M of the
  Teacher's Edition for a lesson plan.)

- *Family Pictures* by Carmen Lomas Garza.
  Children's Press, 1990.

- *City Green* by DyAnne DiSalvo-Ryan.
  William Morrow, 1994.

After students have chosen their books, give each
student a copy of My Reading Log, found on page
R38 in the back of the *Teacher's Edition*. Have
students fill in the information at the top of the
form. Then have them use the log to keep track
of their reading and to record their responses to
the literature.

Conduct student-teacher conferences. Arrange for an individual
conference time with each student to discuss his or her self-selected
reading. Have students bring their Reading Logs to share during the
conference. You may also want to have the stu-
dent choose a favorite passage to read aloud to
you. Then ask questions designed to stimulate discussion. For example, you might ask what information the student learned from a nonfiction text,
how the author structured the text, or how the
artwork helped the student understand the topic.

FLUENCY PERFORMANCE Have students read aloud to you
the passage from "Certain Steps" they have selected and practiced previously with their partners. Keep track of the number of words the student
reads correctly. Ask each student to rate his or her performance on the
1–4 scale. If students aren't happy with their oral reading, give them an
opportunity to practice some more and then to reread the passage
to you.

See *Oral Reading Fluency Assessment* for monitoring progress.

BEFORE

Building
Background
and Vocabulary

Use with

"Little by Little"

Review Phonics: Short Vowel /e/ea

Identify the sound. Have students repeat the following sentence aloud three times: *A heavy shower is heading toward the meadow.* Ask students to identify the words that have the /e/ sound they hear in *thread*. (*heavy, heading, meadow*)

Associate letters to sound. Write on the board the sentence *A heavy shower is headed toward the meadow*. Underline the letters *ea* in the words *heavy, heading,* and *meadow*. Tell students that in these words, the letters *ea* stand for the /e/ sound, or the short e vowel sound.

Word blending. Model how to blend and read the word *bread*. Point to *b* and say /b/. Point to *r* and say /r/. Slide your hand under *ea* and say /e/. Point to *d* and say /d/. Slide your hand under the whole word as you elongate the sounds: /bbrredd/. Then read the word naturally—*bread*. Follow a similar procedure with the words *spread* and *instead*.

INTERVENTION
PRACTICE
BOOK

page 88

Apply the skill. *Vowel Substitution* Write the following words on the board, and have students read each aloud. Make the changes necessary to form the words in parentheses. Have a volunteer read aloud each new word. Try to give every student an opportunity to respond.

had (head)	**sweet** (sweat)	**broth** (breath)
deed (dead)	**throat** (threat)	**father** (feather)

Introduce Vocabulary

PRETEACH **lesson vocabulary.** Tell students they are going to learn six new words that they will see again when they read a story called "Little by Little." Teach each Vocabulary Word using the following process.

Use the following suggestions or similar ideas to give the meaning or context.

> Write the word.
> Say the word.
> Track the word and have students repeat it.
> Give the meaning or context.

polio   The man had polio as a child and now walks with a limp.

decipher   My older brother wrote a long math problem that I could not decipher.

astonished   He was astonished to win the jumping contest because he had not won before.

immobility   The car's headlights made the deer freeze with immobility.

dismay   Because I had expected
an A on my test, I looked with
dismay at the D on my paper.

despised   She despised herself after she
had lied to her friend.

For vocabulary activities, see Vocabulary Games on pp. 2–7.

For vocabulary activities, see Vocabulary Games on pp. 2–7.

Vocabulary Words

polio an infectious disease that often causes paralysis

decipher to read and understand

astonished amazed

immobility the state of not being able to move

dismay feeling of confusion and disappointment

despised disliked; hated

AFTER
Building Background and Vocabulary

Apply Vocabulary Strategies

Use affixes and root words. Write the word *immobility* on the board, and ask a student to read it aloud. Remind them that they can sometimes figure out the meaning of an unfamiliar word by breaking it down into its root word and its prefix and suffix.

> **MODEL** I recognize a part of a word in the middle of this word—*mobil-*. I know that *mobil-* means "able to move." Then I notice the prefix *im-*, which I know can mean "not." The suffix *-ity* refers to a state of being, so *immobility* must mean "the state of being not able to move." I'll check it by looking it up in the dictionary.

Remind students to use this strategy with other unfamiliar words in their reading.

RETEACH **lesson vocabulary.** Be sure each student has a set of vocabulary cards. Read aloud the following sentences, saying "blank" for each blank. Ask students to hold up the correct word card. Reread the sentence with the correct word.

1. After she had had ___(polio)___ , she needed leg braces.
2. We could not _(decipher)_ his bad handwriting.
3. They were _(astonished)_ to see it snow in July.
4. She used her left hand because of the _(immobility)_ in her right hand.
5. We watched in ___(dismay)___ as he did a card trick.
6. We _(despised)_ having to leave the movie before it finished.

FLUENCY BUILDER Use *Intervention Practice Book* page 87. Read aloud each of the words in the first column and have students repeat it. Then have partners read the words to each other. Repeat for the remaining columns. After each partner has had a turn reading aloud the words in each column, have them practice reading the entire list while timing themselves.

INTERVENTION PRACTICE BOOK

page 87

BEFORE

Reading "Little by Little"
pages 514–526

USE SKILL CARD 22A

Focus Skill Author's Purpose and Perspective

PRETEACH the skill. Have students look at **side A of Skill Card 22: Author's Purpose and Perspective**. Read the first explanation aloud. Then direct students' attention to the web. Remind students that to inform is to give facts and information; to persuade is to convince someone of something; and to entertain is to make someone enjoy something. Ask:

- **What are some things you have read that inform?** (Possible responses: a science book; a newspaper)
- **What are some things you have read that entertain?** (Possible responses: the selection "The Fun They Had"; a comic book)
- **What are some things you have read that try to persuade?** (Possible responses: a letter to the editor; a book review)

Then read aloud the second explanation, and direct students' attention to the second illustration. Tell students that another word for *perspective* is *viewpoint.* Discuss how authors show their viewpoints, opinions, and attitudes by choosing their words and ideas carefully.

Prepare to Read: "Little by Little"

Preview. Tell students that they are going to read an autobiography called "Little by Little." Explain that an autobiography tells one's own life story. Then preview the selection.

DISTANT VOYAGES
pages 514–526

- **Pages 514–517:** The illustrations show that this story is about a girl in school. She seems to be paying attention in class. I wonder why school is important in the story.
- **Pages 518–519:** In one illustration, a girl seems to be saying something mean to another girl at recess. In the next illustration the girl is standing alone by a tree. She looks lonely and sad.
- **Pages 522–525:** Now the girl is doing schoolwork, but on the next page she seems to be in some kind of trouble. I wonder if she did something wrong.
- **Page 526:** The teacher is talking to the girl, but the girl looks unsure of herself. I wonder why she looks so unsure.

Set purpose. Model setting a purpose for reading "Little by Little."

MODEL **I want to read this story to find out why the girl in the story seems upset and what finally happens.**

Reread and Summarize

Have students reread and summarize "Little by Little" in sections, as described in the chart below.

Pages 514–517

Let's look again at pages 514–517 to remember what Jean is afraid of as she starts fifth grade.

Summary: Jean likes school and her teacher, but she cannot see the board well. She is given a special desk, but it makes her feel very different from the other students.

Pages 518–521

Let's reread pages 518–521 to see what happens at recess time.

Summary: Jean is excited because her teacher asks a popular girl to help her at recess. When the girl tells Jean to get lost, Jean tries not to cry. In math, the teacher gives a mental math test, but Jean doesn't know her multiplication tables.

Pages 522–525

Reread pages 522–525 to recall what Jean does about the test.

Summary: Jean writes the answers as the teacher says them, but some girls threaten to tell the teacher that she has cheated.

Page 526

Reread page 526 to recall the ending of the story.

Summary: Jean admits to the teacher what she has done and agrees to learn her multiplication tables.

FLUENCY BUILDER Reuse *Intervention Practice Book* page 87. Call attention to the sentences at the bottom of the page. State that the goal is to have each student read each phrase smoothly. Model the appropriate pace, expression, and phrasing as you read aloud each of the sentences. Then have partners practice reading each sentence aloud two or three times.

INTERVENTION PRACTICE BOOK

page 87

Directed Reading: "Quest for a Healthy World," pp. 174–181

TAKE
FLIGHT
pages
174–181

Page 174

Ask a volunteer to read the title. Explain that this selection tells the true story of a famous doctor who made many important discoveries. Have students read page 174 to find out something about Jonas Salk's life.
Ask: **What did Jonas first plan to be?** (*a lawyer*) **IMPORTANT DETAILS**

Page 175

Have students read page 175 to find out what Salk became. (*medical scientist*) **IMPORTANT DETAILS**

Ask: **What did one of Salk's instructors claim?** (*that the method for preventing bacterial illness wouldn't work for illnesses caused by viruses*) **SUMMARIZE**

Page 176

After students read page 176, ask: **Did Salk agree with his instructor? How do you know?** (*No; he tried using a killed-virus vaccine again.*) **DRAW CONCLUSIONS**

Ask: **What did Salk make?** (*a flu vaccine*) **IMPORTANT DETAILS**

Page 177

Read page 177 aloud, having students listen to find out what Dr. Salk decided to do next. (*develop a polio vaccine*) **IMPORTANT DETAILS**

Ask: **Was the vaccine successful? How do you know?** (*Possible response: Yes; Dr. Salk became famous.*) **DRAW CONCLUSIONS**

Page 178

Have students read page 178 to find the reasons Salk didn't want to be rich from his invention. Model using the strategy Self-Question.

> **MODEL** I'm not sure why Salk didn't want to be rich from his invention, so I ask myself what he thought of his work. The story says he hated the idea of making money from a medicine that was needed to save lives.
> (Focus Strategy) **SELF-QUESTION**

Page 179

Have students read page 179 to learn about the people who were important to Dr. Salk. Ask: **Who did Dr. Salk feel was his best teacher, and why?** (*Possible response: His mother; she taught him that it is important to work hard and to go to school.*) **SYNTHESIZE**

Page 180

Have students read page 180 to find out how Dr. Salk thinks people should choose a career. (*by knowing themselves and figuring out how they can help people, and then working for that dream*) **SYNTHESIZE**

What do you think is the author's purpose in writing this story? What is her perspective, or viewpoint? (*To inform: the world is a better place because of the life and work of Salk.*) (Focus Skill) **AUTHOR'S PURPOSE AND PERSPECTIVE**

INTERVENTION PRACTICE BOOK

page 89

Page 181

Summarize the selection. Ask students to think about Salk's life before, during, and after developing flu and polio vaccines. Then have students write three sentences to summarize the selection.

Answers to *Think About It* Questions

1. Salk developed vaccines for influenza and polio. **SUMMARY**

2. Possible response: Salk felt it was important to help people. He may have felt he could help more people by doing medical research than by treating patients. **INTERPRETATION**

3. Responses will vary but should follow the business-letter format and should express appreciation for Dr. Salk's hard work and accomplishments. **WRITE A LETTER**

AFTER

Skill Review
pages 532–533

USE SKILL CARD 22B

(Focus Skill) Author's Purpose and Perspective

Reteach the skill. Have students look at **side B of Skill Card 22: Author's Purpose and Perspective**. Read the skill reminder aloud to them. Remind them that an author may have more than one purpose for writing a selection.

Ask a volunteer to read aloud the story on the card. Tell them this is an interview with an author. Explain that Alzheimer's is a disease that makes people more and more forgetful until they can no longer take care of themselves. Ask them to determine the purpose the author had for writing the story.

Responses for question I will vary but should be supported. Possible responses for question 2: More should be done to find treatments and a cure for Alzheimer's disease; it is very sad for the family of a victim of Alzheimer's disease.

FLUENCY BUILDER Reuse *Intervention Practice Book* page 87. Explain that students will practice the sentences at the bottom of the page by reading them aloud on tape. Assign new partners, and have them take turns reading the sentences aloud to each other and then reading them on tape. After students listen to the tape, have them tell how they have improved their reading. Then have them tape themselves again, focusing on improved pacing and tone.

INTERVENTION PRACTICE BOOK

page 87

Expository Writing: Outline Ideas

Build on prior knowledge. Point out to students that they will select ideas for a research report that are narrow enough to cover and then organize their ideas into an outline. Display these ideas based on "Quest for a Healthy World."

> a report on polio
>
> the use of the iron lung
>
> how Jonas Salk became famous

Construct the text. As a group, discuss the topics given. Cross out the ideas you don't use. Then build on the remaining idea. "Share the pen" with students in a collaborative writing effort. As students dictate ideas, write them on the board. For example:

> **How Salk Became Famous**
> I.   What he studied
> II. What his experiments were
> III. How his experiments worked out
> IV. How his work affected people's lives

Revisit the text. Reread the ideas with students. Ask: **What details could we add under Roman numeral I?** (Possible reponse: A. He started in law; B. He changed to medicine.) Guide students to understand that in an outline, a detail lettered A must be followed by a detail lettered B.

- Tell students that similar information must be grouped together. Ask: **Under what Roman numeral would we add details about how a person was kept from getting the flu because of Salk's vaccine?** (Roman numeral IV)

- Ask: **Why do we list the topic in item I before we list the topic in item IV?** (Topics and details should follow a sequence of events or time order.)

- Read the outline aloud with students.

On Your Own

Have students apply what they have learned to start their outlines for their research reports. Remind them to use correct letter-and-number format and to group similar ideas.

Connect Spelling and Phonics

RETEACH short vowel /e/ea. Write the word *bread* on the board. Explain that in each word you will say, the short e vowel sound is spelled *ea*. Dictate the following words, and have students write them. After students write each word, display the correct spelling so students can proofread their work.

l. healthy*	2. instead	3. ahead*	4. dreaded
5. dead*	6. threat*	7. wealthy	8. spread*

*Word appears in "Quest for a Healthy World."

Dictate the following sentence for students to write: *A pound of lead is not heavier than a pound of feathers.*

Build and Read Longer Words

**INTERVENTION
ASSESSMENT
BOOK**

Write the following words on the board: *deafness, breakfast, threadbare, dreadful.* Remind students that when two consonants appear between two vowels, the word usually is broken into syllables between the consonants. Point out the two consonants in the middle of the word *deafness.* (*f, n*) Then cover the ending, *ness,* and have a volunteer read the first part, *deaf.* Cover *deaf,* and have a volunteer read *ness.* Then draw your hand under the entire word as students read it aloud. Follow a similar procedure with the remaining words. Then have students read *heaviness, feathering,* and *threaten* in the same way.

FLUENCY BUILDER Have students choose a passage from "Quest for a Healthy World" to read aloud to a partner. You may have students choose passages they found particularly interesting, or have them choose one of the following options:

- Read pages 175–176. (From *Jonas Salk did* . . . through . . . *try it again.* Total: 140 words)

- Read page 177. (From *Polio was* . . . through . . . *to do most.* Total: 128 words)

Ask students to read the selection aloud to their partners three times. Have students rate their own readings on a scale of l to 4. Encourage students to note their improvement from one reading to the next by completing the sentence *I know my reading has improved because* _____. Encourage the listening partner to offer positive feedback about improvements.

Review Vocabulary

To revisit the Vocabulary Words prior to the weekly assessment, use these sentence frames. Read the statements aloud, and have students write the answers. Then review the answers, and discuss why they are correct.

1. To keep from getting **polio**, children are given a
   a. trip in the country.   b. vaccine.

2. To **decipher** his secret code, we needed the
   a. key to the code.   b. password.

3. His mother was **astonished** to see that he had
   a. eaten lunch.   b. cleaned his room.

4. People who have **immobility** in their legs can use
   a. new shoes.   b. a wheelchair.

5. The family watched in **dismay** as their house
   a. burned down.   b. was built.

6. The little boy **despised** going to bed and often
   a. kept getting up.   b. slept well.

   Correct responses: lb, 2a, 3b, 4b, 5a, 6a

This is a good time to show the Vocabulary Words and definitions on page 219. Have students copy them to use for studying for the vocabulary test.

INTERVENTION
PRACTICE
BOOK

page 90

⭐(Focus Skill) Author's Purpose and Perspective

To review author's purpose and perspective before the weekly assessment, use *Intervention Practice Book* page 90. Have volunteers read aloud the first three items and suggest answers. Then have partners review the story to identify two examples that show the writer's opinions and attitudes. Remind students that these details show the author's perspective.

Review Test Prep

INTERVENTION
ASSESSMENT
BOOK

✔

Ask students to turn to page 533 of the *Pupil Edition.* Point out the tips for answering the test questions. Tell students that paying attention to these tips can help them answer these and other test questions. Point out that to answer questions about the author's purpose or perspective, they must read the passage carefully and then think about why it was written.

DISTANT
VOYAGES

page 533

Self-Selected Reading

Encourage students to select their own books to read independently. They may choose books from your classroom library shelf, or you may select a group of appropriate books from which your students can choose.

- *The New Girl.* (See page 533K of the *Teacher's Edition* for a lesson plan.)

- *To the Point: A Story About E. B. White* by David R. Collins. Carolrhoda, 1989.

- *Louisa May Alcott: Young Writer* by Laurence Santrey. Troll, 1986.

After students have chosen their books, give each student a copy of My Reading Log, found on page R38 in the back of the *Teacher's Edition*. Have each student fill in the information at the top of the form. Then have students use the log to keep track of their reading and to record their responses to the literature.

Conduct student-teacher conferences. Arrange for individual conference time with each student to discuss his or her self-selected reading. Have students bring their Reading Logs to share during the conference. You may also want to have students choose a favorite passage to read aloud to you. Then ask questions designed to stimulate discussion. For example, you might ask what information the student learned from a nonfiction text, how the author structured the text, or how the artwork helped the student understand the topic.

FLUENCY PERFORMANCE Have students read aloud to you the passage from "Quest for a Healthy World" they have selected and practiced previously with their partners. Keep track of the number of words each student reads correctly. Ask each student to rate his or her performance on the 1–4 scale. If students aren't happy with their oral reading, give them an opportunity to practice some more and to reread the passage to you.

See *Oral Reading Fluency Assessment* for monitoring progress.

Use with

"Dear Mr. Henshaw"

Review Phonics: Long Vowel /ā/*ea, ei, eigh*

Identify the sound. Tell students to listen for /ā/ in these words: *break, eight, weight.* Then have students repeat the following sentence aloud twice: *My neighbor unveiled a great work of art.* Ask students to identify the words with the /ā/ sound. (*neighbor, unveiled, great*)

Associate letters to sound. Write on the board the sentence *My neighbor unveiled a great work of art.* Underline the letters *ea* in *great.* Point out that in the word *great*, the letters *e* and *a* together stand for the long *a* vowel sound. Then underline the *eigh* in *neighbor* and *ei* in *unveiled*, and tell students that the letters *eigh* and *ei* also can stand for the long *a* vowel sound. Explain that the letters *gh* in *eigh* are silent.

Word Blending. Model how to blend *neighbor.* Point to *n* and say /n/. Slide your hand under *eigh* and say /ā/. Point to *b* and say /b/. Point to *or* and say /ôr/. Slide your hand under the whole word as you elongate the sounds: /nnāābbôôrr/. Then say the word naturally: *neighbor.* Repeat the procedure with *unveiled* and *great.*

**INTERVENTION
PRACTICE
BOOK**

page 92

Apply the skill. *Letter Substitution* Write the following words on the board and have students read each aloud. Make the changes necessary to form the words in parentheses. Have volunteers read the new words.

van (vein)	**fright** (freight)	**stack** (steak)
ran (rein)	**wait** (weight)	**brick** (break)

Introduce Vocabulary

PRETEACH **lesson vocabulary.** Tell students they are going to learn seven new words that will help them read a realistic fiction story called "Dear Mr. Henshaw." Teach each vocabulary word using the following process.

Use the following suggestions or similar ideas to give the meaning or context.

submitted	Ask students what kinds of things might be submitted for approval.
refinery	Use a related word, *refine*, in context: *They were asked to* refine *their opening statements for the debate to make their points clearer.*
grade	Point out that this word has other meanings, but this one refers to land.
partition	Mention that this word comes from the Latin word *partire*, which means "to divide."

> Write the word.
> Say the word.
> Track the word and have students repeat it.
> Give the meaning or context.

insulated Tell students that when they wear warm clothing, they are insulating themselves to keep warm.

prowls This word comes from a middle English word, *prollen*, meaning "to move about."

muffle Talk in a loud voice, then cup your hands over your mouth as you continue to speak to demonstrate the meaning of *muffle*.

Decode multisyllabic words. Write *insulated* on the board. Remind students that they can break longer words into syllables to help decode the words. Model the strategy.

MODEL This is a word with several syllables. When I look at it, I can pronounce the prefix *in-* at the beginning of the word and the *-ed* at the end of the word. Now I am left with just the two syllables in the middle of the word. I can pronounce *su*, and I see the *lat* is followed by the vowel *e*, so *a* must have a long vowel sound. I will pronounce the word: *insulated*.

Have students use this strategy with *refinery* and *partition*.

Vocabulary Words

submitted presented for approval

refinery a place where some crude material, such as sugar or petroleum, is made fine or pure

grade a slope, as of a road or track

partition something that divides, as a wall or screen does

insulated surrounded with material that keeps electricity, heat, or sound from leaking out or in

prowls roams around quietly and slyly

muffle to deaden the sound of

AFTER

Building Background and Vocabulary

Apply Vocabulary Strategies

Have each student make a set of word cards for the Vocabulary Words. Read aloud the sentences below and tell students to hold up the word that completes each sentence. Reread each sentence with the correct word in place. Then discuss how the word relates to the context.

1. She ___(submitted)___ a poem to the literary magazine.
2. They took a tour of an oil ___(refinery)___ .
3. They ran as fast as they could up the ___(grade)___ .
4. He peered around the ___(partition)___ to say "hello" to his office neighbor.
5. During the party, she was glad the wall was well ___(insulated)___ .
6. They know their cat goes out at night and ___(prowls)___ .
7. He puts the pillow over his ears to ___(muffle)___ the sound.

FLUENCY BUILDER Have students look at *Intervention Practice Book* page 91. Read aloud each of the words in the first column and have students repeat it. Then have pairs of students read the words aloud to each other. Tell students to follow the same procedure to read the remaining columns. After each partner has practiced reading the words in each column, have them read aloud the entire list.

INTERVENTION PRACTICE BOOK

page 91

★ Focus Skill Text Structure: Compare and Contrast

PRETEACH **the skill.** Explain to students that an important way to understand something is to see how it is like or different from something else. Point out that authors may present facts or story elements in a compare and contrast format.

Have students look at **side A of Skill Card 23: Text Structure: Compare and Contrast.** Have a volunteer read the introductory paragraph and the definitions of *compare* and *contrast*. Ask students to read the paragraph and look at the Venn diagram beneath it. Go over the words in the diagram and discuss how the girls are alike and how they are different. Ask:

- **What kind of text structure did the writer use to organize the text?** (*compare and contrast*)

- **How do you know?** (*Possible response*: *The writer tells about the similarities and differences between the two girls.*)

Prepare to Read: "Dear Mr. Henshaw"

Preview. Tell students that they are going to read a story called "Dear Mr. Henshaw." Explain that realistic fiction has real-life characters but some of the events are made up. Then preview the selection.

DISTANT VOYAGES

pages 536–555

- **Pages 536–537:** I read the title of the story and I think maybe it is about writing. I see an illustration of a boy writing.

- **Pages 538–539:** I see a wanted poster for a lunch thief and plans for a lunch box. I think maybe someone is stealing lunches.

- **Pages 540–541:** The illustrations on these two pages make me think this boy is an inventor.

- **Pages 542–543:** Here is a picture of a lunch box with an alarm. Maybe that is the boy's invention.

- **Pages 546–547:** I see that the boy is writing. Maybe he is writing in his journal.

- **Page 554:** This shows the boy is still writing. I think that he really enjoys writing.

Set Purpose. Remind students that they can set a purpose for their reading, based on their preview. Tell them that a common purpose for reading may be to enjoy a story and to find out more about the characters. Model the thinking:

MODEL From my preview, I think this story is about a boy who is good at inventing things and also enjoys writing. I am going to read to enjoy the story.

Reread and Summarize

Guide students in rereading "Dear Mr. Henshaw."

Pages 536–537
Let's reread pages 536–537 to recall the introduction.

Summary: Leigh is keeping a diary and is writing letters to his favorite author. Leigh has some problems he needs to solve.

Pages 538–541
Let's reread pages 538–541 to recall what Leigh builds.

Summary: Leigh builds an alarm that will go off when the lunch box is opened.

Pages 542–543
As we reread pages 542–543, let's find out what happens when Leigh goes to lunch.

Summary: By lunchtime, his alarm hasn't gone off, so he opens his lunch and it goes off. Everyone is impressed with his invention.

Pages 544–547
Let's reread pages 544–547 to recall Leigh's phone call.

Summary: Leigh's father calls. Leigh misses him, but he feels like his father doesn't really know him.

Pages 548–549
Reread pages 548–549 to recall what Leigh writes about.

Summary: Leigh writes a story about riding on his father's truck. Barry comes over for dinner and envies Leigh's privacy.

Pages 550–551
Let's reread pages 550–551 to recall what happens next.

Summary: Leigh's story wins an honorable mention. His story is published in the yearbook, and he has lunch with a Famous Author.

Pages 552–554
Let's reread pages 552–554 to see how the story ends.

Summary: The author says she liked Leigh's story and calls him an author. Leigh is happy and proud.

FLUENCY BUILDER Use *Intervention Practice Book* page 91. Call attention to the sentences on the bottom half of the page. Model reading aloud the sentences. Have students repeat after you, using the same expression and pace. Then have students practice reading aloud each sentence three times to a partner.

INTERVENTION PRACTICE BOOK

page 91

Directed Reading: "Pete's Great Invention," pp. 182–188

Pages 182–183

Have a volunteer read aloud the title. Help students identify Pete. Then read page 183 while students listen to find out why Pete's face is so red. Ask: **Does Pete feel embarrassed? Why?** (*He is embarrassed because Mark teased him about being late eight days in a row and everybody laughed.*) **CAUSE AND EFFECT**

TAKE
FLIGHT
pp. 182–188

Ask: **What sounds don't waken him? How are they different from his alarm?** (*Freight train, oil refinery—those noises were very loud compared to his clock.*) **TEXT STRUCTURE: COMPARE AND CONTRAST**

Pages 184–185

Read the first two paragraphs on page 185. Then say,

> **MODEL** In the first paragraph, Pete wonders what he can do. I know that Pete is worried about his grades because he is tardy every day. I use this knowledge to predict that Pete will come up with a way to wake up on time. In the next paragraph, I confirm my prediction when I read that Pete wants to invent a super alarm.
> **MAKE AND CONFIRM PREDICTIONS**

Ask: **How does the invention work?** (*When Pete tries to turn off the alarm, he'll knock over the weight, and the rope will jangle the pots and pans.*) **SUMMARIZE**

Pages 186–187

Ask: **What problem does Pete have to solve for his invention to work?** (*He has to make sure the cat doesn't set it off.*) **IMPORTANT DETAILS**

Ask: **Has Pete already used his invention at home? How do you know?** (*Yes, Miss Deighton says that Pete hasn't been late once since he began using his invention.*) **DRAW CONCLUSIONS**

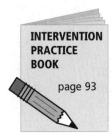

INTERVENTION
PRACTICE
BOOK

page 93

Ask: **Do you think Pete's invention is a good one? Why or why not?** (Possible responses: *Yes, it was easy to make and solved his problems; no, it uses up a lot of pots and pans and is very loud.*) **MAKE JUDGMENTS**

Summarize the selection. Ask students to summarize the story by telling what Pete's problem is and how he solves it. Then have them complete *Intervention Practice Book* page 93.

Answers to *Think About It* Questions

1. Pete invents an alarm clock that makes a lot of noise. Miss Deighton knows the invention is a success because Pete has stopped being late for class. **SUMMARY**

2. Accept reasonable responses. **INTERPRETATION**

3. Accept reasonable responses. Ads should describe the invention accurately and should make the alarm clock seem attractive and effective. **WRITE AN AD**

Skill Review
pages 562–563

USE SKILL CARD 23B

(Focus Skill) Text Structure: Compare and Contrast

RETEACH **the skill.** Have students look at **side B of Skill Card 23: Text Structure: Compare and Contrast.** Read aloud the skill reminder. Ask a volunteer to read the paragraph aloud.

Ask students to note the differences and similarities between the two houses. Ask students to draw a chart like the one on the skill card. Have each student work with a partner and fill in the list.

After students have completed their lists, have a volunteer read his or her list. Help students notice any similarities and differences they have missed.

FLUENCY BUILDER Be sure that students have copies of *Intervention Practice Book*, page 91. Explain that they will practice the sentences on the bottom half of the page by reading them aloud on tape. Have students choose new partners. Tell partners to take turns reading the sentences aloud to each other and then recording them. After listening to the tape, have each student tell how his or her reading has improved. Then have them record the sentences again.

INTERVENTION PRACTICE BOOK

page 91

Expository Writing: Paragraph of Information

Build on Prior Knowledge Tell students that you will be working together to draft a paragraph about the inventor Thomas Edison. Remind students that informational paragraphs contain facts. Display a web like the following on the board:

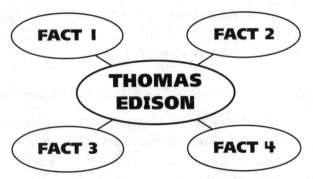

Tell students to use an encyclopedia to find facts about Thomas Edison. As they locate information, have them add their facts to the web. Tell students that they will use the web to help them draft their paragraphs.

Construct the Text. "Share the pen" with students. Use the steps below to guide them through the process.

- Help students write an introductory sentence. The sentence should tell that the paragraph is about Thomas Edison and tell who he was.

- Have students use the facts in the web to write sentences about Thomas Edison. Help students determine which facts should come first.

- Tell students to add a concluding sentence at the end of the paragraph.

Revisit the Text. As you work with students to revise the draft, reread frequently with them and ask them how it can be improved. Tell them to evaluate the sentences to make sure that the facts are stated clearly and are in a logical order. Have students read the completed report aloud.

On Your Own

Have students choose another inventor, or an invention, to write about. Provide simple references for them to use. Remind them that when they write a draft, they should concentrate on writing the most important and interesting facts.

Connect Spelling and Phonics

RETEACH **Long Vowel: /ā/ ea, ei, eigh.** Have students number a sheet of paper 1–8. Dictate the following words and have students write them on their papers. After the students write each word, display the correct spelling of the word so students can proofread their work. Have them draw a line through a misspelled word and write the correct spelling beside it.

1. steak*	2. breakdown	3. veil*	4. reindeer
5. eight*	6. freight*	7. neigh	8. sleigh

*Word appears in "Pete's Great Invention."

Dictate the following sentence, and have students write it: *I had great chow mein at my neighbor's house.*

Build and Read Longer Words

INTERVENTION ASSESSMENT BOOK

Write *underweight* on the board. Have a volunteer identify the letters that come together to form the long *a* sound (*eigh*). Remind students that when reading a longer word with the long *a* sound spelled *ei, ea,* or *eigh,* they should always say the two vowels as one sound: /ā/. Point to each syllable as you say *underweight* (un-der-weight). Have students repeat the syllables and then read the word. Repeat the procedure for the words *breakable* and *unveil.*

FLUENCY BUILDER Have students choose a passage from "Pete's Great Invention" to read aloud to a partner. Tell students they may choose a passage they found interesting, or you can give them the following choices:

- Read page 183. Starting at the top of the page . . . through . . .*really waking up.* (Total: 137 words)

- Read page 185. Starting at the top of the page . . . through . . . *they made!* (Total: 149 words)

Ask students to read the selection aloud to their partners three times. Have students rate their own readings on a scale of 1 to 4. Encourage students to note their improvement from one reading to the next.

Review Vocabulary

Before the weekly assessment, review the core vocabulary words. Have students complete the following statements and then discuss their answers with partners.

I. The architect **submitted** the plans to the building owner. He
   a. presented them for approval.   b. tore them up.

2. The truck carried the crude oil to the **refinery**, which is
   a. where it would be burned.   b. where it would be made pure.

3. The car struggled to get up the **grade**, which was
   a. the bridge.   b. the slope in the road.

4. She built a **partition** in her living room. A partition
   a. divides a room.   b. opens up a room.

5. They **insulated** the house. They
   a. added materials to keep the heat in.   b. decorated the house.

6. The cat **prowls** around the house, which means it
   a. storms around the house.   b. roams around quietly.

7. She wants to **muffle** a loud noise. She wants to
   a. deaden the noise.   b. amplify the sound.

Correct responses: Ia, 2b, 3b, 4a, 5a, 6b, 7a

 ## Review Text Structure: Compare and Contrast

INTERVENTION PRACTICE BOOK

page 94

Review text structure: compare and contrast before the weekly assessment by having students tell how authors structure text to show the similarities and differences between characters, settings, or events. Then have them complete *Intervention Practice Book* page 94. Students should see that both Leigh and Pete are creative and use that creativity to solve problems.

Review Test Prep

Ask students to turn to page 563 of the *Pupil Edition*. Have a volunteer read the tips for answering the test questions. Tell students that these tips can help them answer not only the questions on this page but also other test questions.

DISTANT VOYAGES

page 563

INTERVENTION ASSESSMENT BOOK

Have students follow along as you read aloud each test question and its tip. For the first item, help students understand that finding the same information in both diary entries will show students how the entries are similar. For the second item, point out the details in each entry. Explain that the writer describes how each student feels about the same event.

Self-Selected Reading

Encourage students to select their own books to read on their own. They may choose books from your classroom library shelf, or you may select a group of appropriate books from which your students can choose. Titles might include:

- *A Drummer's Dream* by Kimberly Jackson. See page 563M of the *Teacher's Edition* for an independent reading lesson.

- *Messages in the Mailbox: How to Write a Letter* by Loreen Leedy. Holiday House, 1991

- *The Toothpaste Millionaire* by Jean Merrill. Houghton Mifflin, 1994

You might also suggest additional books that are the same genre, are by the same author, or have the same kind of text structure as the selection.

After students have chosen their books, give each student a copy of "My Reading Log," found on page R38 in the back of the Teacher's Edition. Have students fill in the information at the top of the form. Then have them use the log to keep track of their reading and to record their responses to the literature.

Conduct Student-Teacher Conferences. Arrange for an individual conference time with each student when you can discuss his or her self-selected reading. Have students bring their books and Reading Logs to share during the conference. Tell students to choose a favorite passage to read aloud to you. Then ask questions designed to stimulate discussion.

FLUENCY PERFORMANCE Have students read aloud to you the passage from "Pete's Great Invention" that they practiced. Observe students' pronunciation, intonation, and phrasing. Ask each student to rate his or her performance on the 1–4 scale. Give students an opportunity for additional practice if they are not satisfied with their performance.

See *Oral Reading Fluency Assessment* for monitoring progress.

Use with

"Frindle"

Review Phonics: Silent Letters *b, h, t, n*

Identify the sound. Have students repeat the following sentence aloud three times: *Honestly, those boys often climb that column.* Ask: **What sound does the word** *climb* **end with?** (/m/) **What sound do you hear in the middle of** *often***?** (/f/) **What sound does the word** *column* **end with?** (/m/). **Does the word** *honestly* **begin like** *honey* **or like** *on***?** (on)

Associate letters to sounds. Write this sentence: *Honestly, those boys often climb that column.* Underline the letter *H* in *Honestly*, the *t* in *often*, the *b* in *climb*, and the *n* in *column*. Ask students what sound each of these letters stands for in these words. (*None: they are silent.*) Tell students that in the letter combinations *mn* and *mb*, the *n* and *b* are usually silent. *H* is silent at the beginning of a few words, such as *honest* and *honor*; and *t* is sometimes silent after *s* and *f*, as in *listen* and *often*.

Word blending. Write the words *thumb, honor, soften,* and *solemn* on the board, and model how to blend and read them. For *thumb,* slide your hand under the whole word as you elongate sounds: /thuumm/. Then read the word naturally—*thumb.* Repeat the process for the remaining words.

Apply the skill. *Letter Substitution* Write the following words on the board, and have students read each aloud. Make the changes necessary to form the words in parentheses. Have a volunteer read aloud each new word. Try to give every student an opportunity to respond.

soft (soften)   **plum** (plumber)   **list** (listen)   **number** (numb)

INTERVENTION PRACTICE BOOK

page 96

Introduce Vocabulary

PRETEACH **lesson vocabulary.** Tell students they are going to learn six new words that they will see again when they read a story called "Frindle." Teach each vocabulary word using the following process.

Use the following suggestions or similar ideas to give the meaning or context.

		Write the word.
beaming	As she came onto the stage to accept her award, she was beaming with pride.	Say the word. Track the word and have students repeat it. Give the meaning or context.
reputation	Dogs have a reputation for hating cats, but our dog loves our cat.	
sidetrack	The boy didn't want to shop for clothes, so he tried to side-track his dad into going to the toy store.	

absorbed	Because I was absorbed in my homework, I didn't see mom come into my room.
aisle	He walked down the aisle of the theater and sat in the front row.
oath	In court, the judge asked the man to take an oath that he would tell the truth.

For vocabulary activities, see Vocabulary Games on pages 2–7.

For vocabulary activities, see Vocabulary Games on pages 2–7.

Vocabulary Words

beaming smiling very warmly

reputation overall character as judged by people in general

sidetrack to distract; to take attention away from

absorbed took the full attention of

aisle hallway or passage

oath formal statement promising something

AFTER

Building Background and Vocabulary

Apply Vocabulary Strategies

Decode Multisyllabic Words. Write the word *sidetrack* on the board. Remind students that they can often decode an unfamiliar word by breaking it into familiar parts, pronouncing the parts separately, and then putting the parts together until it sounds familiar.

> **MODEL** Inside this word I see two familiar smaller words: *side* and *track*. I can pronounce the familiar parts and then put the parts together and say the whole word.

Tell students to use this strategy as they encounter other unfamiliar words in their reading. Remind them that they may use a dictionary or glossary to confirm pronunciations.

RETEACH **lesson vocabulary.** Be sure each student has a set of vocabulary cards. Read aloud the following sentences. Say the word "blank" as you come to each blank, and have students hold up the correct word card. Reread the sentence with the appropriate word.

1. She was ___(beaming)___ at me after I gave her the gift.
2. His ___(reputation)___ as a good teacher was well deserved.
3. They tried to ___(sidetrack)___ their mother so she would forget about their report cards.
4. He was so ___(absorbed)___ in his book that he forgot to eat lunch.
5. I asked the man at the market which ___(aisle)___ the bread was on.
6. Club members had to swear an ___(oath)___ of secrecy.

FLUENCY BUILDER Use *Intervention Practice Book* page 95. Read aloud each of the words in the first column and have students repeat it. Then have partners take turns reading the words to each other. Follow the same procedure with each of the remaining columns. Then have partners practice reading the entire list themselves.

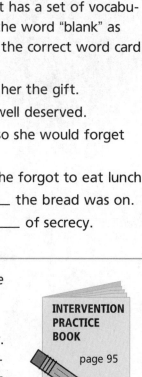

INTERVENTION PRACTICE BOOK

page 95

Author's Purpose and Perspective

PRETEACH the skill. Have students look at **side A of Skill Card 24: Author's Purpose and Perspective.** Ask a volunteer to read aloud the text in the speech balloon. Then point out the boxes below the illustration which list authors' purposes. If necessary, guide students to understand the terms *inform, persuade,* and *entertain.* Ask students to tell which purposes the man in the illustration had. (to inform and to persuade)

Then direct attention to the section about author's perspective, and tell students that *perspective* means "viewpoint." Ask students to tell what they think the author's perspective is on smoking. (Possible response: It's bad for the health; it's harmful; it's hard to quit.) Point out that a person's experiences help form his or her perspectives. For example, perhaps a relative of this man became ill from smoking cigarettes.

Prepare to Read: "Frindle"

Preview. Tell students that they are going to read "Frindle." Explain that this is a realistic fiction selection, which means that the characters and events seem like those in real life, but that the story was made up.

DISTANT VOYAGES
pages 566–574

- **Pages 566–567:** The title of the story interests me, partly because the letters are made out of pens, and partly because it is a word I don't recognize. Maybe it is this boy's name.

- **Pages 568–569:** I can see that the boy likes to be involved in the classroom because he has his hand up. I wonder what he wants to say.

- **Pages 570–571:** Now the boy is going home from school, but he doesn't look like he is worrying about homework. He looks like he is having fun. I wonder what the girl is doing and what she is looking at so closely.

- **Pages 572–573:** This scene seems to be in a candy store. The lady behind the counter looks really surprised. I wonder what the boy has said or done and how the candy store connects to school.

Set purpose. Model setting a purpose for reading "Frindle."

MODEL This story seems to be about a boy who is clever and fun. I will read to enjoy the story and to see what the boy is up to. I also want to find out what pens have to do with the story.

Reread and Summarize

Have students reread and summarize "Frindle" in sections, as described in the chart below.

Pages 566–569

Let's look again at pages 566–569 to remember the introduction to this story.

Summary: Nicholas Allen gets attention in school for his ideas. When Nick questions why d-o-g means *dog*, his teacher gives a lecture on word meanings and the dictionary, but it doesn't stop her from getting to their assignment.

Pages 570–571

As we reread pages 570–571, let's pay attention to what Nick thinks about what his teacher has said.

Summary: As he walks home from school with Janet, Nick thinks about his baby-talk word for *music* and how the word made sense to him at the time. Just then, Janet's pen drops.

Pages 572–573

Let's reread pages 572–573 and see Nick's scheme.

Summary: Nick calls Janet's pen a *frindle* and persuades others to use the word, too. In time, even the store clerk knows what it means.

Page 574

Reread page 574 to remember how Nick continues to try to change the language.

Summary: Nick asks five friends to swear they will use the word. What his teacher said is true: People decide what words mean.

FLUENCY BUILDER Reuse *Intervention Practice Book* page 95. Call attention to the sentences at the bottom of the page. State that the goal is to have each student read each phrase smoothly. Model the appropriate pace, expression, and phrasing as you read aloud each of the sentences. Then have students practice reading aloud each sentence two or three times to a partner.

INTERVENTION
PRACTICE
BOOK

page 95

Directed Reading: "One of a Kind," pp. 190–197

Ask a volunteer to read aloud the title of the story.
Then help students identify Mr. Lee, Jenna, and Andy,
the leader of the opposite team, in the illustration.

Take Flight
pages
190–197

Pages 190–191

Have students read page 190. Ask: **How is the widget
game played?** (*Possible response: The teacher thinks of
an object, and teams ask questions until someone guesses what it is.*)
MAIN IDEA

Pages 192–193

Point out that the author says that some of the kids think the game is
dumb. Ask: **What do you think the author's perspective is on whether
the game is dumb?** (*Possible response:* She thinks the game is fun because
she is telling the story of a person who thinks it is fun.) (Focus Skill) **AUTHOR'S
PURPOSE AND PERSPECTIVE**

Before students read this page, direct their attention to the word *kazoo*,
in the fifth line. Model using the strategy Use Decoding/Phonics:

> **MODEL** I am not sure what this word is, but I will try to sound it
> out. I see the familiar word *zoo* in it, and I know it is pronounced /zoo/.
> I also know that a single vowel between consonants often has the
> schwa sound, so I will try pronouncing the word /kə-zoo/. This sounds
> like a word I know. (Focus Strategy) **USE DECODING/PHONICS**

Have a volunteer read page 193. Ask: **What happens when a class member thinks he or she knows the answer?** (*Possible response: He or she has
to blow a kazoo, but if the guess is wrong, the team is out of the game.*)
SUMMARIZE

Ask: **What do you think the widget is?** (*Responses will vary.*)

Pages 194–195

Have students look at the illustration on page 194 and describe what they
think is happening. (*Possible response: Jenna looks as if she wants to
guess the answer, because she is diving for her kazoo.*) **DRAW
CONCLUSIONS**

Have students read page 195 to find out whether Jenna makes a guess.
What do you think of Jenna's answer? (*Responses will vary.*) **EXPRESS
PERSONAL OPINIONS**

Page 196

Before students read page 196, have them look at the illustration and
make a prediction about whether Jenna's answer is correct. Ask: **Is the
ending of the story believable? Why or why not?** (*Responses will vary.*)
MAKE JUDGMENTS

Summarize the selection. Ask students to think about what happened during the beginning, middle, and end of the widget game. Then have students write three sentences to summarize the story.

Page 197

INTERVENTION PRACTICE BOOK

page 197

Answers to *Think About It* Questions

1. She puts the fact that Mr. Lee is one of a kind together with other facts. **SUMMARY**

2. Possible response: Before she gives her answer, she worries that she might be wrong. After she gives her answer, she feels proud. **INTERPRETATION**

3. Responses will vary. Sentences should identify classroom objects, and questions should elicit useful information. **WRITE SENTENCES**

AFTER

Skill Review
pages 580–581

USE SKILL CARD 24B

(Focus Skill) Author's Purpose and Perspective

RETEACH the skill. Have students look at **side B of Skill Card 24: Author's Purpose and Perspective.** Read the skill reminder aloud to them.

Ask a student to read the paragraph aloud. Then ask students to answer the first question (Possible response: *to entertain*) and then to write three sentences about attitudes and opinions. If necessary, prompt responses by asking questions such as these. (Possible responses *are given*.)

- **How does the author feel about heights?** (The author is secretly afraid of heights.)

- **How does the author deal with being scared?** (The author thinks he or she should get over his or her fear by facing it.)

- **What does the author feel about mornings?** (He or she thinks morning is a nice time of day.)

FLUENCY BUILDER Reuse *Intervention Practice Book* page 95. Explain that each student will practice the sentences at the bottom of the page by reading them aloud on tape. Assign new partners, and have them take turns reading the sentences aloud to each other and then reading them on tape. After students listen to the tape, have them tell how they have improved their reading. Then have them tape themselves again, focusing on improved pacing and tone.

INTERVENTION PRACTICE BOOK

page 95

Research Report: Editing a Paragraph

Build on prior knowledge Tell students that they will edit a sample paragraph to put ideas in order, to make the ideas clear, and to add or remove words and sentences. Display the following questions:

> **Are my sentences in the best order?**
>
> **Are all of my ideas clear?**
>
> **Do I need to change any of the words?**

Construct the text. Write this sample paragraph on the board:

Families in the park play their radio too loud. Teenagers on the streets play their radio too loud. We should all do our part to cut down on the racket. Some people shout when they should talk quietly. Scientists have found that loud noise damages my hearing. Loud noise also causes stress. I like to listen to quiet piano music.

Revisit the text. Read the sample paragraph aloud with students. Take each sentence or idea at a time, and work with students to make revisions.

- Ask: **How can we combine the first two sentences into one? What other changes should we make in those sentences?** (Possible response: Combine the two subjects and say *Families in the park and teenagers on the streets*; fix the subject-verb agreement to read *play their radios*.)

- Ask: **Does the third sentence belong where it is? If not, where should it go?** (Possible response: No; after *also causes stress*.)

- Ask: **How should we change the sentence that begins *Scientists have found . . .*?** (Possible response: It should end with *damages the hearing* or *damages people's hearing*.)

- Ask: **Does the final sentence belong in the paragraph? Why or why not?** (No; it is off the subject.)

- After the corrections are made, read the paragraph aloud with students.

On Your Own

Ask students to write the revised paragraph and add some sentences of their own. They may reorganize it, add details, or use more vivid words. Ask volunteers to share their paragraphs.

Connect Spelling and Phonics

RETEACH **silent letters b, h, t, n.** Write the words *doubt*, *herb*, *fasten*, and *column* on the board. Tell students that all the words you will say have silent *b, h, t,* or *n.* Dictate the words, and have students write them. After each one, display the correct spelling so students can proofread their work.

1. comb*	2. dumb*	3. limb	4. listening*
5. whistle	6. solemn*	7. condemn	8. honor*

***Word appears in "One of a Kind."**

Dictate the following sentence, and have students write it:
I listened to the lambs.

Build and Read Longer Words

Write the words: glisten, subtle, and condemn on the board. Remind students that when two or more consonants appear between two vowels, the word is usually broken into syllables between the consonants. Point to the word *glisten.* Cover the word part *ten,* and have a volunteer read *glis.*

> **glisten**
> **subtle**
> **condemn**

Then cover *glis,* and ask a volunteer to read *ten.* Point out that in this word, *t* is silent. Draw your hand under the whole word as students read it aloud. Call on volunteers to read the remaining two words aloud, and tell how they figured them out. Then have students read the words *fastener, doubtless,* and *honorable.*

FLUENCY BUILDER Have students choose a passage from "One of a Kind" to read aloud to a partner. You may have students choose passages they found particularly interesting or have them choose one of the following options:

- Read page 192. (From *The teams took . . .* through . . . *Another no.* Total: 122 words)

- Read pages 195–196. (From *Everyone laughed . . .* through . . . *one of a kind.* Total: 130 words)

Ask students to read the selection aloud to their partners three times. Have students rate their own readings on a scale of 1–4. Encourage students to note their improvement from one reading to the next by completing the sentence *I know my reading has improved because* _____. Encourage listeners to offer positive feedback about improvements.

Review Vocabulary

To revisit the Vocabulary Words prior to the weekly assessment, use these sentence frames. Read the items aloud to students, and have them write the answers. Go over the answers, and discuss why they are correct.

1. The students began **beaming** when the teacher said they could
   a. have a test tomorrow.   b. have a pizza party.

2. The man's **reputation** for being selfish changed when he
   a. started a business.   b. saved someone's life.

3. "Don't **sidetrack** me from my fishing," Dad said. "I want to
   a. catch a big one."   b. go home now."

4. If you are **absorbed** in your art project, you have probably
   a. cleaned up your mess.   b. lost track of time.

5. Our teacher walked up and down each **aisle** as she
   a. helped us write.   b. wrote on the board.

6. The mayor of our city took an **oath** of office. This means she
   a. promised to do her best.   b. said bad words.

Correct responses: lb, 2b, 3a, 4b, 5a, 6a

This is a good time to show the Vocabulary Words and definitions on page 239. Have students copy them to use for studying for the vocabulary test.

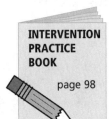

**INTERVENTION
PRACTICE
BOOK**

page 98

⭐ Focus Skill Author's Purpose and Perspective

To review author's purpose and perspective before the weekly assessment, use *Intervention Practice Book*, page 98. Have volunteers read the first three items aloud, and discuss answers with the class. Then direct students' attention to the following section. Explain that especially in fiction, an author doesn't always state his or her perspective. Instead, readers must figure it out by noticing details.

In the next section, guide students to identify events in the story that show that school and learning are fun. (Possible responses: the widget game; the pizza reward; Mr. Lee's joking) After students complete the next question, have them identify the author's attitudes and opinions. (Possible responses: Learning and school can be fun; it is good to have a goal; students should care about things.)

Review Test Prep

**INTERVENTION
ASSESSMENT
BOOK**

✔

Ask students to turn to page 581 of the *Pupil Edition*. Point out the tips for answering the questions. Tell students that paying attention to the tips can help them answer these and other test questions.

**DISTANT
VOYAGES**

page 581

Point out that in some multiple-choice questions, one answer choice is the opposite of the correct answer. They can eliminate that choice first and then eliminate other unlikely ones.

Self-Selected Reading

Encourage students to select their own books to read on their own. They may choose books from your classroom library shelf, or you may select a group of appropriate books from which your students can choose.

- *The Graceful Bull and Other Stories*. (See page 58IM of the *Teacher's Edition* for a lesson plan.)

- *The Hand-Me-Down Horse* by Marion Hess Pomeranc. Albert Whitman, 1996.

- *Donavan's Word Jar* by Monalisa DeGross. HarperCollins, 1998.

After students have chosen their books, give each student a copy of My Reading Log, found on page R38 in the back of the *Teacher's Edition*. Have each student fill in the information at the top of the form. Then have students use the log to keep track of their reading and to record their responses to the literature.

Conduct student-teacher conferences. Arrange for an individual conference time with each student when you can discuss his or her self-selected reading. Have students bring their Reading Logs to share during the conference. You may also want to have each student choose a favorite passage to read aloud to you. Then ask questions designed to stimulate discussion. For example, you might question what information the student learned from a nonfiction text, how the author structured the text, or how the artwork helped the student understand the topic.

FLUENCY PERFORMANCE Have students read aloud to you the passage from "One of a Kind" they have selected and practiced previously with their partners. Keep track of the number of words each student reads correctly. Ask each student to rate his or her performance on the I–4 scale. If students aren't happy with their oral reading, give them an opportunity to practice some more and then to reread the passage to you.

See *Oral Reading Fluency Assessment* for monitoring progress.

Use with

"The Fun They Had"

Review Phonics: Letter Pattern *ough*

Identify the sound. Have students repeat the following sentence aloud two times: *He bought enough flour to make the dough.* Ask students to identify the word that rhymes with *thought* (*bought)* and the word that rhymes with *stuff.* (*enough*) Ask students which word rhymes with *go.* (*dough*)

Associate letters to sounds. Write the sentence from above on the board. Underline the letters *ough* in *bought, enough,* and *dough.* Explain that the letters *ough* can stand for the /ô/ sound in *bought,* the /uf/ sound in *enough,* and the /ō/ sound in dough. Also explain that the letters *ough* can stand for the /o͞o/ sound in *through.*

Apply the skill. *Sorting the Sounds* Write *bought, tough,* and *dough* as column headings on the board. Have a volunteer read the words aloud and identify the sound that *ough* stands for in each word. Have students sort the following words into the appropriate columns of the chart: *cough, enough, thought, though, rough, although,* and *trough.* Have them line up the letters *ough* in each column.

Apply the skill. *Letter Substitution* Write each of the following words on the board and have students read each aloud. Then make the changes necessary to form the words in parentheses. Have a volunteer read aloud each new word. Try to give every student an opportunity to respond.

**INTERVENTION
PRACTICE
BOOK**

page 100

cuff (cough)	**both** (bought)	**toad** (tough)	**dug** (dough)
enroll (enough)	**threat** (thought)	**throat** (through)	**those** (though)

Introduce Vocabulary

PRETEACH **lesson vocabulary.** Tell students they are going to learn six new words that they will see again when they read a story called "The Fun They Had." Teach each vocabulary word using the following process.

Use the following sentences or similar ideas to give the meaning or context.

dispute	No one will dispute that reading is a very important skill.
nonchalantly	Dad asked him to hang his coat up, but he threw it nonchalantly on his bed instead.

> Write the word.
>
> Say the word.
>
> Track the word and have students repeat it.
>
> Give the meaning or context.

loftily	"There is a big difference between my fine painting and your scribbles," the artist said loftily.
sorrowfully	Mom told us sorrowfully that Grandma was very sick.
adjusted	Many years ago, children wore metal roller skates that could be adjusted to fit different people.

For vocabulary activities, see Vocabulary Games on pp. 2–7.

For vocabulary activities, see Vocabulary Games on pp. 2–7.

Vocabulary Words

dispute to argue about something

nonchalantly acting with cool indifference

loftily in a haughty, overbearing manner

sorrowfully in a very sad way

adjusted adapted or changed

AFTER

Building Background and Vocabulary

Apply Vocabulary Strategies

Use prefixes and suffixes. Write the word *nonchalantly* on the board, and read it aloud. Tell students that a good strategy for figuring out unfamiliar words is to look for prefixes and suffixes.

> **MODEL** I see the prefix *non-* and the suffix *-ly*. The prefix *non-* means "not," and the suffix *-ly* means "like" or "in a certain way." I'm not sure what the root *-chalant-* means, but the prefix and suffix help me know that it is "not like" something else. I will look up the word to help me understand all of it.

Remind students to use this strategy as they read the selection.

RETEACH lesson vocabulary. Give students vocabulary cards, and read these sentences aloud. Say "blank" for each blank. Have students hold up the correct card. Then read the sentence aloud with the correct word.

1. The candidates will __(dispute)__ each other until the election.
2. He tossed the paper cup __(nonchalantly)__ into the trash can.
3. The man said __(loftily)__, "I shall someday be President."
4. We looked __(sorrowfully)__ in the grass for Mom's lost ring.
5. I __(adjusted)__ the angle of my paper and began to write.

FLUENCY BUILDER Use *Intervention Practice Book* page 99. Read aloud each of the words in the first column and have students repeat it. Then have students work in pairs and take turns reading the words to each other. Follow the same procedure with each of the remaining columns. After each partner has had a turn reading aloud the words in each column, have them practice reading the entire list while timing themselves.

INTERVENTION PRACTICE BOOK

page 99

(Focus Skill) **Draw Conclusions**

PRETEACH **the skill.** Have students look at **side A of Skill Card 25: Draw Conclusions.** Ask a student to read the explanation aloud. Then direct students' attention to the illustration. Discuss how students can observe the angry boy slamming the door and use their own experience to draw the conclusion that the boy is angry.

Next, have students read the sentences about Shanna. Discuss the fact and the conclusion given, and invite volunteers to discuss whether their own experiences support the conclusion.

Prepare to Read: "The Fun They Had"

Preview. Tell students that they are going to read a selection called "The Fun They Had." Explain that this is a science fiction story. In science fiction, an author tells the story of something that could happen or exist in the future, sometimes a long time from now.

DISTANT VOYAGES
pages
584–592

- **Pages 584–585:** Judging by the robot, the stars, and the rocket, I think this is going to be about something in the future. Maybe it is also in outer space.

- **Pages 586–587:** I can tell from these pictures that these people are interested in the book about school. They look like they live in a future time and maybe on another planet. I am curious about what their lives are like.

- **Pages 588–589:** It looks like the student has a robot teacher. I wonder why the girl looks so surprised.

- **Pages 590–591:** This illustration shows what school looks like now. I wonder if the story compares today's schools and schools of the future.

- **Page 592:** The story seems to end on another planet. I wonder what happens to the characters there.

Set Purpose. Model setting a purpose for reading "The Fun They Had."

MODEL I think this selection tells how schools of the future might be different from schools of today. I want to read to find out how the author thinks they will be different.

Reread and Summarize

Have students reread and summarize "The Fun They Had" in sections, as described in the chart below.

Pages 584–587

Let's reread pages 584–587 to discover the setting of the story and how the story begins.

Summary: The story opens in the future, perhaps on another planet. Tommy finds a real printed book in his house and shows it to Margie. Margie says that her grandfather's grandfather said that in the past, all books were printed. Margie's and Tommy's books are on computers.

Pages 588–589

Let's reread pages 588–589 to see what Margie's school is like.

Summary: Someone comes to repair the problems with Margie's mechanical teacher, but she wishes the person would take it away instead. Margie wants to know what Tommy learns in the printed book, which is written about school.

Pages 590–591

Let's reread pages 590–591 to find out what school was like when people used real books.

Summary: Margie is surprised to learn that school used to be held in buildings with lots of students and human teachers. She wants to read more about this.

Page 592

Let's reread page 592 to see what Margie thinks of the old schools and how they did things.

Summary: Margie gets back to work with her mechanical teacher. She imagines what school must have been like, with the kids and the teachers getting together. She thinks it would've been fun.

FLUENCY BUILDER Reuse *Intervention Practice Book* page 99. Call attention to the sentences at the bottom of the page. State that the goal is to have each student read each phrase smoothly. Model the appropriate pace, expression, and phrasing as you read aloud each of the sentences. Then have students practice reading aloud each sentence two or three times to a partner.

INTERVENTION PRACTICE BOOK

page 99

Directed Reading: "What a Time It Was!" pp. 198–205

Ask a volunteer to read aloud the title of the story. Ask: **What do the illustrations on this page tell you about the time of this story?** (*Possible response: This is set in the future.*) **GRAPHIC AIDS**

TAKE FLIGHT
pp. 198–205

Page 198

Ask students to read page 198. Ask: **What form of writing is used in this selection?** (*diary*) **AUTHOR'S CRAFT**

Ask: **Why does the writer seem to dislike the Detroit assignment?** (*The writer thinks it would be more interesting and useful to be on the moon-orbiter project.*) **IMPORTANT DETAILS**

Page 199

Read page 199 aloud. Ask students to follow along and decide how to summarize what the writer has discovered so far. Model using the Summarize strategy.

> **MODEL** After I read this page, I think about all the details the writer tells me about and retell just the main points in a shorter way. I learn that he has discovered that cars were used in the past for transportation but that they seem uncomfortable to him. (*Focus Strategy*) **SUMMARIZE**

Ask: **How are cars different from jet tubes?** (*In a jet tube, you don't sit upright.*) **MAKE COMPARISONS**

Page 200

Ask a volunteer to read aloud page 200. Ask: **Why doesn't the writer like cars?** (*Possible response: They are small, uncomfortable, and slow.*) (*Focus Skill*) **DRAW CONCLUSIONS**

Ask: **What does the writer think an airbag is?** (*a breathing device*) **IMPORTANT DETAILS**

Page 201

Have students read page 201. Then ask: **How long do people at the writer's time live?** (*200 years*) (*Focus Strategy*) **DRAW CONCLUSIONS**

Page 202

Read page 202 aloud. Ask students to listen to find out what the person discovers about cars. Ask: **What does the writer discover about how cars traveled?** (*They traveled on two-way open roads where accidents would happen.*) **IMPORTANT DETAILS**

Ask: **How do you know that accidents aren't a problem in the writer's time?** (*Possible response: Jet tubes go one at a time through one-way tunnels.*) **SYNTHESIZE**

Page 203

Ask: **What is most interesting to the writer about the camper?** (*Possible response: It was like a home on wheels, which makes his own home seem boring.*) **CHARACTERS' EMOTIONS**

Have a volunteer read the text on page 204. Ask: **How does the writer feel about the music and dancing?** (*excited; pleased*) **CHARACTERS' EMOTIONS**

Summarize the selection Ask students to think about the things that the diary writer discovers about life as it used to be. Then have students write three or four sentences to summarize how the writer's world is different from the world of the past.

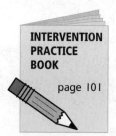

INTERVENTION PRACTICE BOOK

page 101

Answers to *Think About It* Questions

1. They discovered the car and decided it was inefficient but fun. They discovered music CDs and dancing, which were also fun. **SUMMARY**

2. Possible response: He liked the music most and the uncomfortable cars least. **INTERPRETATION**

3. Responses will vary. Encourage students to think about the fashions and customs of today. **WRITE IDEAS**

AFTER

Skill Review
pages 596–597

 Draw Conclusions

RETEACH the skill. Have students look at **side B of Skill Card 25: Draw Conclusions.** Ask a student to read aloud the skill reminder. Discuss the illustrated version of this concept.

USE SKILL CARD 25B

Ask a volunteer to read the paragraph aloud. Then read the instructions below the paragraph. Have students discuss what the author says, what the character does, and what they know. Ask students to write their own conclusions. (Possible responses: The man is guilty of doing something wrong; he has stolen something and is trying to hide from the police.)

Students may wish to discuss their responses to the final instruction. Remind students that sometimes, even good readers draw conclusions that turn out to be wrong but that they can always change their ideas later in a story.

FLUENCY BUILDER Reuse *Intervention Practice Book* page 99. Explain that each student will practice the sentences at the bottom of the page by reading them aloud on tape. Assign new partners, and have them take turns reading the sentences aloud to each other and then reading them on tape. After students listen to the tape, have them tell how they have improved their reading. Then have them tape themselves again, focusing on improved pacing and tone.

INTERVENTION PRACTICE BOOK

page 99

Research Report: Publish a Graphic Aid

Build on prior knowledge. Tell students that they will produce a bar graph based on information in the story "What a Time It Was!" Explain that they will practice changing written information into a visual, or graphic, form. Have students turn to page 200 of "What a Time It Was!" and read aloud the second paragraph. Have students dictate sentences telling the speeds of the 2002 convertible and the junior jet tube. Ask students to suppose there is a senior jet tube, and make up a sentence about its speed. For example:

> The 2002 convertible went at a top speed of 180 miles per hour.
>
> A junior jet tube goes at a top speed of 300 miles per hour.
>
> A senior jet tube goes at a top speed of 500 miles per hour.

Construct the text. "Share the pen" with students in a collaborative effort to construct the bar graph. You may wish to use a chart-paper grid or a transparency of a grid. Discuss the elements of a bar graph, such as labels for the top and sides, increments for the scale, and the heights of the bars.

Revisit the text. Go back and reread the sentences with students, and review the bar graph. Ask: **How can we make sure we show the facts correctly in the graph?** (Possible response: Reread the sentences and check the graph to make sure the information matches.)

- Guide students to see whether they have included all labels and have written a title for the graph.

- Ask: **Do we need a caption to explain our bar graph?** (Responses will vary.)

- Ask: **Have we begun the scale at zero?** Make any necessary changes.

On Your Own

Have students apply the skill to their graphic aids for their research reports. Tell them to refer to graphic aids in their language, math, science, or social studies textbooks for ideas.

Connect Spelling and Phonics

RETEACH **letter pattern *ough*.** Tell students that each word you will say contains a vowel sound spelled *ough*. Dictate the words below, and have students write them. After they write each word, display the correct spelling so students can proofread their work.

I. roughly*   2. tough*   3. dough   4. ought

5. bought   6. thoroughly*   7. through   8. although*

*****Word appears in "What a Time It Was!"**

Dictate the following sentences, and have students write them: *Jon thought his sister played rough. Did you put the dough through the trough?*

Build and Read Longer Words

Write these words on the board: *doughnut, thoughtful.* Explain to students that the letter pattern *ough* always stays together in a syllable. Point to *doughnut* and ask students which part of the word stands for the /dō/ sound and which part stands for the /nut/ sound. Follow a similar procedure for *thoughtful.* Then ask students to read *afterthought, sourdough,* and *thoroughfare* and explain how they figured them out.

INTERVENTION
ASSESSMENT
BOOK

FLUENCY BUILDER Have students choose a passage from "What a Time It Was!" to read aloud to a partner. You may have students choose passages they found particularly interesting or have them choose one of the following options:

- Read pages 199–200. (From *It seems the . . .* through . . . *junior jet tube.* Total: 167 words)

- Read pages 201–202. (From *The manual was . . .* through . . . *than I thought!* Total: 139 words)

Ask students to read the selection aloud to their partners three times. Have students rate their own readings on a scale of 1–4. Encourage students to note their improvement from one reading to the next by completing the sentence *I know my reading has improved because* _____. Encourage listeners to offer positive feedback about improvements.

Review Vocabulary

Read the statements to students to revisit the Vocabulary Words prior to the weekly assessment, use these sentence frames, and ask them to write the correct answers on their papers. Go over the answers, and discuss why they are correct.

1. The two settlers had an angry **dispute** over who

    a. grew the flowers.   b. owned the land.

2. When she said **nonchalantly** that they had had an accident, I knew

    a. it was not very bad.   b. it was very bad.

3. The magazine advertisement praised the cars **loftily**. This means that

    a. they were not liked.   b. they were well liked.

4. When mom took Grandma to the airport, mom said **sorrowfully**,

    a. "I'll miss you!"   b. "I'll see you tomorrow."

5. Our car's brakes had to be **adjusted** because they were

    a. working very well.   b. not working well.

    Correct responses: 1b, 2a, 3b, 4a, 5a

This is a good time to show the Vocabulary Words and definitions on page 249. Have students copy them to use for studying for the vocabulary test.

 Draw Conclusions

**INTERVENTION
PRACTICE
BOOK**

page 102

To review drawing conclusions before the weekly assessment, use *Intervention Practice Book* page 102. Have volunteers read the first two sentences aloud and suggest answers.

Direct students' attention to the next section. Ask students to refer to "What a Time It Was!" if they need help in answering these questions. Read aloud the sentence that is the first conclusion, and ask students to write the facts that support that conclusion. Then ask volunteers to share their answers. Follow this same procedure with the next conclusion.

Review Test Prep

Ask students to turn to page 597 of the *Pupil Edition*. Point out the tips for answering the test questions. Tell students that paying attention to these tips can help them answer these and other test questions.

**DISTANT
VOYAGES**

page 597

**INTERVENTION
ASSESSMENT
BOOK**

Remind students that when they are asked for the definition of a word used in a passage, they should look for context clues in the passage to decide its meaning. Also remind them that when they are asked for conclusions about a passage, they should be sure to note the details in the passage.

Self-Selected Reading

Encourage students to select their own books to read on their own. They may choose books from your classroom library shelf or you may select a group of appropriate books from which your students can choose.

- *Fun with Robots.* (See page 597K of the *Teacher's Edition* for a lesson plan.)

- *Don't Read This Book, Whatever You Do! More Poems About School* by Kalli Dakos. Aladdin, 1998.

- *Destination: Jupiter* by Seymour Simon. William Morrow, 1998.

After students have chosen their books, give each student a copy of My Reading Log, found on page R38 in the back of the *Teacher's Edition*. Have each student fill in the information at the top of the form. Then have students use the log to keep track of their reading and to record their responses to the literature.

Conduct student-teacher conferences. Arrange for an individual conference time with each student when you can discuss his or her self-selected reading. Have students bring their Reading Logs to share during the conference. You may also want to have students choose a favorite passage to read aloud to you. Then ask questions designed to stimulate discussion. For example, you might question what information the student learned from a nonfiction text, how the author structured the text, or how the artwork helped the student understand the topic.

FLUENCY PERFORMANCE Have students read aloud to you the passage from "What a Time It Was!" they have selected and practiced previously with their partners. Keep track of the number of words each student reads correctly. Ask each student to rate his or her performance on the 1–4 scale. If students aren't happy with their oral reading, give them an opportunity to practice some more and to reread the passage to you.

See *Oral Reading Fluency Assessment* for monitoring progress.

Use with

"Across the Wide Dark Sea"

Review Phonics: Prefixes *un-, re-, dis-*

Identify the meaning. Have students repeat the following sentence aloud two times: *I stared in disbelief at my little brother's untied shoes. I had just retied them for the sixth time.* Ask: **What does** *retied* **mean?** (*"tied again"*) **Which word is the opposite of** *belief*? (*disbelief*) **Which word is the opposite of** *tied*? (*untied*)

Associate prefixes to meanings. Write the sentences from above on the board, and underline the prefixes. Explain that a prefix is a word part that is added to the beginning of a word and that changes its meaning. Use the word *retied* to explain how a prefix changes the meaning of a word. Explain that *re-* means "again" and that *retied* means "tied again." Repeat for the remaining prefixes.

Apply the skill. *Prefix Addition* Write the following words on the board, and have students read each one aloud. Make the changes necessary to form the words in parentheses. Have a volunteer read aloud each new word and explain its meaning.

INTERVENTION PRACTICE BOOK

page 104

pay (repay)	**reliable** (unreliable)	**placed** (displaced)
heated (reheated)	**satisfied** (dissatisfied)	**did** (undid)

Introduce Vocabulary

PRETEACH **lesson vocabulary.** Tell students they are going to learn seven new words that they will see again when they read "Across the Wide Dark Sea." Teach each vocabulary word using the following process.

Use the following suggestions or similar ideas to give the meaning or context.

> Write the word.
> Say the word.
> Track the word and have students repeat it.
> Give the meaning or context.

rigging	It was scary to see the sailor climb into the rigging of the ship's tall masts.
furl	At the end of every day someone would take the flag down and furl it.
huddled	As the tornado hit, our family huddled together in the basement.
vast	When seen from land the Earth looks vast, but when seen from the moon it looks small.
beams	The long beams stretched from the front of the ship to the back and supported the deck.

| lurked | Three mountain lions lurked behind the trees, waiting for the deer to come closer. |
| settlement | A pioneer settlement usually had a store, a church, and homes. |

For vocabulary activities, see Vocabulary Games on pp. 2–7.

AFTER
Building Background and Vocabulary

Apply Vocabulary Strategies

Use word, sentence, and paragraph context. Write the word *rigging* on the board and say it aloud. Remind students that they can often figure out the meaning of an unfamiliar word by looking at the meaning of the entire sentence and the other words in the sentence.

> **MODEL** I will look at how this word is used in the selection to try to figure out its meaning. The sentence says that the sailors were "hauling on ropes, climbing in the *rigging*, and perched at the very top of the mast." From this, I think that the *rigging* must refer to the sails and the ropes on the ship.

Have students use this strategy as they encounter other unfamiliar words when they read.

RETEACH lesson vocabulary. Be sure each student has a set of vocabulary cards. Read aloud the following sentences, saying "blank" for each blank. Ask students to hold up the correct word card, and then reread the sentence with the appropriate word.

1. From high up in the ship's __(rigging)__ , the sailor shouted, "Land!"
2. The sailors worked to __(furl)__ the sails and put them away.
3. The fox puppies __(huddled)__ in their winter den.
4. On a clear night you can see a __(vast)__ number of stars.
5. Up in the attic I could see the __(beams)__ that held the roof.
6. The monster in the movie __(lurked)__ behind the buildings.
7. The farmer rode his horse 20 miles to the __(settlement)__ .

FLUENCY BUILDER Use *Intervention Practice Book* page 103. Read aloud each of the words in the first column and have students repeat it. Then have partners read the words to each other. Repeat with the remaining columns. After partners have read aloud each column, have them read the entire list and time themselves.

INTERVENTION PRACTICE BOOK

page 103

(Focus Skill) **Connotation and Denotation**

PRETEACH the skill. Explain that the words in a passage can tell a lot about the feelings and ideas the author wants to share. The feelings and ideas words carry can tell more than just the dictionary meanings do. Have students look at **side A of Skill Card 26: Connotation and Denotation.** Ask volunteers to read the definitions and the explanation aloud.

Then call attention to the chart. Discuss how the words that mean "interested" carry different feelings and ideas. Ask:

- **What feelings do you have about the *curious* neighbor?** (Possible response: Positive feelings; he or she wonders about others.)

- **What feelings do you have about the *nosy* neighbor?** (Possible response: Negative feelings; he or she seems like a troublemaker or a busybody.)

Continue through the chart for the other words. Then help students compare the feelings they have from the sentences using the word *thin*.

Prepare to Read: "Across the Wide Dark Sea"

Preview. Tell students that they are going to read a selection called "Across the Wide Dark Sea." Explain that this is historical fiction, or a story set in the past. In this case the story is based on a real event, but the author has made up surrounding events and characters.

DISTANT VOYAGES
pages 602–617

- **Pages 602–603:** When I see the illustration of the old ship with huge sails, I can tell that the story is set in the past. I think it will be about explorers or about settlers coming across the sea to America.

- **Pages 604–607:** This picture shows a family waving good-bye from a ship. The people look a little sad, so maybe they are going away forever. On the next page the people are inside the ship, but it looks crowded and not very comfortable.

- **Pages 608–611:** It looks like there is a storm on the sea. I think the boy is safe, though, because I see him on the next page. I think a man gets swept into the sea. I wonder if he is saved or lost.

Set Purpose. Model setting a purpose for reading "Across the Wide Dark Sea."

MODEL I want to read this story to find out why the boy's family takes the trip and how they start a new home.

Reread and Summarize

Have students reread and summarize "Across the Wide Dark Sea" in sections, as described in the chart below.

Pages 602–605

Let's reread pages 602-605 to recall the characters and the beginning of the trip.

Summary: A family leaves its home to go to a new land. They board a ship and wave good-bye to their friends.

Pages 606–609

As we reread pages 606-609, let's recall the start of the trip.

Summary: The ship is very crowded with other people and their belongings. One day they hit a storm.

Pages 610–611

When we reread pages 610-611, let's notice what life is like and what scary thing happens.

Summary: People spend the days trying to sleep and stay dry and eating simple meals. A man is washed into the sea but is saved.

Pages 612–613

Let's reread pages 612-613 to recall the big problem.

Summary: The ship begins to leak, but the sailors repair it. After many long weeks at sea, someone finally sees land.

Pages 614–615

Reread pages 614-615 to recall the arrival on land.

Summary: The ship enters a bay, and some men row to shore to see what is there. When they come back, everyone goes to shore.

Pages 616–617

Reread the end of the story to find out what happens on land.

The people find fresh food and wash their clothes. As winter comes, the people find a good place to build a settlement.

FLUENCY BUILDER Reuse *Intervention Practice Book* page 103. Call attention to the sentences at the bottom of the page. State that the goal is to have each student read each phrase smoothly. Model the appropriate pace, expression, and phrasing as you read aloud each of the sentences. Then have students practice reading aloud each sentence two or three times to a partner.

INTERVENTION PRACTICE BOOK

page 103

Directed Reading: "A Safe Harbor" pp. 206–212

Making Connections *pages 620–621*

Page 206

Read aloud the title of the story, and preview the illustrations with the students. Explain that this story is a work of historical fiction: it is a made-up story based on an event that really happened. Read aloud page 206 as students follow along. Ask: **Which real person is mentioned in the story?** (*Christopher Columbus*) **IMPORTANT DETAILS**

TAKE FLIGHT pp. 206–212

Page 207

Ask students to read page 207 to find out whether Manolo gets to sail with Christopher Columbus. Ask: **How does it happen that Manolo gets to sail with Columbus?** (*His father is hired as a cook on the ship, and Manolo gets to go along to help.*) **MAIN IDEA**

Ask: **Why do you think Mamá doesn't want Manolo to go on the voyage?** (*Possible response: She is worried that the trip will be dangerous.*) **SUMMARIZE**

Page 208

Call on volunteers to read page 208 aloud. Ask: **What does Manolo do on the ship?** (*Possible response: He helps Papá cook, scrubs the deck, ties and unties ropes, and carries buckets of water.*) **SUMMARIZE**

Ask: **How can you tell by the author's use of the word *teased* that the sailors are being friendly and not cruel?** (*Possible response: Teasing has the connotation of good-natured and friendly joking. If the sailors had been cruel or mean, the author might have used* picked on, tormented, *or* harassed.) (Focus Skill) **DENOTATION/CONNOTATION**

Page 209

Read page 209 aloud, and ask students to use the details to form mental pictures of the storm. Model using the strategy Create Mental Images:

> MODEL The lively details about the storm help me picture it in my mind. I can imagine the water flooding the deck and the ship tipping wildly back and forth. I can picture the gust of wind that almost tips the boat over. These mental pictures help me understand how dangerous the storm is. (Focus Strategy) **CREATE MENTAL IMAGES**

Page 210

Ask students to read page 210 to find out who saves the ship. Ask: **Who saves the ship?** (*Manolo*) **MAIN IDEA**

Ask: **What does he do that no one else on the ship will do?** (*He is the only person brave enough to climb the rigging and lower the sails.*) **MAKE COMPARISONS**

Page 211

Read aloud page 211, and ask students to think about how Manolo feels. Ask: **How would you feel if Columbus had thanked you for saving the ship?** (*Possible response: I would feel proud and would remember the day forever.*) **IDENTIFY WITH CHARACTERS**

Summarize the selection. Ask students to discuss what happens during Manolo's voyage with Columbus and what Manolo learns. Then have them summarize the story in two or three sentences.

Page 212

INTERVENTION PRACTICE BOOK

page 105

Answers to *Think About It* Questions

1. Manolo saves the *Santa María* and its crew when he climbs the mast and lowers the sails during a storm. **SUMMARY**

2. Possible response: No, because the teasing was just in fun. It had not discouraged Manolo. **INTERPRETATION**

3. Responses will vary but should be written in the first person, from the point of view of Manolo's father. They should describe the storm and Manolo's actions. **WRITE A DIARY ENTRY**

AFTER

Skill Review
pages 622–623

USE SKILL CARD 26B

(Focus Skill) Connotation and Denotation

RETEACH **the skill.** Have students look at **side B of Skill Card 26: Connotation and Denotation.** Read the skill reminder aloud. Have volunteers read aloud the example paragraph, and then discuss the feelings they have about the underlined words. (Possible responses for the first sentence: I have a good feeling about the words *very best friend*, because it's nice to be good friends with someone. The words *moved away* give me a sad feeling.)

Direct students' attention to the numbered sentences, and make sure they understand the directions. As students copy the chart, tell them to add as many rows as there are underlined words. Have dictionaries available for the denotations. The first word is already done as an example.

FLUENCY BUILDER Reuse *Intervention Practice Book* page 103. Explain that each student will practice the sentences at the bottom of the page by reading them aloud on tape. Assign new partners, and have them take turns reading the sentences aloud to each other and then on tape. After students listen to the tape, have them tell how they have improved their reading. Then have them tape themselves again, focusing on improved pacing and tone.

INTERVENTION PRACTICE BOOK

page 103

Writing: Two-Line Rhymes

Build on prior knowledge. Tell students that they will identify rhyming words and write two-line rhyming poems. Help students brainstorm rhyming words. If necessary, have students refer to their spelling books or Reading Logs for word lists or to "Across the Wide Dark Sea" or "A Safe Harbor" for ideas. Display their suggestions on the board.

Construct the text. "Share the pen" with students in a collaborative writing effort. As students dictate lines, write them on the board or on chart paper. Guide the process by making suggestions as needed. Here are four examples based on "Across the Wide Dark Sea."

> **I held on to my father's hand**
> **As we left for the unknown land.**
>
> **When one of the beams began to crack,**
> **The sailors used an iron jack.**
>
> **A sailor said, "There's land ahead,"**
> **So onto shore the rowboat sped.**
>
> **We went ashore, and now we'll stay**
> **So we can worship our own way.**

Revisit the text. Go back and reread each two-line poem with students. Ask them to notice whether each line in the couplet has the same rhythm. Ask: **How can you make the rhythm, or beat, of both lines the same?** (*Possible answer*: *change verbs; reorder some of the words; add descriptions*)

- Guide students to notice the rhythms they have used. For example, underline accented syllables, use colored chalk to write the different syllables, or help students clap the rhythm.

- Help students review the adjectives and verbs. Ask questions such as these: **What stronger or more vivid verb can we use? How can we make this description come alive? What detail can we add to appeal to the sense of sight, hearing, taste, smell, or touch?**

- Have each student choose a couplet to read aloud alone or with you.

On Your Own

Have students write three or four two-line rhyming poems of their own. The rhymes may be serious or silly. Ask volunteers to share their rhymes with the class.

Connect Spelling and Phonics

RETEACH prefixes *un-, re-, dis-*. Write the words *undone*, *reread*, and *dislike* on the board, and draw students' attention to them. Then dictate the words below, and have students write them. After they write each word, display the correct spelling so students can proofread their work.

I. distaste   2. reheated   3. unmatched   4. unsteady*

5. unsafe*   6. disliked*   7. unhappy*   8. repay*

*Word appears in "A Safe Harbor."

Dictate the following sentences, and have students write them: *I was displeased with Nan. She would not repay the cash I had loaned her. Nan was unreliable.*

Build and Read Longer Words

Write *dissatisfied* on the board. Tell students that when breaking a word with a prefix, the letters of the prefix stay together. Point to *dissatisfied*, and ask students which part of the word stands for the /dis/ sound, which part stands for the /sat/ sound, which part stands for the /əs/ sound, and which part stands for the /fīd/ sound. Make sure students understand that the prefix forms the first syllable of the word. Then ask them to read these words and explain how they figured them out: *unrewarded, recaptured, reunited, distasteful, unbelievable, disenchanted.*

INTERVENTION
ASSESSMENT
BOOK

FLUENCY BUILDER Have students choose a passage from "A Safe Harbor" to read aloud to a partner. You may have students choose passages they found particularly interesting or you can have them choose one of the following options:

- Read pages 207–208. (From *Papá was hired* . . . through . . . *vast blue sea*. Total: 136 words.)

- Read pages 209–210. (From *One day a* . . . through . . . *as a monkey*. Total: 132 words.)

Ask students to read the selection aloud to their partners three times. Have students rate their own readings on a scale of 1–4. Encourage students to note their improvement from one reading to the next by completing the sentence *I know my reading has improved because* _____ . Encourage listeners to offer positive feedback about improvements.

Review Vocabulary

To revisit the Vocabulary Words prior to the weekly assessment, use these sentence frames. Read the statements aloud, and ask students to write the answers. Then discuss why the answers are correct.

1. The sailor climbed high up into the ship's **rigging** to
   a. check on the sails. b. eat dinner.

2. At sunset, the man would **furl** the flag and
   a. let it flutter. b. put it away folded.

3. The kittens were **huddled** in a basket. They looked like
   a. they were climbing out. b. a ball of fur.

4. The astronaut has a **vast** knowledge of rockets. She knows
   a. a couple of facts. b. a great deal about them.

5. The **beams** that support a ship are used as
   a. lights. b. part of the frame.

6. The little boy was afraid of what he thought **lurked**
   a. under his bed. b. on the kitchen table.

7. The pioneer **settlement** was a place where people
   a. boarded ships. b. built their homes.

Correct responses: 1a, 2b, 3b, 4b, 5b, 6a, 7b

This is a good time to show the Vocabulary Words and definitions on page 259. Have students copy them to use for studying for the vocabulary test.

Review Connotation and Denotation

INTERVENTION PRACTICE BOOK

page 106

To review connotation and denotation before the weekly assessment, use *Intervention Practice Book* page 106. Have volunteers read the first three items aloud and suggest answers.

Ask a volunteer to read aloud the paragraph from "A Safe Harbor." Then work through the four examples with students. Have dictionaries available for students.

Review Test Prep

INTERVENTION ASSESSMENT BOOK

✔

Ask students to turn to page 623 of the *Pupil Edition*. Point out the tips for answering the test questions. Tell students that paying attention to these tips can help them answer these and other test questions. Remind students to read true-or-false statements carefully before they answer.

DISTANT VOYAGES

page 623

Self-Selected Reading

Encourage students to select their own books to read on their own. They may choose books from your classroom library shelf or you may select a group of appropriate books from which your students can choose.

- *The Stowaway.* (See page 623M of the *Teacher's Edition* for a lesson plan.)

- *How Many Days to America?* by Eve Bunting. Clarion, 1998.

- *How My Family Lives in America* by Susan Kuklin. Simon & Schuster, 1992.

After students have chosen their books, give each student a copy of My Reading Log, found on page R38 in the back of the *Teacher's Edition*. Have each student fill in the information at the top of the form. Then have students use the log to keep track of their reading and to record their responses to the literature.

Conduct student-teacher conferences. Arrange for an individual conference time with each student when you can discuss his or her self-selected reading. Have students bring their Reading Logs to share during the conference. You may also want to have the student choose a favorite passage to read aloud to you. Then ask questions designed to stimulate discussion. For example, you might question what information the student learned from a nonfiction text, how the author structured the text, or how the artwork helped the student understand the topic.

FLUENCY PERFORMANCE Have students read aloud to you the passage from "A Safe Harbor" they have selected and practiced previously with their partners. Keep track of the number of words each student reads correctly. Ask each student to rate his or her performance on the 1–4 scale. If students aren't happy with their oral reading, give them an opportunity to practice some more and to reread the passage to you.

See *Oral Reading Fluency Assessment* for monitoring progress.

Use with

"Name This American"

Review Phonics: Suffixes *-ly*, *-ful*, *-able*, *-less*

Identify the meanings. Have students repeat the following sentence aloud twice: *Sandy said loudly that the bike was fixable.* Ask: **What does loudly mean?** (*"in a way that is loud"*) Ask: **What does fixable mean?** (*"able to be fixed"*) Then have students repeat this sentence twice: *I'm hopeful of a painless visit to the dentist.* Ask: **Which word means "full of hope"?** (*hopeful*) Ask: **Which word means "free of pain"?** (*painless.*)

Associate suffixes to meanings. Write the sentences from above on the board. Explain that a suffix is a word part that is added to the end of a word and that changes the word's meaning. Explain that the suffix *-ly* means "in a way that is" and that *loudly* means "in a way that is loud." Follow a similar procedure for the suffixes *-able* ("able to be"), *-ful* ("full of" or "with"), and *-less* ("without").

Apply the skill. *Suffix Addition* Write each of the following words on the board, and have students read it aloud. Then make the changes necessary to form the words in parentheses. Have a volunteer read aloud each new word. Try to give every student an opportunity to respond.

delight (delightful)   **read** (readable)   **fear** (fearless)
safe (safely)   **help** (helpful)   **treat** (treatable)

Introduce Vocabulary

PRETEACH **lesson vocabulary.** Tell students that they are going to learn eight new words that they will see again when they read "Name This American." Teach each vocabulary word using the following process.

Use the following suggestions or similar ideas to give the meaning or context.

guarantee	The store's guarantee means that you can take its products back if you don't like them.
distinguished	The men shown on our money are great and distinguished leaders.
stumps	If a problem in your math book stumps you, ask your teacher for help.
misleading	The advertisements showing a flying bicycle are misleading.

> Write the word.
> Say the word.
> Track the word and have students repeat it.
> Give the meaning or context.

indebted	Americans are indebted to people who have fought for freedom.
interpreter	We needed an interpreter to understand the man who spoke Greek.
suffrage	The women's suffrage movement helped women gain the right to vote.
anthem	Our national anthem is "The Star-Spangled Banner."

For vocabulary activities, see Vocabulary Games on pp. 2–7.

AFTER

Building Background and Vocabulary

Apply Vocabulary Strategies

Use affixes and roots. Write the word *misleading* on the board and read it aloud. Remind students that they can sometimes figure out the meaning of an unfamiliar word by breaking it into its root, prefix, and suffix.

MODEL I see the word *lead* in the middle of this word, and I know that *lead* means "to show the way." Then I see the prefix *mis-*, and I think it means "wrong." I think the entire word has to do with giving wrong ideas about something.

RETEACH lesson vocabulary. Be sure each student has a set of vocabulary cards. Read aloud the following sentences, saying "blank" for each blank. Then ask students to hold up the correct word card.

1. The __(interpreter)__ translated for each of our guests.
2. We sang the national __(anthem)__ at the beginning of the game.
3. The __(distinguished)__ scientist had won many honors.
4. "There is no __(guarantee)__ for this car," the salesman said.
5. My great-grandmother worked for women's __(suffrage)__.
6. The __(misleading)__ ad seemed to promise sparkling teeth.
7. This riddle __(stumps)__ me, so I need help.
8. We are __(indebted)__ to our parents for their love and care.

FLUENCY BUILDER Use *Intervention Practice Book* page 107. Read aloud each of the words in the first column and have students repeat it. Then partners read the words to each other. Repeat with the remaining columns. Then have them practice reading the entire list while timing themselves.

INTERVENTION PRACTICE BOOK

page 107

★ Focus Skill — Cause and Effect

PRETEACH the skill. Point out that understanding causes and effects is a skill that helps readers understand why things happen. Have students look at **side A of Skill Card 27: Cause and Effect.** Ask a volunteer to read the explanation aloud. Then direct students' attention to the illustration. Ask:

- **What is a different effect that could happen?** (Possible response: The boy could stumble but not fall.)

- **What could have caused the boy to fall?** (Possible response: Someone could have pushed him.)

Ask volunteers to read the text at the bottom of the card. Discuss other possible causes and effects of the things in the list. For example, melting snow can cause the rivers to overflow; many days of rain can ruin crops.

Prepare to Read: "Name This American"

Preview. Tell students that they will read "Name This American," a play. Remind students that plays are written to be performed. Explain that this play tells about some famous Americans. Then preview the play.

- **Pages 626–627:** I see the illustration of Uncle Sam. I think that in this selection I am going to learn about American history, and I think it will be in a fun format.

DISTANT VOYAGES
pages
626–639

- **Pages 628–629:** The illustration on these two pages is very interesting. Uncle Sam is in the middle. There is a man with a beard, who is dressed from some earlier time. On the right are three young people, one with her hand up. This looks like a quiz show with Uncle Sam as the host. I wonder who that other man is.

- **Pages 630–631:** I know this is an illustration of Mount Rushmore. I don't know who the man in front is. He seems to have a jackhammer, so I wonder if he was involved in creating the carvings on Mount Rushmore.

Set Purpose. Model setting a purpose for reading "Name This American."

MODEL I want to read this play to find out who these historic people are. I also want to perform the play on stage.

Reread and Summarize

Have students reread and summarize "Name This American" in sections, as described in the chart below.

Pages 626–629

Let's reread pages 626–629 to see who is in the play and how it begins.

Summary: Uncle Sam has eight guests on a quiz show, but I recognize the names of only some of them. The panelists ask questions and learn that the first guest is Walter Hunt, inventor of the safety pin.

Pages 630–633

Let's reread to find out who the next three guests are.

Summary: Panelists ask questions of the next three guests and find out that they are Gutzon Borglum, sculptor of Mount Rushmore; Maria Mitchell, an astronomer who discovered a new comet; and Dolley Madison, wife of the fourth President, James Madison.

Pages 634–635

Let's reread to find out about the fifth guest.

Summary: Panelists discover that the fifth guest is Sacajewea, the Native American guide and interpreter for the Lewis and Clark expedition.

Pages 636–639

Reread pages 636–639 to remember the last three guests.

Summary: Panelists find that two guests are Elizabeth Cady Stanton, who worked toward women's suffrage, and the baseball legend Babe Ruth. The final guest is Queen Liliuokalani, of Hawaii.

FLUENCY BUILDER Reuse *Intervention Practice Book* page 107. Call attention to the sentences at the bottom of the page. State that the goal is to have each student read each phrase smoothly. Model the appropriate pace, expression, and phrasing as you read aloud each of the sentences. Then have students practice reading aloud each sentence two or three times to a partner.

INTERVENTION PRACTICE BOOK

page 107

Directed Reading: "The Mystery Guest," pp. 214–221

TAKE FLIGHT
pages
214–221

Pages 214–215

Read aloud the title of the story. Discuss the conventions of a play. Have students read pages 214 and 215 silently. Ask: **Who are the characters?** (*Lucretia Mott, James Mott, Beth, Harriet Tubman, three or four escaped slaves*) **IMPORTANT DETAILS**

If necessary, tell students that Harriet Tubman was a real person who risked her life to help slaves escape to freedom. Ask: **Where and when does the play take place?** (*at the Mott home in Pennsylvania, in 1850*) **IMPORTANT DETAILS**

Page 216

Read page 216 aloud as students follow along. Then have volunteers reread the characters' dialogue aloud. Ask: **Why do you think Lucretia keeps the guest's identity a secret?** (*Possible response: It may be dangerous for a young girl to know who the guest is.*) **SPECULATE**

Page 217

Read page 217 aloud as students follow along. Ask: **How does James feel about Beth's becoming involved in the plans?** (*He is upset.*) **CHARACTERS' EMOTIONS**

Ask: **What do you think James will do in the cellar?** (*Possible response: Perhaps he will get food for the guest.*) **SPECULATE**

Page 218

Call on volunteers to read aloud page 218. Remind students to follow the stage directions, too. Ask: **Why do you think Lucretia is making food bundles?** (*Possible response: Perhaps the guest is hungry and needs to eat in secret.*) **SPECULATE**

Page 219

Read page 219 aloud, and ask students to predict what will happen after Lucretia, Beth, and James put the food outside for the guests. Model using the strategy Make and Confirm Predictions.

> **MODEL** I read that the three characters put the food outside for the guests. Now I wonder what will happen next. Lucretia and James have made such careful and secret plans that I think the guest will come to eat the food safely. I will read the last page of the play to find if I am right. (*Focus Strategy*) **MAKE AND CONFIRM PREDICTIONS**

Page 220

Read aloud page 220. Ask: **Who is the distinguished guest?** (*Harriet Tubman*) **IMPORTANT DETAILS**

Ask: **What do you think causes Lucretia and James to help this guest? What is the effect of their helping the guest?** (*Possible response: Lucretia and James want to help slaves escape. The effect is that it helps Harriet Tubman lead the escaped slaves to freedom.*) (*Focus Skill*) **CAUSE AND EFFECT**

Summarize the selection. Ask students to discuss how Lucretia and James get ready for the mysterious guest and how Beth helps. Then have students summarize the play in two or three sentences.

Answers to *Think About It* Questions

1. The mystery guest is Harriet Tubman. She and the escaped slaves must stay hidden, so they are going to stay in the cellar. **SUMMARY**

2. Possible response: She slips out because she wants to see who the mystery guest is. When Beth sees Harriet Tubman, she is probably excited. **INTERPRETATION**

3. Responses will vary but should be written in play format. They should present a discussion of the previous night's events and perhaps plans for activities to come. **WRITE A SCENE**

(Focus Skill) Cause and Effect

RETEACH **the skill.** Have students look at **side B of Skill Card 27: Cause and Effect.** Ask a student to read aloud the first two sentences. Then ask for a second volunteer to read the next two. Tell students to copy the charts onto their own papers.

Read the cause in the first set of boxes. Ask students to write a possible effect. Ask a volunteer to read his or her answer. (Possible response: *the car hits another car.*) Point out that a cause may have more than one effect. Ask for another possible effect. (Possible response: *a police officer will stop the driver and issue a ticket.*)

Read the effect in the next set of boxes, and ask students to fill in a cause explaining what made the electricity go out. (Possible response: *Lightning hit an electric pole nearby.*) Allow students to suggest alternative causes. Have students fill in the rest of the boxes on their own.

FLUENCY BUILDER Reuse *Intervention Practice Book* page 107. Explain that each student will practice the sentences at the bottom of the page by reading them aloud on tape. Assign new partners, and have them take turns reading the sentences aloud to each other and then on tape. After students listen to the tape, have them tell how they have improved their reading. Then have them tape themselves again, focusing on improved pacing and tone.

Various Forms: Vivid Sentences

Build on prior knowledge. Tell students that they will work with you to change ordinary sentences into ones that are vivid and lively. Write on the board a few sentences such as these based on "The Mystery Guest."

> We will take the food outside.
>
> We will put the bundles by the woodshed.
>
> We can see without a light.

Construct the text. "Share the pen" with students in a collaborative writing effort. First, help students brainstorm vivid verbs, adjectives, and nouns that could be added or substituted. As students suggest words and phrases to add, write them on the board or on chart paper. Guide the process by making suggestions as needed. For example:

1. We will sneak this mouth-watering food outside.
2. We will tuck the bundles around the stacks of wood.
3. The full moon will help us see without a lantern.

Revisit the text. Go back and reread the sentences with students. Discuss the various words that were added and the effect they have on the sentences. Ask: **Why is it more interesting to say *mouth-watering food*?** (Possible response: It appeals to our sense of taste.)

- Guide students to revise any sets of sentences that begin in the same way, such as sentences 1 and 2 above. Ask: **How can we change one of these sentences so they don't begin in the same way?** (Possible response: Begin by saying *First* and *Next*; begin one with *Let's* and the other with *Now*.)

- Guide students to check their sentences for correct spelling, capitalization, and punctuation.

- Read the sentences aloud with students.

On Your Own

Ask students to look through a selection of their choice to find at least three ordinary sentences that they would like to revise. Remind students to replace ordinary verbs, adjectives, and nouns with vivid words.

Connect Spelling and Phonics

RETEACH suffixes *-ly, -ful, -able, -less.* Write the words *fairly, wishful, returnable,* and *toothless* on the board, and remind students that they have learned words with the suffixes *-ly, -ful, -able,* and *-less.* Then dictate the following words, and have students write them. After each word, display the correct spelling for students to proofread against.

1. **quietly***   2. **grateful***   3. **careful***   4. **assuredly***

5. **suitable***   6. **comfortable***   7. **useful***   8. **careless***

***Word appears in "The Mystery Guest."**

Dictate the following sentence, and have students write it: *The watchful teacher quickly grabbed the breakable vase before the careless student could drop it.*

Build and Read Longer Words

INTERVENTION
ASSESSMENT
BOOK

Write these words on the board: *restful, weightless, secretly,* and *laughable.* Explain to students that the letters of a suffix stay together when the word is broken into syllables. Point to *restful,* and ask students which part of the word stands for /rest/ and which part stands for /fəl/. Follow a similar procedure with the other words. Then have students read the following words: *suspiciously, excitedly, dutiful, plentiful, recyclable, reusable, shameless,* and *boundless.*

FLUENCY BUILDER Have students choose a passage from "The Mystery Guest" to read aloud to a partner. You may have students choose passages they found particularly interesting, or have them choose one of the following options:

- Page 216. (From *Lucretia and her . . .* through *. . . behind the door.* Total: 146 words)

- Page 220. (From *Now it's time . . .* through *. . . whispers along.* Total: 151 words)

Ask students to read the selection aloud to their partners three times. Have students rate their own readings on a scale of 1 to 4. Encourage students to note their improvement from one reading to the next by completing the sentence *I know my reading has improved because _____.* Encourage listeners to offer positive feedback about improvements.

Review Vocabulary

To revisit the Vocabulary Words prior to the weekly assessment, use these sentence frames. Read each statement aloud, and ask students to write the answers. Go over the answers, and discuss why they are correct.

1. The owner of the bike shop can **guarantee** that my bike
   a. will last 25 years. b. will be beautiful.

2. The judge in the courtroom looked **distinguished** and
   a. important. b. messy.

3. If it **stumps** you how to start your research report, you should
   a. get some advice. b. not say anything

4. I followed the **misleading** instructions, and my model looked
   a. perfect. b. all wrong.

5. The hungry man was **indebted** to us for
   a. not helping b. giving him food.

6. I need an **interpreter** to understand someone who speaks
   a. my language. b. another language.

7. The **suffrage** movement was all about getting people the
   a. right to vote. b. right to pray.

8. The Pledge of Allegiance is spoken, and the national **anthem** is
   a. shouted. b. sung.

Correct responses: lb, 2a, 3a, 4b, 5b, 6b, 7a, 8b

This is a good time to show the Vocabulary Words and definitions on page 269. Have students copy them to use for studying for the vocabulary test.

Cause and Effect

To review cause and effect before the weekly assessment, use *Intervention Practice Book* page 110. Call attention to the title Cause and Effect. Have volunteers read aloud the sentences and fill in the blanks. Allow one sentence per volunteer.

Direct students' attention to the next section. Mention that these refer to "The Mystery Guest." Guide students through the items, and have volunteers share their answers.

INTERVENTION PRACTICE BOOK

page 110

Review Test Prep

Ask students to turn to page 647 of the *Pupil Edition*. Point out the tips for answering the test questions. Tell students that paying attention to these tips can help them answer these and other test questions.

INTERVENTION ASSESSMENT BOOK

DISTANT VOYAGES

page 647

Have students follow along as you read aloud the passage and the tips. Point out that focusing on the cause and then the effect will help them answer the questions.

Self-Selected Reading

Encourage students to select their own books to read on their own. They may choose books from your classroom library shelf, or you may select a group of appropriate books from which your students can choose.

- *Susan B. Anthony.* (See page 647M of the *Teacher's Edition* for a lesson plan.)

- *Rooftop Astronomer: A Story About Maria Mitchell* by Stephanie Sammartino. Carolrhoda, 1990.

- *Why Don't You Get a Horse, Sam Adams?* by Jean Fritz. Coward-McCann, 1974.

After students have chosen their books, give each student a copy of My Reading Log, found on page R38 in the back of the Teacher's Edition. Have each student fill in the information at the top of the form. Then have students use the log to keep track of their reading and to record their responses to the literature.

Conduct student-teacher conferences. Arrange for an individual conference time with each student when you can discuss his or her self-selected reading. Have students bring their Reading Logs to share during the conference. You may also want to have students choose a favorite passage to read aloud to you. Then ask questions designed to stimulate discussion. For example, you might question what information the student learned from a nonfiction text, how the author structured the text, or how the artwork helped the student understand the topic.

FLUENCY PERFORMANCE Have students read aloud to you the passage from "The Mystery Guest" they have selected and practiced previously with their partners. Keep track of the number of words the student reads correctly. Ask each student to rate his or her performance on the 1–4 scale. If students aren't happy with their oral reading, give them an opportunity to practice some more and to reread the passage to you.

See *Oral Reading Fluency Assessment* for monitoring progress.

Use with

"What's the Big Idea, Ben Franklin?"

Review: Prefixes *im-, non-, pre-*

Identify the meaning. Have students repeat the following sentence aloud two times: *Nick found it impossible to put down the new nonfiction book about prehistoric animals.* Ask: **What does** *impossible* **mean?** (*not possible*) **What word means "not fiction"?** (*nonfiction*) Have a volunteer identify the word that means "before recorded history." (*prehistoric*)

Associate prefixes to meanings. Write on the board *Nick found it impossible to put down the new nonfiction book about prehistoric animals.* Explain that a prefix is a word part that is added to the beginning of a word and that changes its meaning. Underline the prefixes in the words in which they appear. Then use *impossible* to explain how a prefix changes the meaning of the word. Cover up *im-*, and ask a volunteer to identify the word that remains. (*possible*) Then cover up the word *possible*, and have a volunteer identify the prefix. Explain that this prefix means "the opposite of" or "not" and that *impossible* means "not possible." Repeat the procedure for *non-* and *pre-*.

INTERVENTION PRACTICE BOOK

page 112

Apply the skill. *Prefix Addition* Write the following words on the board and have students read each aloud. Make the changes necessary to form the words in parentheses. Have a volunteer read aloud each new word.

heat (preheat)   **stop** (nonstop)   **perfect** (imperfect)   **pay** (repay)
fat (nonfat)   **patient** (impatient)   **set** (reset)   **polite** (impolite)

Introduce Vocabulary

PRETEACH **lesson vocabulary.** Tell students they are going to learn six new words that they will see again when they read a story called "What's the Big Idea, Ben Franklin?" Teach each Vocabulary Word using the process shown in the box.

Use the following suggestions or similar ideas to give the meaning or context.

honors	Relate to ways your school recognizes student achievements.
contraption	Tell students that the first cars were called contraptions by the people who didn't understand how they worked.
edition	Explain that changes and corrections are made to one edition of the book before the next one is published.
repeal	Make up a rule and then tell students you have repealed it.

> Write the word.
> Say the word.
> Track the word and have students repeat it.
> Give the meaning or context.

suspended	Point out an object in your classroom that is suspended from something.
treaty	Explain that the governments of England and the United States signed an agreement called a treaty to end the war in which we won independence.

For vocabulary activities, see Vocabulary Games on pp. 2–7.

Vocabulary Words

honors glory, reputation, or credit for fine or heroic acts

contraption an odd or puzzling device or gadget

edition the total of all copies of a book published at the same time and printed from the same plates

repeal to cancel

suspended hung by a support from above

treaty a formal agreement between two or more countries in reference to peace or other matters

AFTER

Building Background and Vocabulary

Apply Vocabulary Strategies

Use context. Write *almanac* on the board and read it aloud. Tell students that they can sometimes figure out the meaning of a word by using context.

Ask students to listen carefully as you read these sentences aloud: *Every family bought an almanac each year. People read it to find out the holidays, the weather forecast, the schedule of tides, the time the sun came up and went down, when the moon would be full, when to plant what.*

> **MODEL** I'm not sure what *almanac* means, so I look for clues in the other words and sentences around it. The second sentence tells me what people used an almanac for, and this gives me its meaning: "a book published each year and containing useful information."

RETEACH **lesson vocabulary.** Provide a set of word cards for each student. Write on the board the meaning of one of the Vocabulary Words and the first letter in that word. Students match the correct word card to the definition. Continue until students have matched all the words.

FLUENCY BUILDER Use *Intervention Practice Book* page 111. Read aloud each of the words in the first column and have students repeat it. Then have students work in pairs and take turns reading the words to each other. Follow the same procedure with each of the remaining columns. After each partner has had a turn reading aloud the words in each column, have students time themselves as they practice reading the entire list.

INTERVENTION PRACTICE BOOK

page 111

BEFORE

Reading "What's
the Big Idea, Ben
Franklin?"
pages 650–667

USE SKILL CARD 28A

(Focus Skill) Connotation and Denotation

PRETEACH the skill. Point out that understanding connotation and denotation will help students create stronger mental images of the characters and events in a selection. Have students look at **side A of Skill Card 28: Connotation and Denotation.** Ask a volunteer to read the explanation aloud.

Ask a student to read the first box on the left. Ask: **When you hear** *said* **what do you think of? How does the person feel?** (Possible response: *You can't tell.*) Point out the first box on the right. Mention that we know that *said* means *talked.* That is the denotation. It doesn't give you any emotional clues about the speaker.

Continue with the other versions of the sentence, leading the students to realize how the use of *pleaded* or *demanded* give entirely different mental images.

Prepare to Read: "What's the Big Idea, Ben Franklin?"

Preview. Tell students that they are going to read a selection called "What's the Big Idea, Ben Franklin?" Explain that this is a biography, the story of someone's life and why this person was important.

DISTANT VOYAGES
pages
650–667

- **Pages 650–651:** I notice a man flying a kite. Then I notice the title and the author's name. I think I will be finding out about Ben Franklin and why he is flying a kite.

- **Pages 652–657:** I can tell from the clothing in these pictures that this takes place long ago. I see a lot of people reading the same little book, Ben Franklin sitting on the ground, a man in a little house on top of a tower, and a stagecoach. I am curious as to how all these relate.

- **Pages 658–664:** The illustration on pages 658 and 659 shows how Franklin dressed and what his room looked like. The illustration of men talking on pages 660 makes me think these pages might be about some of the things he did for our government.

- **Pages 664–667:** On page 666 Franklin is in bed and being taken care of by a maid. I wonder how long he lived and how he felt about his life when he was old.

Set Purpose. Model setting a purpose for reading "What's the Big Idea, Ben Franklin?"

MODEL One purpose for reading a biography is to find out more about a particular person. I'll read to get an idea of what Ben Franklin was like as a person.

Reread and Summarize

Have students reread and summarize "What's the Big Idea, Ben Franklin?" in sections, as described in the chart below.

Pages 652–653

Let's look again at pages 652–653 to remember what Benjamin Franklin did at the beginning of his life.

Summary: Franklin publishes an almanac that includes his proverbs. He sells many copies of the book and does this for twenty-five years.

Pages 654–657

As we read pages 654–657 again, let's recall what happens with Franklin's experiments with electricity and what other important things he did.

Summary: Franklin learns as much as he can about electricity and then tries his own experiments. He knocks himself unconscious once. Then he wants to prove that lightning is electricity.

Franklin uses a key and a kite to prove his idea about lightning. He goes on to do other important things. He was Postmaster General and improved mail service.

Pages 658–661

Let's reread pages 658–661 and see what role Franklin had in the new country of America.

Summary: Franklin goes to England to represent his colony, but he is treated badly. He goes home and finds a war in progress. He helps write the Declaration of Independence.

Page 662–667

Reread pages 662–667 and let's remember that Franklin continued to serve this country in important ways.

Summary: Franklin goes to France to get money to help this country with the war. He becomes very popular there. He is known for eating too much, playing too much, and being messy. He comes back to America and helps write the Constitution.

FLUENCY BUILDER Reuse *Intervention Practice Book* page 111. Call attention to the sentences on the bottom half of the page. State that students' goal will be to read each phrase smoothly. Model appropriate pace, expression, and phrasing as you read aloud each sentence. Then have students practice reading aloud each sentence two or three times to a partner.

INTERVENTION PRACTICE BOOK

page 111

Directed Reading: "Who Was Poor Richard?" pp. 222–229

TAKE FLIGHT
pp. 222–229

Page 222

Ask a volunteer to read aloud the title of the story. Help students identify the colonial American setting in the illustration on page 222. Ask: **What is the family reading?** (*a newspaper*) Have a volunteer read page 222 while other students listen to find out what American colonists read in the early 1700s. **What is an almanac?** (*a book containing calendars, lists of holidays, weather forecasts, and other bits of information*) **NOTE DETAILS**

Page 223

Ask students to read page 223 to find out more about Ben Franklin. Ask: **What is a pen name, and who was Richard Saunders?** (*Possible response: A pen name is a name that an author uses to disguise his or her true identity. Richard Saunders was a name and character made up by Franklin.*) **IMPORTANT DETAILS**

Page 224

Have students read page 224 to find out what the character Richard Saunders was like. **What was Poor Richard's reason for starting an almanac?** (*Possible response: His wife was nagging him to do something useful, and they needed the money.*) **CHARACTERS' MOTIVATIONS**

Page 225

Ask volunteers to read the proverbs on page 225. Ask: **What is a proverb?** (*Possible response: a short, humorous saying that gives advice*) **DRAW CONCLUSIONS**

Page 226

Read page 226 aloud. Ask students to listen to find out more about the history of *Poor Richard's Almanak*. Ask: **How do you know that *Poor Richard's Almanak* was popular with colonial Americans?** (*Possible response: The author says on page 224 that the book was an immediate hit. On page 225 the author says that the proverbs brought nods and smiles from readers.*) **SYNTHESIZE**

Page 227

Ask students why people were afraid Franklin might hide a joke in the Declaration of Independence. Model using the strategy of rereading to clarify

> **MODEL** I don't know why anyone would put a joke in an important document like this. I'll go back through the selection to see why someone would worry that Franklin would do it. Now I remember: On page 215 the author refers to Franklin's use of the pen name Richard Saunders as a joke he would keep to himself. The fact that he also wrote funny proverbs says he has a sense of humor. (Focus Strategy) **REREAD TO CLARIFY**

Page 228

INTERVENTION
PRACTICE
BOOK

page 113

Have volunteers read the text and proverbs on page 228. Ask: **How does Franklin make good use of language and meanings of words in his proverbs?** (*Possible response: He uses strong words with connotations that make the writing even more vivid.*) (Focus Strategy) **CONNOTATION/DENOTATION**

Summarize the Selection Ask students to think about events in Ben Franklin's life, including the publishing of *Poor Richard's Almanak*. Have them write a paragraph summarizing his life and contributions.

Answers to *Think About It* Questions

1. Benjamin Franklin used the pen name Richard Saunders to write and publish *Poor Richard's Almanak*, in which he told stories, predicted the weather, and gave advice. **SUMMARY**

2. Accept reasonable responses. Possible response: He knew that people were more likely to read and remember short, humorous sayings than serious statements or long explanations. **INTERPRETATION**

3. Accept reasonable responses. Newspaper articles should explain that the last edition is being published and that it contains a special preface. They should discuss the popularity of all the editions of the almanac and should give some basic information about "Richard Saunders." **WRITE A STORY**

AFTER

Skill Review
pages 674–675

USE SKILL CARD 28B

(Focus Skill) Connotation and Denotation

RETEACH the skill. Have students look at **side B of Skill Card 28: Connotation and Denotation.** Ask a student to read aloud the skill reminder. Point to the boxed word *say* and then to its denotations underneath. Read those aloud. Ask students to look at the list of words. Point out that these words are fairly similar to *say* but that their connotations are different.

Have students read aloud together the list of words on the skill card. Then ask them to work in pairs and, on their own papers, group the ones that have similar connotations. Give the example that *bellow* and *shout* have similar connotations. Provide dictionaries if students need help. (*Answers will vary on these. Possible response*: Bellow, shout, yell, *and* bark *belong together.* Cry *and* scream *belong together.* Answer *and* respond *belong together.* Assert, debate, *and* argue *belong together.* Utter, express, declare, *and* pronounce *belong together.*)

Point out that a writer can use words with different connotations to make his or her writing more vivid. A good reader will think about the connotations of words to understand a deeper meaning of the writing.

FLUENCY BUILDER Use *Intervention Practice Book* page 111. Explain that today each student will practice the sentences on the bottom half of the page by reading them aloud on tape. Assign a new partner for each reader. Have students take turns reading the sentences aloud to each other and then reading them on tape. After students listen to the tape, have each person tell how he or she has improved the reading. Then have students do the activity again, focusing on improved pacing and tone as they read the sentences aloud on tape.

INTERVENTION PRACTICE BOOK

page 111

Expressive Writing: Scene

Build on prior knowledge. Tell students that in this exercise you are going to work together as a group to write a short scene for a play about Benjamin Franklin. The scene will be about Franklin flying his kite.

Remind students that they need to write the directions for where the action will take place—the setting. They also need to determine the plot: the conflict or problem that needs to be solved. Finally, they need to decide who the characters are in addition to Franklin. Suggest a limit of four. Remind students that in this scene they will need to write dialogue for the characters.

Construct the text. Write Setting on the board. Share the pen with students, guiding them to write a sentence describing the setting, offering suggestions and asking questions as needed. Then ask them to tell you to describe the action. (*Possible response: The sky is dark and cloudy and the field has few trees but lots of high grass. Ben Franklin walks out into the middle of the field, carrying a kite and a large spool of kite string.*) Explain that students have written stage directions.

Next, ask students to dictate the dialogue for the scene. Write it in the correct format for a play, pointing this out as you do so. Also mention that they need to write out in sentence or paragraph form any action that happens.

Revisit the text. When you have finished writing the scene as students dictated it, ask them to look over the dialogue and see if everything is spelled correctly.

- Ask: *Have we included stage directions so the actors know what to do or how to speak?*

- *Does this scene tell a story? Is there a problem and a solution to it?*

- Have students take the roles of the various characters to read this aloud.

On Your Own

Ask students to write a script for the scene in which Franklin knocks himself out at the picnic where he is cooking with electricity. Ask them to refer to the story to remind themselves of the details. Have a volunteer present his or her script, with classmates reading the parts of the other characters.

Connect Spelling and Phonics

RETEACH prefixes *im-, non-, pre-*. Have students number a sheet of paper 1 through 8. Dictate the words below, and have students write them. After they write each word, display the correct spelling so students can proofread their work. Have them draw a line through a misspelled word and write the correct spelling beside it.

1. nonfat	2. improper	3. impractical*	4. presuppose
5. impossible*	6. nonsense	7. preschool	8. nonexistent*

*Word appears in "Who Was Poor Richard?"

Dictate the following sentences, and have students write them: *Ashley talked nonstop during the movie previews. Carl told her she was being impolite.*

Build and Read Longer Words

Write these words on the board: *imbalance, nonverbal.* Remind students that in a word with a prefix, the letters of the prefix stay together when the word is broken into syllables. Point to *imbalance*, and ask students which part of the word stands for the /im/ sound, which part stands for the /bal/ sound, and which part stands for the /ən(t)s/ sound. Follow a similar procedure for *nonverbal*, asking students which part of the word stands for the /non/ sound, which part stands for the /vər/ sound, and which part stands for the /bəl/ sound. Then ask them to read these words and explain how they figured them out: *immovable, nonexistent, prepackage, replacement, dissatisfied.* Encourage students to build other longer words with the prefixes *im-, non-,* and *pre-*.

INTERVENTION ASSESSMENT BOOK ✔

FLUENCY BUILDER Have students choose a passage from "Who Was Poor Richard?" to read aloud to a partner. You may have students choose a passage that they found particularly interesting, or you can assign them a particular passage, such as one of these:

- Pages 222–223. (From In the early . . . *through* . . . *Richard Saunders.*) Total: 163 words

- Pages 226–227. (From Ben Franklin . . . *through* . . . *peace treaty.*) Total: 164 words

Ask students to read the selection aloud to their partners three times and to rate their own readings on a scale of 1 to 4. Encourage students to note their improvement from one reading to the next by completing the sentence *I know my reading has improved because* _____. Encourage the listening partner to offer positive feedback about improvements.

Review Vocabulary

To revisit Vocabulary Words prior to weekly assessment, have students listen as you read aloud each of the following sentence beginnings. Call on a volunteer to complete each sentence so that it makes sense. Alternatively, you might write the sentence beginning on the board with the Vocabulary Words underlined, and have volunteers read aloud and complete the sentence.

1. The students who received **honors** at the assembly were _____.

2. When my dad saw the **contraption** we had built, he said _____.

3. Every book that was printed as part of the first **edition** has the same _____.

4. We think the principal should **repeal** the rule against having classroom pets because _____.

5. The mobile was **suspended** from the ceiling by _____.

6. In the **treaty**, both countries agreed that _____.

This is a good time to show the Vocabulary Words and definitions on page 279. Have students copy them to use for studying for the vocabulary test.

Review Connotation and Denotation

To review connotation and denotation before the weekly assessment, use *Intervention Practice Book*, page 114. Call attention to the title, Connotation and Denotation. Have a student read aloud the definitions.

Direct students' attention to the next section. Mention that this is a paragraph from "Who Was Poor Richard?" Go over each underlined word with the class. Ask for volunteers to propose alternative words. Write the words on the board. Ask how the connotation of the suggested alternative word is different from the word it replaces. Try to involve each student in this answer-and-discussion time.

**INTERVENTION
PRACTICE
BOOK**

page 114

Review Test Prep

Ask students to turn to page 675 of the *Pupil Edition*. Point out the tips for answering the test questions. Tell students to pay attention to these tips because they can help them answer not only the test questions on this page but also other test questions like these. Mention to students that when they are asked to read a selection and substitute one word for another, they need to look at the context for clues as to the correct meaning of the word they will be replacing.

**DISTANT
VOYAGES**

page 675

**INTERVENTION
ASSESSMENT
BOOK**

Self-Selected Reading

Have students select their own books to read independently. They may choose books from your classroom library shelf, or you may select a group of appropriate books from which students can choose. Titles might include the following:

- *Wise Men.* (See page 675 of the *Teacher's Edition* for a lesson plan.)

- *How My Family Lives in America* by Susan Kuklin. Aladdin, 1998.

- *Storms* by Seymour Simon. Morrow/Avon, 1992

In addition, you may want to choose additional books that are the same genre or by the same author, or those that have the same kind of text structure as the selection.

After students have chosen their books, give each student a copy of My Reading Log, found on page R38 in the back of the *Teacher's Edition*. Have each student fill in the information at the top of the form. Then have students use the log to keep track of their reading and to record their responses to the literature.

Conduct student-teacher conferences. Arrange for an individual conference time with each student when you can discuss his or her self-selected reading. Have students bring their Reading Logs to share during the conference. You may also want to have the student choose a favorite passage to read aloud to you. Then ask questions designed to stimulate discussion. For example, you might ask what information the student learned from a nonfiction text, how the author structured the text, or how the artwork helped the student understand the topic.

FLUENCY PERFORMANCE Have students read aloud to you the passage from "Who Was Poor Richard?" they selected and practiced previously with their partners. Keep track of the number of words the student reads correctly. Ask each student to rate his or her performance on the 1–4 scale. If students aren't happy with their oral reading, give them an opportunity to practice some more and then to reread the passage to you.

See *Oral Reading Fluency Assessment* for monitoring progress.

LESSON 29

"Lewis and Clark"

BEFORE

Building Background and Vocabulary

Review Phonics: Word Parts/Suffixes /shən/ -*tion*, -*sion*; /yən/ -*ion*

Identify the sounds. Have students repeat the following sentence aloud three times: *In your opinion, is the action movie about the space mission worth seeing?* Ask students to identify words with the /shən/ sound they hear in *caution*. (*action, mission*) Read the sentence again. Ask students to identify the word with the /yən/ sound they hear in *trillion*. (*opinion*)

Associate letters to sounds. Write the sentence from above on the board. Point out the -*sion* pattern in *mission* and the -*tion* pattern in *action*. Tell students that these letter patterns usually stand for the /shən/ sound. Explain that -*tion* and -*sion* are suffixes, and remind students that suffixes change the meanings of words. Also point out that the -*ion* pattern in *opinion* stands for the /yən/ sound.

Word blending. Write these words on the board: *devote, devotion, decide, decision*. Read aloud the word *devote*. Then model how to blend and read *devotion*. Point to *de* and say /di/. Point to *vo* and say /vō/. Slide your hand under *tion* and say /shən/. Then model how to blend the syllables together to read the entire word. Follow a similar procedure with the words *decide* and *decision*.

INTERVENTION PRACTICE BOOK

page 116

Apply the skill. *Suffix Substitution* Write the following words on the board and have students read each aloud. Make the changes necessary to form the words in parentheses. Have a volunteer read aloud each new word.

note (notion)　**institute** (institution)　**decide** (decision)　**tense** (tension)

Introduce Vocabulary

RETEACH **lesson vocabulary.** Tell students that they are going to learn six new words that they will see again when they read a story called "Lewis and Clark." Teach each Vocabulary Word using the following process.

Use the following suggestions or similar ideas to give the meaning or context.

profusely	Mention that this word comes from the Latin *profusus*, meaning "to pour forth."
dismal	The Latin term *dies mali* meant "evil days."
terrain	Mention a related term in context: *terrarium. They planted ferns in the terrarium and then put in some pebbles.*

> Write the word.
>
> Say the word.
>
> Track the word and have students repeat it.
>
> Give the meaning or context.

ordeal	Point out that in England, *ordeal* by fire and *ordeal* by water were once used to establish the guilt or innocence of a person.
peril	The Latin word *periculum* means "trial, test, danger."
esteem	Refer to a related word, *estimate*, which means "to determine an approximate value of something."

For vocabulary activities, see Vocabulary Games on pp. 2–7.

For vocabulary activities, see Vocabulary Games on pp. 2–7.

Vocabulary Words

profusely in great amount; abundantly

dismal gloomy

terrain an area of land

ordeal a difficult adventure or experience

peril danger

esteem to value, respect, or hold in high regard

AFTER

Building Background and Vocabulary

Apply Vocabulary Strategies

Use word origins. Tell students that much of the English language is derived from other languages, especially ancient Latin and Greek. It helps to be able to spot the parts of words that are from other languages when you are trying to decode words. Write the word *terrain* on the board and model the strategy.

> **MODEL** To figure out the meaning of the word *terrain*, I'll try to break the word down into parts that might be more familiar. The first part of the word, *terra-*, I've seen before, in words like *terrarium* and *terrestrial*. From those words, I know *terra-* means "earth" or "land." So the word *terrain* probably has something to do with land or an area of land.

Encourage students to use this strategy as they encounter other unfamiliar words when they read.

RETEACH **lesson vocabulary.** Read aloud the following sentences. Ask students to hold up the word card with the word that completes the sentence. Reread the sentence with the appropriate word choice.

1. We were thanked (profusely) by the owner of the dog.
2. It was a (dismal) day before the sun broke through the clouds.
3. This (terrain) makes me think of the land where I grew up.
4. Getting caught in the storm had been quite an (ordeal).
5. He apologized for having put their lives in (peril).
6. She wanted the teachers to (esteem) her highly.

FLUENCY BUILDER Use *Intervention Practice Book* page 115. Read aloud each of the words in the first column and have students repeat it. Then have students read the words aloud. Follow the same procedure with each of the remaining columns. After students have read aloud the words in each column, have them practice reading the entire list.

INTERVENTION PRACTICE BOOK

page 115

USE SKILL CARD 29A

(Focus Skill) **Cause and Effect**

PRETEACH the skill. Mention to students that good readers try to decide why something happens in a story (the cause), as well as what happens as a result (the effect).

Have students look at **side A of Skill Card 29: Cause and Effect**. Ask a volunteer to read the first two lines aloud. Then have another student read the next two lines. Ask students to look at the illustration on the card. Ask: **What is the event that has happened?** (*A car crashed into a tree.*) **What are the causes for this event?** (*a bad rainstorm, a signal light that is out of order, and brakes that don't work*)

Remind students that there may be words in the text that indicate whether something is a cause or an effect. Ask students to fill in the blank in this sentence: _____ *the brakes were broken, the car wouldn't stop.* Ask: **What word or words could be used in that blank?** (*because* or *since*) Ask students what word or words could be used before an effect in the sentences *The brakes were broken.* _____ , *the car wouldn't stop.* (*therefore* or *as a result*)

Prepare to Read: "Lewis and Clark"

Preview. Tell students that they are going to read a selection called "Lewis and Clark." Explain that this is a biography. In a biography, an author tells the story of someone's life and why this person was important.

DISTANT VOYAGES
pages 678–691

- **Pages 678–679:** I read the title, and then I see two photographs. I think these men must be Lewis and Clark. I remember that they were explorers, but I don't really know much about them, so I am interested in finding out more.

- **Pages 680–681:** I can see the photograph of a very large bear. I wonder if Lewis and Clark encountered bears on their travels.

- **Pages 682–683:** When I see these illustrations of more Native Americans, I wonder what kind of experiences Lewis and Clark had. Were they scared at times?

Set Purpose. Model setting a purpose for reading "Lewis and Clark."

MODEL From previewing these pages, I think I will learn a lot more about Lewis and Clark and their travels and why they were important. I know that one reason people read biographies is to be more informed about a particular person. I will read to learn more about Lewis and Clark's adventures and the danger they faced.

Reread and Summarize

Have students reread and summarize "Lewis and Clark" in sections, as described in the chart below.

Pages 678-681

Let's look again at pages 678-681 to remember what problems Lewis and Clark have at the start of their journey.

Summary: President Jefferson sent the explorers to the Pacific Ocean. They were joined by Sacagawea, an Indian woman. They crossed rivers and then they came to the Rocky Mountains.

Pages 682–685

As we read pages 682–685, let's recall some of the ordeals that Lewis and Clark encounter.

Summary: With Sacagawea as a guide, the expedition is able to find the way around difficult obstacles and to get horses and another guide from the Shoshone, a tribe in which Sacagawea lived as a child. Snowstorms slow their progress through the Rocky Mountains, but eventually they get through and use canoes to travel over rivers to the Pacific.

Pages 686-687

Let's reread pages 686-687 and see how the explorers get back to St. Louis.

Summary: Although the president said he would pay for their ship travel, they could find no ships to take them, so they went back over land. It took six months and they left Sacagawea in her home village along the way.

Pages 688-691

Reread pages 688-691 and let's remember how the explorers are greeted across the country.

Summary: The explorers were treated as heroes on their way to Washington. The President was pleased, and they had wonderful stories to tell of their achievements.

FLUENCY BUILDER Reuse *Intervention Practice Book* page 115. Call attention to the sentences on the bottom half of the page. Model the appropriate pace, expression, and phrasing as you read aloud each of the sentences. Then have students practice reading aloud each sentence two or three times to a partner.

INTERVENTION PRACTICE BOOK

page 115

Directed Reading: "The Mission of the Pony Express" pp. 230–237

TAKE FLIGHT
pp. 230–237

Point out the word *expeditions* on page 230. Model the Use Decoding/Phonics strategy to help students determine the meaning of the word:

Page 230

> **MODEL** Since I don't recognize the word *expeditions*, I'll try breaking it up into smaller parts and looking for prefixes or suffixes I recognize. When I break the word up into syllables, I see the word part *ex-*, which I recognize from words like *exit* and *external*. I know *ex-* means "outside." I also recognize the word part *ped-* from words like *pedal* and *pedestrian*, so it probably has something to do with "feet" or "traveling." Finally, I see the suffix *-tion*, which I know from words like *action* and *motion* to mean "in a state of." Blending all of them together, I think the word must have something to do with traveling or being on a journey. ⭐ **USE DECODING/PHONICS**

Page 231

Ask students to read page 231 to find out more about mail service to the West. Ask: **Why was there a need for faster mail service?** (*Possible response: Many people who went west for the gold rush settled there and wanted news and mail from home.*) **DRAW CONCLUSIONS**

Page 232

Have students read page 232 to discover what the Pony Express system was like. Ask: **How far did a Pony Express rider go?** (*A rider would go as fast as he could for seventy-five miles, changing horses at each station.*) **NOTE DETAILS**

Ask: **What other work opportunities were created by the Pony Express?** (*Other workers were hired to feed the horses and riders and take care of the stations.*) ⭐ **CAUSE-EFFECT**

Page 233

Ask a volunteer to read aloud page 233. Ask: **Why were the riders greatly respected?** (*Possible response: The riders had to be brave and face danger from wild animals and robbers.*) **DRAW CONCLUSIONS**

Page 234

Read page 234 aloud. Ask students to listen to find out more about that first Pony Express trip. Ask: **What was the difference in mail delivery time between stagecoach and Pony Express?** (*It took weeks for stagecoach but only ten days to deliver mail by Pony Express.*) **COMPARE/CONTRAST**

Ask: **How was the first rider greeted when he arrived in Sacramento?** (*with bands and a cheering crowd*) **NOTE DETAILS**

Page 235

Read page 235 aloud to students so they can notice the reason for the end of this system. Ask: **Why did the Pony Express last only nineteen months?** (*Possible response: The telegraph and railroad to California provided faster ways of communicating.*) **SUMMARIZE**

Page 236

Have a volunteer read the text on page 236. Ask: **How did William F. Cody distinguish himself as a rider?** (*Once he rode 384 miles without a rest.*) **NOTE DETAILS**

Ask: **Why did William F. Cody become famous?** (Possible response: *because he had been brave as a rider, hunter, and scout, and was a good storyteller*) **EXPRESS PERSONAL OPINIONS/MAKE JUDGMENTS**

Summarize the selection. Ask students to think about what happened before, during, and after the Pony Express, and how it affected people. Then have students write three or four sentences to summarize this selection.

INTERVENTION PRACTICE BOOK

page 117

Page 237

Answers to *Think About It* Questions

1. Riders rode as fast as they could through bad weather and dangerous situations to get mail to the next rider. **SUMMARY**
2. Accept reasonable responses. Possible response: They were probably proud of what they did because they regularly faced difficult ordeals. **INTERPRETATION**
3. Accept reasonable responses. Letters should be written in the first person and include details about the excitement and dangers of the ride. **WRITE A LETTER**

AFTER

Skill Review
pages 696–697

USE SKILL CARD 29B

(Focus Skill) Cause and Effect

RETEACH **the skill.** Have students look at **side B of Skill Card 29: Cause and Effect**. Ask a volunteer to read aloud the skill reminder.

Then read to students the paragraph about the factory closing. Explain that this is a cause and that this cause can have a number of effects. Ask students to create boxes like those on the skill card. Then have them work with a partner to fill in the boxes.

After students have finished, go over their answers. As they propose effects, list them on the board.

Go over the words that are clues for causes (*because* and *since*) and words that signal effects (*as a result of* and *therefore*).

FLUENCY BUILDER Reuse *Intervention Practice Book*, page 115. Explain that each student will practice the sentences on the bottom half of the page by reading them aloud on tape. Assign new partners. Have students take turns reading the sentences aloud to each other and then reading them on tape.

INTERVENTION PRACTICE BOOK

page 115

Expressive Writing: Tall Tale

Build on Prior Knowledge Tell students that in this exercise they need to remember how to effectively structure a story. They will have to develop a character and a conflict, as well as use vivid language.

Construct the Text. Inform students that you are going to write a tall tale, which is a story that may have been based on an actual event. In a tall tale, the story is exaggerated with impossible events and larger-than-life characters. These tales are often humorous.

"Share the pen" with students as you construct a tall tale about a Pony Express rider. Ask students to pretend they used to be Pony Express riders and are telling about things that happened to them. Write the tale on the board as the students develop it. You may want to help the class get started by writing an opening line on the board: *Once, when I was riding with the Pony Express, I . . .*

As students start building the tale, remind them to exaggerate and to use vivid verbs in the writing. As they add another sentence, ask: **And what happened next?** If students suggest a line that has a weak descriptive word, such as *big* in the phrase "a big bear," ask them to rephrase that. Perhaps say "a bear as big as a mountain," or something similar.

Revisit the text. After you have created this tale, ask students to look back and identify the verbs they have used. Ask if they can come up with more vivid, more active verbs. Change as many verbs as necessary. Have students copy this story on their papers. Ask a volunteer to read the final version aloud.

On Your Own

Ask students to tell something that happened to them or someone they know as a tall tale. This can be something that happened at school or at home. It could be a story from a student's grandparents. Remind them to create larger-than-life characters.

Connect Spelling and Phonics

RETEACH word parts/suffixes /shən/-*tion, -sion*; /yən/*ion*. Have students number a piece of paper 1 through 4. Tell students that the first word you will say has the suffix -*tion* as in *perfection*. Dictate the word and have students write it. Then tell students that the next two words you will say have the suffix -*sion* as in *mission*. Dictate words 2 and 3, and have students write them on their paper as before. Finally, tell students that the last word you will say has the word part -*ion* as in *opinion*. Dictate the last word, and have students write it as before. Help students proofread their work.

1. invention*   2. passion   3. procession   4. dominion

*Word appears in "The Mission of the Pony Express."

Dictate the following sentence, and have students write it: *An expression of pure elation crossed the champion's face.*

Build and Read Longer Words

Remind students that they have learned how to decode words with the word parts/suffixes -*tion, -sion*, and -*ion*.

Write *collection* and *intention* on the board. Remind students that the letters that make up a suffix stay together when the word is broken into syllables. Point to *collection*, and ask students which part of the word stands for the /kəl/ sound, which part stands for the /lek/ sound, and which part stands for the /shən/ sound. Repeat this procedure with the word *intention*. (/in/+/ten/ + /shən/).

INTERVENTION
ASSESSMENT
BOOK

FLUENCY BUILDER Have students choose a passage from "The Mission of the Pony Express" to read aloud to a partner. You may have students choose passages they found particularly interesting, or you can assign them a particular passage, such as:

- Pages 232–233. (From *The way the . . .* through *. . . of good pay.* Total: 156 words)

- Pages 234–235. (From *The first pony . . .* through *. . . to send mail.* Total: 138 words)

Ask students to read the selection aloud to their partners three times. Have students rate their own readings on a scale of 1 to 4.

Review Vocabulary

Read the statements to students and ask them to write the correct answers on their papers. Go over the answers and discuss why the answers are correct.

I. He talked **profusely** when he was nervous. That means
a. he talked once in a while.   b. he talked a lot.

2. The last day of school seemed rather **dismal**, meaning it was
a. exciting.   b. gloomy.

3. That state is known for its flat **terrain**, meaning its flat
a. land.   b. economy.

4. Going to the emergency room was quite an **ordeal**. It was
a. well organized.   b. a difficult experience.

5. The amusement park ride made her feel like she was in **peril**. That means she was in
a. danger.   b. heaven.

6. They were told they should **esteem** their elders. That means they should
a. iron their shirts.   b. hold them in high regard.

Correct responses: lb, 2b, 3a, 4b, 5a, 6b

This is a good time to show the Vocabulary Words and definitions on page 289. Have students copy them to use for studying for the vocabulary test.

★ Focus Skill Cause and Effect

INTERVENTION
PRACTICE
BOOK

page 118

To review cause and effect before the weekly assessment, use *Intervention Practice Book*, page 118. Call attention to the title Cause and Effect. Have a student read the first sentence aloud and fill in the blank. Continue with the next sentence and the two true and false questions.

Direct students' attention to the next section. Tell students to use "The Mission of the Pony Express" to answer the questions.

Review Test Prep

Ask students to turn to page 697 of the *Pupil Edition*. Point out the tips for answering the test questions. Tell students to pay attention to these tips because they can help them answer not only the test questions on this page but also other test questions like these.

DISTANT
VOYAGES
page
697

INTERVENTION
ASSESSMENT
BOOK

Have students follow along as you read aloud each test question and the tip that goes with it. Mention that these questions require that you look back at the passage and find places in the text that support what you think is the right answer. If you can't support it from the text, then you may have the wrong answer.

Self-Selected Reading

Encourage students to select their own books to read independently. They may choose books from your classroom library shelf, or you may select a group of appropriate books from which your students can choose.

- Cross Country (See page 697K of the *Teacher's Edition* for a lesson plan.)

- *Powwow* by George Ancona, Harcourt, 1993

- *Cassie's Journey: Going West in the 1860's* by Brett Harvey, Holiday House, 1988

After students have chosen their books, give each student a copy of My Reading Log, found on page R38 in the back of the Teacher's Edition. Have each student fill in the information at the top of the form. Then have students use the log to keep track of their reading and to record their responses to the literature.

Conduct student-teacher conferences. Arrange for an individual conference time with each student when you can discuss his or her self-selected reading. Have students bring their Reading Logs to share during the conference. You may also want to have each student choose a favorite passage to read aloud to you. Ask questions about the reading to stimulate discussion. For example, you might ask what information the student learned from a nonfiction text, how the author structured the text, or how the artwork helped the student understand the topic.

FLUENCY PERFORMANCE Have students read aloud to you the passages they have selected and practiced previously with their partners. Keep track of the number of words each student reads correctly. Ask each student to rate his or her performance on the 1–4 scale. If students aren't happy with their oral reading, give them additional opportunities to practice and to reread the passage to you.

See *Oral Reading Fluency Assessment* **for monitoring progress.**

BEFORE

Building
Background
and Vocabulary

Use with

"Black Frontiers"

Review Phonics: Syllable Patterns

Identify the syllables. Remind students that a syllable is a word part that can be said by itself and that every syllable has one vowel sound. Say the following words aloud, and have students hold up one, two, three, or four fingers to show how many syllables each word has: *carpet, weightlessness, coolly, pointer, graphics, poise, distastefully, portray.*

Associate letters to sounds. Write *carpet* on the board. Ask which part of the word stands for the /cär/ sound and which part stands for the /pət/ sound. Remind students that when two consonants come together in the middle of a two-syllable word, the word is usually broken between them. Also remind students that when *r* follows a vowel, the vowel + *r* stay together when the word is divided. Then write *portray* on the board, and have students divide it into syllables. Follow a similar process with the words below.

**INTERVENTION
PRACTICE
BOOK**

page 120

weightlessly	(The letters *eigh* stay together when dividing.)
coolly	(Divide between the double consonants.)
graphics	(The letters *ph* stay together.)
replace	(The prefix *re-* forms a syllable. *Re-* means "again.")
bicep, polar	(The first syllable has a long vowel sound; the word is divided after the vowel.)
necktie	(This word is made up of smaller words *neck* and *tie*.)

Apply the skill. Write the following words on the board. Have students read each word aloud and identify its syllable pattern: *hitting, win, misplace, minor, undertow.*

Introduce Vocabulary

Tell students that they are going to learn five new words that they will see again when they read a story called "Black Frontiers." Teach each Vocabulary Word using the process shown in the box.

Use the following suggestions or similar ideas to give the meaning or context.

designated	The root comes from the Latin word *signare*, which means "to mark."
installments	This is most often connected with repayment of debt, as in installment payments.

> Write the word.
>
> Say the word.
>
> Track the word and have students repeat it.
>
> Give the meaning or context.

exodus	Point out that the prefix *ex-* means "out."
migrated	Use a related word, *migration*, in context: The biologists were concerned about the massive migration of foxes.
burrowed	Point out that the noun form of *burrow* means "a hole" or "a tunnel."

For vocabulary activities, see Vocabulary Games on p. 2–7.

AFTER

Building
Background
and Vocabulary

Apply Vocabulary Strategies

Use word origins and derivation. Write the word *migrated* on the board and read it aloud. Ask students if they know its meaning. Remind students that it's fun to learn the origin of a word and its derivation—where it comes from. This helps one understand it better and remember the meaning. Model using the strategy.

> **MODEL** The word *migrated* looks familiar, but I am not quite certain of its meaning. I look it up in the dictionary to find its origin. I discover that this word comes from the Latin word *migrare*, "to change or move." I also discover the related words *emigrate* and *immigrate* which are actions of people and imply a permanent move.

Have students use this strategy as they encounter other unfamiliar words when they read.

RETEACH lesson vocabulary. Be sure each student has a set of word cards. Read aloud the following sentences. Ask students to hold up the card with the word that should go in that blank. Reread the sentence with the appropriate word.

1. He was the __(designated)__ driver.
2. She paid off the debt in __(installments)__ .
3. There was a whole __(exodus)__ of people leaving the city.
4. The birds __(migrated)__ to Alaska from Florida every spring.
5. The animal had __(burrowed)__ under the porch.

Vocabulary Words

designated appointed or set aside for a definite duty or purpose

installments payments made on a debt at definite times

exodus a departure or going away from a place

migrated moved from one region or climate to another

burrowed dug

FLUENCY BUILDER Use *Intervention Practice Book* page 119.
Read aloud each of the words in the first column and have students repeat it. Then have students work in pairs and take turns reading the words to each other. Follow the same procedure with each of the remaining columns. After each partner has had a turn reading aloud the words in each column, have students practice reading the entire list and time themselves.

INTERVENTION
PRACTICE
BOOK

page 119

Summarize and Paraphrase

PRETEACH **the skill.** Mention to students that there are some methods for increasing understanding of their reading. These are important skills that they will use often.

Have students look at **side A of Skill Card 30: Summarize and Paraphrase.** Ask volunteers to read the two sentences aloud. Mention to students that *summarize* and *paraphrase* are not opposites. They are similar, but they also have important differences. Direct students' attention to the chart. Ask: **How are these two skills alike?** (*Possible response: You need to read carefully to do each; both are a sort of retelling; both help you understand a selection.*) **How are these two skills different?** (*Possible response: One is based on main points that are retold; the other tells the whole thing in very different words. One is short; the other is longer.*)

Tell students that the main thing to remember is that the summary is the main point and the paraphrase is the whole selection in the reader's own words.

Prepare to Read: "Black Frontiers"

Preview. Tell students that they are going to read a selection called "Black Frontiers." Explain that this is expository nonfiction. It gives information about real people, places, or events. Then preview the selection.

DISTANT VOYAGES

pages 700–710

- **Pages 700–701:** I read the title and subtitle. I notice the photograph and realize I know nothing about African Americans in the old West.

- **Pages 702–705:** On these pages I see a frontier house and a person using horses to help with his work. I am sure that life was hard. I wonder if it was harder for black pioneers because of their race. On pages 704 and 705 I see photos of people. One photo seems to be of a very large family. I wonder if they were very crowded in their house.

- **Pages 706–707:** From the handbill I think these pages will tell me about people who went west looking for homes of their own. I think they were called homesteaders and I am curious whether they included former slaves.

- **Pages 708–709:** From these pages I think that I will learn about African American communities that were formed.

Set purpose. Model setting a purpose for reading "Black Frontiers."

MODEL From my previewing, I think this nonfiction selection is about the experience of African American settlers on the frontier. I'll read to get information about what life was like for them.

Reread and Summarize

Have students reread and summarize "Black Frontiers" in sections,
as described in the chart below.

Pages 700–703

**Let's look again at pages 700–703 to remember what the settlers'
homes were like.**

Summary: Homesteaders in Kansas and Nebraska had to build houses
out of clumps of sod. They needed a mule, a plow, and seed.

Pages 704–705

**As we read pages 704–705 again, let's recall how homesteaders
fared in different climates.**

Summary: In cold North and South Dakota, settlers built homes in
the ground. Sometimes they had to make fires in holes with buffalo
droppings as fuel. In desert regions, they made houses out of mud
and straw. Wherever they were, black pioneers were lonely.

Pages 706–707

**When we reread pages 706–707, let's pay attention to the story
of one man who led people to freedom and their own homes.**

Summary: Benjamin Singleton bought land in Kansas and organized
a campaign to get black homesteaders to settle in that area. The result
was the formation of two black communities with more than 800
homesteaders.

Pages 708–710

**Let's reread pages 708–710 and see how the town of Nicodemus
grew.**

Summary: Early settlers in Nicodemus had it rough, but neighboring
white farmers helped them, and the town ultimately grew to 8,000
homesteaders by the turn of the century. The town is also known
for its baseball team.

FLUENCY BUILDER Use *Intervention Practice Book*
page 119. Call attention to the sentences on the bottom
half of the page. State that the goal is to have each
student read each phrase smoothly. Model appropriate
pace, expression, and phrasing as you read aloud each
of the sentences. Then have students practice reading
aloud each sentence two or three times to a partner.

INTERVENTION
PRACTICE
BOOK

page 119

Directed Reading: "Frontier Children," pp. 238–244

TAKE FLIGHT
pp. 238–244

Page 238

Read aloud the title and tell students that the story is based on historical events. Read aloud page 238 as students follow along. Ask: **How do the children help out in the morning?** (*They do chores.*) **IMPORTANT DETAILS**

What chores do you think they have to do? (*Possible response: Maybe they have to make breakfast or take care of the animals.*) **MAKE PREDICTIONS**

Page 239

Ask students to read page 239 silently. Ask: **How are the girl's chores different from the boy's chores?** (*The girl has indoor chores; the boy has outdoor chores.*) **MAKE COMPARISONS/CONFIRM PREDICTIONS**

How can you tell that the children like going to school? (*Possible response: They hurry to get their chores done; they will be sad when it is too snowy to go to school.*) **DETERMINE CHARACTERS' EMOTIONS**

Pages 240–241

Ask volunteers to read pages 240–241 aloud. Remind students to pay attention to the time-order words. Ask: **Why did the family come to the West?** (*They wanted to find good farming land.*) **SUMMARIZE**

What does the word *desolate* **mean?** Model using the strategy Use Context to Confirm Meaning.

> **MODEL** I don't know what *desolate* means so I'll look at the rest of the sentence for clues. I see that the place is empty and that not even trees grow there. *Desolate* must mean bare and useless.
> (Focus Strategy) **USE CONTEXT TO CONFIRM MEANING**

What did the family do in their first spring, summer, and fall in the West? (*The family built a house of sod and then planted and harvested crops. They set some foods aside for winter and sold the rest.*) (Focus Strategy) **SUMMARIZE/PARAPHRASE**

Why doesn't the family build an adobe house or a log cabin? (*Possible response: The plains regions don't have the resources to build these kinds of houses.*) **SUMMARIZE**

Page 242

Ask students to read page 242 to learn how the children get ready for school. Ask: **What is special about the food the children eat?** (*The girl picked the berries for the jam they are having for breakfast. The boy gathered the eggs they will have for lunch.*) **SYNTHESIZE**

How can you tell that the children like living on the frontier now? (*They like playing with their friends at school.*) **DRAW CONCLUSIONS**

INTERVENTION PRACTICE BOOK

page 121

Why is it important for frontier families to form a community? (*Possible response: They can help each other out and feel less lonely.*) **INTERPRET THEME**

Summarize the selection. Ask students to discuss how the children get used to living in a frontier community. Then have them summarize the story in three sentences.

Answers to *Think About It* Questions

1. Their old house was in a town in the East. Their frontier home is made of sod and is on a farm, miles away from the next house. **SUMMARY**

2. Possible response: They don't mind doing the chores because they can see that they are a real help to the family. **INTERPRETATION**

3. Accept reasonable responses. Letters should follow the friendly-letter format and should describe the family's new home and way of life from the girl's point of view. **WRITE SENTENCES**

AFTER

Skill Review
pages 714–715

USE SKILL CARD 30B

(Focus Skill) Summarize and Paraphrase

RETEACH the skill. Have students look at **side B of Skill Card 30: Summarize and Paraphrase.** Read the skill reminder aloud to them.

Ask a volunteer to read aloud the paragraph below the skill reminder. Then ask students to read the two other versions silently. After they have finished, have a student reread version 1 aloud. Ask: **Is this a summary or a paraphrase?** (*paraphrase*) **How do you know?** (*Possible response: It is as long as the original and has the same idea in different words.*)

Ask another volunteer to read the second version. Ask: **Is this a summary or paraphrase?** (*summary*) **How do you know?** (*Possible response: It is shorter than the original and has just the main ideas.*)

FLUENCY BUILDER Use *Intervention Practice Book* page 119. Explain that each student will practice the sentences on the bottom half of the page by reading them aloud on tape. Assign a different partner for each reader. Have students take turns reading the sentences aloud to each other and then reading them on tape. After students listen to the tape, have each person tell how his or her reading has improved. Then have students repeat the process, focusing on improved pacing and tone as they read the sentences aloud on tape.

INTERVENTION PRACTICE BOOK

page 119

Expressive Writing: Friendly Letter

Build on prior knowledge. Tell students that being able to write a letter is an important skill. Remind them of the parts of a friendly letter. You may wish to display this list on the board.

- a heading
- a greeting
- the body of the letter
- a closing and a signature

Tell students that you are going to work as a group to write a friendly letter to students in another school in a place that is different than yours. (For example, write to a classroom in a rural area if your class is in the city, to a class in the north if you are in the south, or to a class that lives inland if you are on the ocean.) Tell the class that in the letter you want to explain what the climate and surroundings are like where you live and to ask about the other class's surroundings.

Construct the text. "Share the pen" with students in a collaborative group writing effort. Guide the process by asking questions and offering suggestions as needed. Write on the board the heading, which is the address of the school and the date. Write a greeting, such as "Dear Students," and then construct the body of the letter. Remind students that the purpose is to inform another class what life is like for your class. Finish with an appropriate closing.

Revisit the text. Have students read the completed letter aloud. Ask:

- **Have we left out any commas that should be there?**

Remind students to look for longer prepositional phrases or a group of two phrases at the beginning of a sentence. These need to be set off by a comma.

On Your Own

Write a friendly letter to a relative, a pen pal, or someone you know in another school or community. Describe what you do on a typical weekend. Include a sentence with a long prepositional phrase that needs to be set off by a comma.

Connect Spelling and Phonics

RETEACH **syllable patterns.** Have students number a sheet of paper 1 through 8. Dictate the following words, and have students write them. After they write each word, display the correct spelling so students can proofread their work.

1. quickly*   2. trustingly*   3. humanity   4. pailful*

5. photograph   6. comfortable*   7. assuredly   8. endless*

*Word appears in "Frontier Children."

Dictate the following sentence, and have students write it:
Sally found a hammer, a screwdriver, and several nails in the toolshed.

Build and Read Longer Words

Write these words on the board:

humankind   neighborly   needlessly

nonflammable   prehistoric   successfully

Have students read each word aloud. Guide them in explaining the syllable pattern or patterns that enable them to figure out each word.

INTERVENTION ASSESSMENT BOOK

FLUENCY BUILDER Have students choose a passage from "Frontier Children" to read aloud to a partner. You may have students choose a passage they found particularly interesting, or you can assign them a particular passage, such as:

- Page 238 and the first two paragraphs on page 239. (Starting with *In the predawn . . .* through *. . . trustingly.* Total: 144 words)

- Page 242. (Starting with *Breakfast . . .* through *. . . it is home.* Total: 144 words)

Ask students to read the selection aloud to their partners three times. Have students rate their own readings on a scale of 1 to 4. Encourage them to note their improvement from one reading to the next by completing the sentence *I know my reading has improved because* _____. Encourage the listening partner to offer positive feedback.

Vocabulary Review

To review the Vocabulary Words prior to the weekly assessment, read the following statements to students and ask them to write the correct answers on their papers. Go over the answers and discuss why each answer is correct.

1. He was *designated* as the hall monitor. That means he was
   a. appointed to that job.
   b. asked to do the job.

2. I couldn't make the *installments* so I called the banks. These installments were
   a. time payments on a loan.
   b. special interest rates.

3. When she left, it started a whole *exodus*. That was a
   a. trend.
   b. departure or going away by many.

4. She had *migrated* north to escape the heat, meaning she had
   a. moved to a different climate.
   b. flown north.

5. The gopher *burrowed* into the ground and went to sleep. It
   a. dug a hole.
   b. climbed a tree for shelter.

Correct responses: 1a, 2a, 3b, 4a, 5a

This is a good time to show the Vocabulary Words and definitions on page 299. Have students copy them to use in studying for the vocabulary test.

 ## Review Summarize and Paraphrase

To review summarizing and paraphrasing before the weekly assessment, use *Intervention Practice Book* page 122. Call attention to the title Summarize and Paraphrase. Have a student read aloud the first sentence and fill in the blank. Have a second student read the second sentence, completing the blank. Then guide students through the activity, reading the items and then writing first a summary, and then a paraphrase.

**INTERVENTION
PRACTICE
BOOK**

page 122

Review Test Prep

Ask students to turn to page 715 of the *Pupil Edition*. Call attention to the Tips for answering the test questions. Tell students to pay attention to these tips because they can help them answer not only the test questions on this page but also other test questions like these. Ask students to read the passage. Go over the two questions that follow the selection. Ask for a volunteer to read each question and possible answers. Discuss with the class which is the best answer for each and why.

**DISTANT
VOYAGES**

page 715

**INTERVENTION
ASSESSMENT
BOOK**

Self-Selected Reading

Encourage students to select their own books to read on their own. They may choose books from your classroom library shelf, or you may select a group of appropriate books from which to choose. Titles might include the following.

- *A Big Day in Nicodemus* by Kate Fisher. (See page 715M of the *Teacher's Edition* for a lesson plan.)

- *Heartland* by Diane Siebert. HarperCollins, 1989.

- *Thimble Summer* by Elizabeth Enright. Dell, 1987

You may also want to choose additional books that are the same genre, that are by the same author, or that have the same kind of text structure as the selection.

After students have chosen their books, give each student a copy of My Reading Log, found on page R38 in the back of the *Teacher's Edition*. Have each student fill in the information at the top of the form. Then have students use the log to keep track of their reading and to record their responses to the literature.

Conduct student-teacher conferences. Arrange for an individual conference time with each student when you can discuss his or her self-selected reading. Have students bring their Reading Logs to share during the conference. You may also want to have the student choose a favorite passage to read aloud to you. Then ask questions designed to stimulate discussion. For example, you might question what information the student learned from a nonfiction text, how the author structured the text, or how the artwork helped the student understand the topic.

FLUENCY PERFORMANCE Have students read aloud to you the passage from "Frontier Children" they have selected and practiced previously with their partners. Keep track of the number of words the student reads correctly. Ask each student to rate his or her own performance on the 1–4 scale. If students aren't happy with their oral reading, give them an opportunity to practice some more and then to reread the passage to you.